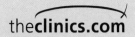

MAGNETIC RESONANCE IMAGING CLINICS

Selected Topics in MR Neuroimaging

May 2006 • Volume 14 • Number 2

ELSEVIER
SAUNDERS

An imprint of Elsevier, Inc
PHILADELPHIA LONDON TORONTO MONTREAL SYDNEY TOKYO

W.B. SAUNDERS COMPANY
A Divison of Elsevier Inc.

Elsevier Inc. ● 1600 John F. Kennedy Boulevard ● Suite 1800 ●
Philadelphia, Pennsylvania 19103-2899

http://www.mri.theclinics.com

MRI CLINICS OF NORTH AMERICA Volume 14, Number 2
May 2006 ISSN 1064-9689, ISBN 1-4160-3891-4

Editor: Barton Dudlick

Reprints: For copies of 100 or more, of articles in this publication, please contact the Commercial Reprints Department, Elsevier Inc., 360 Park Avenue South, New York, New York 10010-1710. Tel. (212) 633-3813, Fax: (212) 462-1935, email: reprints@elsevier.com.

The ideas and opinions expressed in *Magnetic Resonance Imaging Clinics of North America* do not necessarily reflect those of the Publisher. The Publisher does not assume any responsibility for any injury and/or damage to persons or property arising out of or related to any use of the material contained in this periodical. The reader is advised to check the appropriate medical literature and the product information currently provided by the manufacturer of each drug to be administered to verify the dosage, the method and duration of administration, or contraindications. It is the responsibility of the treating physician or other health care professional, relying on independent experience and knowledge of the patient, to determine drug dosages and the best treatment for the patient. Mention of any product in this issue should not be construed as endorsement by the contributors, editors, or the Publisher of the product or manufacturers' claims.

The Magnetic Resonance Imaging Clinics of North America (ISSN 1064-9689) is published quarterly by W.B. Saunders, 360 Park Avenue South, New York, NY 10010-1710. Months of publication are February, May, August, and November. Business and Editorial Offices: 1600 John F. Kennedy Boulevard, Suite 1800, Philadelphia, PA 19103-2899. Accounting and Circulation Offices: 6277 Sea Harbor Drive, Orlando, FL 32887-4800. Periodicals postage paid at New York, NY and additional mailing offices. Subscription prices are $205.00 per year (US individuals), $305.00 per year (US institutions), $100.00 per year (US students), $230.00 per year (Canadian individuals), $375.00 per year (Canadian institutions), $135.00 per year (Canadian students), $280.00 per year (international individuals), $375.00 per year (international institutions), and $135.00 per year (international students). International air speed delivery is included in all *Clinics* subscription prices. All prices are subject to change without notice. **POSTMASTER:** Send address changes to *The Magnetic Resonance Imaging Clinics of North America*, Elsevier Periodicals Customer Service, 6277 Sea Harbor Drive, Orlando, FL 32887-4800. **Customer Service: 1-800-654-2452 (US). From outside of the US, call 1-407-345-4000.**

Magnetic Resonance Imaging Clinics of North America is covered in the *RSNA Index of Imaging Literature, Index Medicus, MEDLINE,* and *EMBASE/Excerpta Medica.*

Printed in the United States of America.

SELECTED TOPICS IN MR NEUROIMAGING

CONTRIBUTORS

SAMEER A. ANSARI, MD, PhD
Resident, Department of Radiology, University of Illinois at Chicago Medical Center; and Chief, Section of Head and Neck Radiology, Department of Radiology, University of Illinois at Chicago, Chicago, Illinois

RICHARD A. BRONEN, MD
Professor, Diagnostic Radiology and Neurosurgery, Yale University School of Medicine, New Haven, Connecticut

WILIAM A. COPEN, MD
Clinical Assistant (Radiology), Massachusetts General Hospital, Boston, Massachusetts

L. CELSO HYGINO CRUZ, Jr, MD
Clínica de Diagnóstico por Imagem, Multi-ImagemRessonância Magnética, Rio de Janeiro, Brazil

R. GILBERTO GONZALEZ, MD, PhD
Director, Massachusetts General Hospital; and Professor (Radiology), Harvard Medical School, Boston, Massachusetts

P. ELLEN GRANT, MD
Chief, Division of Pediatric Radiology, Massachusetts General Hospital, Boston, Massachusetts

STEVEN M. GREENBERG, MD, PhD
Associate Professor (Neurology), Harvard Medical School; Associate Professor (Neurology), and Co-Director, Neurology Clinical Trials Unit, Massachusetts General Hospital, Boston, Massachusetts

AFSHIN KARIMI, MD, PhD, JD
Resident, Department of Radiology, University of Illinois Hospital at Chicago, University of Illinois College of Medicine, Chicago, Illinois

HAROLD KEYSERLING, MD
Assistant Professor, Department of Radiology, Emory University School of Medicine, Atlanta, Georgia

MICHAEL H. LEV, MD
Director, Emergency Neuroradiology and Neurovascular Laboratory, Department of Radiology, Massachusetts General Hospital; and Associate Professor (Radiology), Harvard Medical School, Boston, Massachusetts

MAHMOOD F. MAFEE, MD, FACR
Medical Director, MRI Center; Professor, Department of Radiology, University of Illinois at Chicago Medical Center; and Chief, Section of Head and Neck Radiology, Department of Radiology, University of Illinois at Chicago, Chicago, Illinois

SRINIVASAN MUKUNDAN, Jr, MD, PhD
Assistant Professor, Department of Radiology, Duke University Medical Center; and Assistant Professor, Department of Biomedical Engineering, Pratt School of Engineering, Duke University, Durham, North Carolina

MARK RAPOPORT, BS
Medical Student, Department of Radiology, University of Illinois Hospital at Chicago, University of Illinois College of Medicine, Chicago, Illinois

JONATHAN ROSAND, MD, MS
Assistant Professor (Neurology), Vascular and Critical Care Neurology, Massachusetts General Hospital; and Assistant Professor (Neurology), Harvard Medical School, Boston, Massachusetts

A. GREGORY SORENSEN, MD
Co-Director, Athinoula A. Martinos Center for Biomedical Imaging, Department of Radiology, Massachusetts General Hospital, Boston; and Division of Health Sciences and Technology, Harvard-MIT, Boston, Massachusetts

PAMELA W. SCHAEFER, MD
Associate Director (Neuroradiology); Director (MRI), Massachusetts General Hospital; and Associate Professor (Radiology), Harvard Medical School, Boston, Massachusetts

JAI D. SHAH, MD, MBA, MPH
Medical Student, Department of Radiology,
University of Illinois Hospital at Chicago,
University of Illinois College of Medicine,
Chicago, Illinois

JACK H. SIMON, MD, PhD
Professor (Radiology, Neurology, Neurosurgery,
and Psychiatry); and Vice Chairman (Research),
Department of Radiology, University of Colorado
Health Sciences Center, Denver, Colorado

ERIC E. SMITH, MD, FRCPC
Instructor (Neurology), Vascular and Critical Care
Neurology, Massachusetts General Hospital; and
Instructor (Neurology), Harvard Medical School,
Boston, Massachusetts

VENKATRAMANA R. VATTIPALLY, MD
Clinical Instructor, Yale University School of
Medicine, New Haven, Connecticut

DAVID YU, MD
Shields MRI Health Care Group, Brockton,
Massachusetts

SELECTED TOPICS IN MR NEUROIMAGING

Volume 14 • Number 2 • May 2006

Contents

may provide an improved way to monitor intraoperative surgical procedures as well as their effects. Evaluation of the response to treatment with chemotherapy and radiation therapy may also become possible. Although DTI has some limitations, its active investigation and further study are clearly warranted.

GOAL STATEMENT

The goal of *Magnetic Resonance Imaging Clinics of North America* is to keep practicing radiologists and radiology residents up to date with current clinical practice in radiology by providing timely articles reviewing the state of the art in-patient care.

ACCREDITATION

The Magnetic Resonance Imaging Clinics of North America is planned and implemented in accordance with the Essential Areas and Policies of the Accreditation Council for Continuing Medical Education (ACCME) through the joint sponsorship of the University of Virginia School of Medicine and Elsevier. The University of Virginia School of Medicine is accredited by the ACCME to provide continuing medical education for physicians.

The University of Virginia School of Medicine designates this educational activity for a maximum of 60 AMA PRA Category 1 Credits™. Physicians should only claim credit commensurate with the extent of their participation in the activity.

The American Medical Association has determined that physicians not licensed in the US who participate in this CME activity are eligible for AMA PRA Category 1 Credits™.

Category 1 credit can be earned by reading the text material, taking the CME examination online at http://www.theclinics.com/home/cme, and completing the evaluation. After taking the test, you will be required to review any and all incorrect answers. Following completion of the test and evaluation, your credit will be awarded and you may print your certificate.

FACULTY DISCLOSURE/CONFLICT OF INTEREST

The University of Virginia School of Medicine, as an ACCME accredited provider, endorses and strives to comply with the Accreditation Council for Continuing Medical Education (ACCME) Standards of Commercial Support, Commonwealth of Virginia statutes, University of Virginia policies and procedures, and associated federal and private regulations and guidelines on the need for disclosure and monitoring of proprietary and financial interests that may affect the scientific integrity and balance of content delivered in continuing medical education activities under our auspices.

The University of Virginia School of Medicine requires that all CME activities accredited through this institution be developed independently and be scientifically rigorous, balanced and objective in the presentation/discussion of its content, theories and practices.

All authors/editors participating in an accredited CME activity are expected to disclose to the readers relevant financial relationships with commercial entities occurring within the past 12 months (such as grants or research support, employee, consultant, stock holder, member of speakers bureau, etc.). The University of Virginia School of Medicine will employ appropriate mechanisms to resolve potential conflicts of interest to maintain the standards of fair and balanced education to the reader. Questions about specific strategies can be directed to the Office of Continuing Medical Education, University of Virginia School of Medicine, Charlottesville, Virginia.

The authors/editors listed below have identified no financial or professional relationships for themselves or their spouse/partner:

Sameer A. Ansari, MD, PhD; Richard A. Bronen, MD; William A. Copen, MD; L. Celso Hygino Cruz, Jr., MD; Barton Dudlick, Acquisitions Editor; R. Gilberto Gonzalez, MD, PhD; P. Ellen Grant, MD; Steven M. Greenberg, MD, PhD; Afshin Karimi, MD, PhD, JD; Harold Keyserling, MD; Mahmood F. Mafee, MD; Srinivasan Mukundan, Jr., MD, PhD; Mark Rapoport, BS; Jonathan Rosand, MD, MS; Pamela W. Schaefer, MD; Jai D. Shah, MD, MBA, MPH; Jack H. Simon, MD, PhD; Eric E. Smith, MD, FRCPC; Venkatramana R. Vattipally, MD; and, David Yu, MD.

The authors/editors listed below have identified the following professional or financial affiliations for themselves or their spouse/partner:

Michael H. Lev, MD is on the speaker's bureau for GE Medical Services and Bracco Diagnostics.

A. Gregory Sorensen, MD is on the speaker's bureau for Siemens Medical Solutions, is a consultant for Berlex Laboratories, Epix Pharmaceuticals, and BiogenIdec, and receives research support from National Institutes of Health, Siemens Medical Solutions, General Electric Healthcare, GlaxoSmithKline, Novartis Pharmaceuticals, Merck (USA), BiogenIdec, WorldCare, RadPharm, PerkinElmer, StemCells, Inc., Ono Pharmaceuticals, and MDS Pharma Services.

Disclosure of Discussion of Non-FDA Approved Uses for Pharmaceutical and/or Medical Devices.
The University of Virginia School of Medicine, as an ACCME provider, requires that all authors identify and disclose any "off label" uses for pharmaceutical and medical device products. The University of Virginia School of Medicine recommends that each physician fully review all the available data on new products or procedures prior to clinical use.

TO ENROLL

To enroll in the Magnetic Resonance Imaging Clinics of North America Continuing Medical Education program, call customer service at 1-800-654-2452 or visit us online at www.theclinics.com/home/cme . The CME program is available to subscribers for an additional fee of $175.00.

MAGNETIC
RESONANCE
IMAGING CLINICS

Magn Reson Imaging Clin N Am 14 (2006) 127–140

Imaging of Hemorrhagic Stroke

Eric E. Smith, MD, FRCPC[a,b,*], Jonathan Rosand, MD, MS[a,b],
Steven M. Greenberg, MD, PhD[b,c]

Hemorrhagic stroke accounts for approximately 15% of all stroke and is classified according to anatomic compartmentalization as intracerebral hemorrhage (ICH) (approximately two thirds) or subarachnoid hemorrhage (SAH) (approximately one third) [1]. This article discusses the use of CT and MR imaging for the differential diagnosis of ICH; for a detailed review of SAH, which is typically attributed to aneurysm rupture or severe trauma, the reader is referred elsewhere [2]. Topics to be discussed include the CT and MR imaging appearance of ICH, the differential diagnosis of ICH by location, and the imaging evaluation of acute stroke with regard to hemorrhage.

CT appearance of intracerebral hemorrhage

The CT appearance of hemorrhage is determined by the degree of attenuation of the x-ray beam, which is proportional to the density of hemoglobin protein (relative to plasma concentration) within the hematoma.

This article was originally published in *Neuroimaging Clinics of North America* 2005;15(2):259–72. This work was supported by National Institutes of Health Grant K23 NS046327.
[a] Vascular and Critical Care Neurology, Massachusetts General Hospital, Boston, MA, USA
[b] Harvard Medical School, Boston, MA, USA
[c] Neurology Clinical Trials Unit, Massachusetts General Hospital, Boston, MA, USA
* Corresponding author. Stroke Service, VBK 802, Massachusetts General Hospital, 55 Fruit Street, Boston, MA 02114.
E-mail address: eesmith@partners.org (E.E. Smith).

Immediately following vessel rupture, the hematoma consists of a collection of red blood cells, white blood cells, platelet clumps, and protein-rich serum that has a heterogeneous appearance on CT with attenuation in the range of 30–60 Hounsfield units (HU), depending on the degree of plasma extrusion [3]. In this hyperacute phase, hemorrhage may be difficult to distinguish from normal cortex because of similar attenuation. Over minutes to hours, a fibrin clot forms with an increase in attenuation to 60–80 HU (Fig. 1A) [3]. Clot retraction and extrusion of serum can further increase attenuation to as high as 80–100 HU in the center of the hematoma. The degree of attenuation may be reduced in patients with severe anemia [4], impaired clot formation due to coagulopathy, or volume averaging with adjacent tissue. Vasogenic edema evolves around the hematoma within hours and may continue to increase for up to 2 weeks after hemorrhage onset [5].

Over the following days, cells and protein are broken down and scavenged by macrophages, leading to slowly decreasing attenuation, with the greatest decrease at the periphery of the hematoma and more gradual evolution toward the center (Fig. 1B and C) [6]. Within 4 to 9 days, the hematoma attenuation decreases to that of normal cortex, and within 2 to 3 weeks to that of normal white matter [3].

The CT recognition of subacute intracerebral hematoma can be challenging because the attenuation is similar to that of normal brain tissue, although mass effect may still be present. MR imaging can confirm subacute hematoma. As time goes on, attenuation continues to decrease to levels below that of the normal brain. Eventually, the hematoma resolves into a fluid-filled or slit-like cavity that may be difficult to visualize on CT (Fig. 1D). Contrast enhancement is not present in the initial days following ICH but may develop at the periphery in weeks to months [7], sometimes leading to diagnostic confusion with brain tumor or abscess.

A blood-fluid level may be seen in medium to large ICH within the first hours after onset; the dependent portion displays higher attenuation (Fig. 2) due to sedimentation of cellular elements [8]. This finding may be more common in ICH caused by anticoagulation [9], but it is not specific and has also been described in ICH due to hypertension, trauma, tumor, or arterial-venous malformation. The association with shorter time interval from ICH onset, and in some cases with anticoagulation, has led to speculation that incomplete clotting is required for blood-fluid level formation.

MR appearance of intracerebral hemorrhage

The physics of MR imaging of hemorrhage is complex; multiple reviews have covered this topic in detail [10,11]. A brief explanation is warranted here, however, because an understanding of the signal characteristics of hemorrhage, as well as their

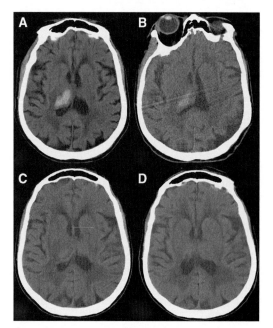

Fig. 1. CT appearance of hemorrhage. Serial CT scans of right thalamic hematoma. (*A*) Acute ICH in the right thalamus with mean attenuation 65 HU. (*B*) CT performed 8 days later than (*A*); the periphery of the hematoma is now isodense to the brain while the center of the hematoma has mean attenuation 45 HU. (*C*) CT performed 13 days later than (*A*) shows continued evolution of the hematoma with decreasing attenuation. (*D*) CT performed 5 months later than (*A*) shows a small area of encephalomalacia in the location of the previous hemorrhage.

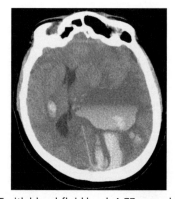

Fig. 2. CT with blood-fluid level. A 77-year-old woman was admitted with coma of 4 hours' duration. CT scan shows massive left hemispheric hematoma with blood-fluid level. No history of anticoagulation or coagulopathy.

evolution over time, is essential for radiologic interpretation.

The MR signal intensity of hemorrhage is dependent on both the chemical state of the iron atoms within the hemoglobin molecule and the integrity of the red blood cell membrane [12]. Iron can be either diamagnetic or paramagnetic, depending on the state of its outer electron orbitals. In the paramagnetic state, it alters the T1 and T2 relaxation times of water protons through magnetic dipole–dipole interactions and susceptibility effects. Dipole–dipole interactions shorten both the T1 and T2 relaxation times but have a greater effect on T1. Susceptibility effect is present when iron atoms are compartmentalized within the red cell membrane, causing magnetic field inhomogeneity, with resulting loss of phase coherence and selective shortening of the T2 relaxation time. After degradation of red cell membranes, the iron becomes more homogenously distributed, and this effect is nullified. Other factors that influence signal characteristics to a lesser extent include protein content, brain edema, oxygen tension, blood–brain barrier breakdown, thrombus formation, and clot retraction [11].

Both the chemical environment surrounding the hemoglobin iron atom and red cell membrane integrity undergo relatively predictable changes after ICH. The following section enumerates these changes in MR signal characteristics during the different phases of ICH evolution (Fig. 3 and Table 1).

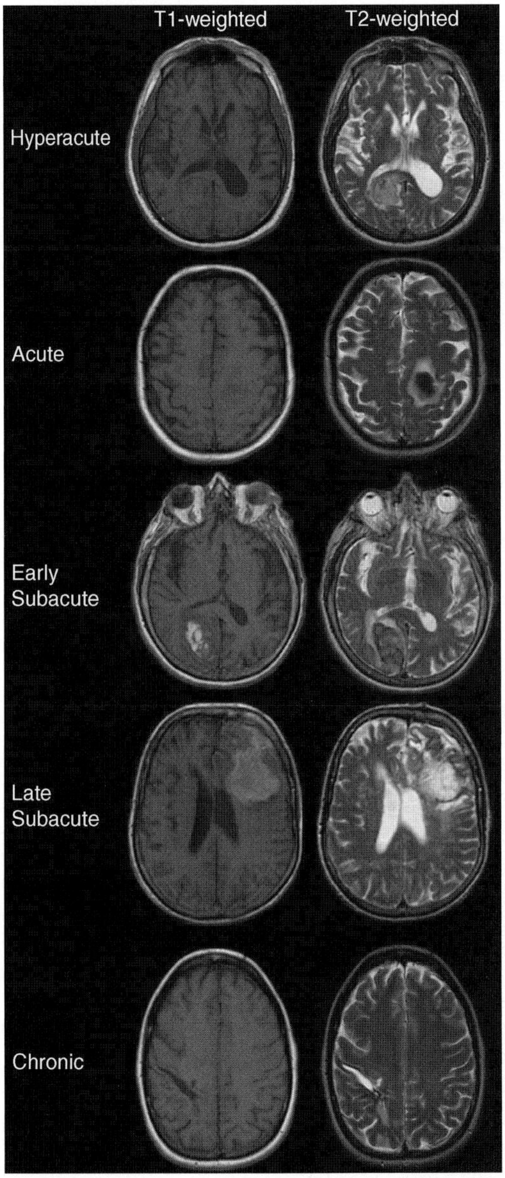

Fig. 3. MR imaging appearance of hemorrhage on T1-weighted (*left column*) and T2-weighted (*right column*) sequences for the different stages of hematoma (*rows*). Examples are selected from various patients. Hyperacute: There is relative isointensity on the T1-weighted and hyperintensity on the T2-weighted sequence of this right occipital hematoma. A small degree of vasogenic edema surrounds the hematoma. On the T2-weighted sequence there is a thin rim of hypointensity that is barely detectable in the periphery; this is caused by susceptibility effect from deoxy-hemoglobin. Acute: The marked hypointensity on the T2-weighted sequence of this left frontal hematoma is caused by susceptibility effect from deoxy-hemoglobin. Early subacute: The hyperintensity on the T1-weighted sequence of this right occipital hematoma is caused by the oxidation of deoxy-hemoglobin to met-hemoglobin. Late subacute: The hyperintensity on the T2-weighted sequence of this large left frontal hematoma results from the loss of susceptibility effect caused by degradation of the red cell membranes. The degree of vasogenic edema is lesser compared with earlier phases. Chronic: A former large right frontal hematoma has resolved into a slit-like cavity with a rim of hypointensity on the T2-weighted sequence caused by hemosiderin deposition.

Table 1:   **Evolution of MR imaging signal characteristics with time**

Phase	Time	Iron-containing molecule	Iron oxidation state	Red cell membranes	T1	T2	T2*
Hyperacute	Hours	Oxyhemoglobin	Fe^{2+}	Intact	↓	↑	
Acute	Hours to days	Deoxyhemoglobin	Fe^{2+}	Intact	iso, ↓	↓	↓
Early subacute	Days to 1 week	Methemoglobin	Fe^{3+}	Intact	↑↑	↓	
Late subacute	1 week to months	Methemoglobin	Fe^{3+}	Degraded	↑↑	↑	
Chronic	≥ months	Hemosiderin	Fe^{3+}	Degraded	iso, ↓	↓	↓

Abbreviations: Fe, iron; iso, isointense relative to normal brain; ↑, hyperintense relative to brain, ↓, hypointense relative to brain.

Effect of hematoma evolution on MR imaging appearance of intracerebral hemorrhage

Hyperacute phase

The hyperacute phase of the hematoma is seen immediately following extravasation of blood into the brain parenchyma. At this stage the red cell membrane is intact, and the hemoglobin molecule is normally saturated with oxygen (oxy-hemoglobin). Specifically, the iron atoms contained within the heme portions of the hemoglobin molecule are bound to oxygen. This is the only phase of hematoma in which the iron atoms have no unpaired electrons in their outer orbitals and are therefore "diamagnetic," without exaggerated T1 relaxation or susceptibility effects. The ICH signal characteristics are thus not primarily attributable to iron but instead to the increased spin density of the hematoma relative to uninvolved brain tissue. Hyperacute hematoma appears slightly hypointense or iso-intense on T1-weighted images and slightly hyperintense on T2-weighted images (see Fig. 3); this pattern resembles that of many other pathologic conditions of the brain. Even early in the hyperacute phase, however, there is often deoxy-hemoglobin at the periphery of the hematoma, which appears as a thin rim of T2 hypointensity. This pattern can help differentiate hyperacute hematoma from other brain pathologies [13–16].

Acute phase

The acute phase, which begins within hours of ICH, is characterized by deoxy-hemoglobin. Deoxygenation occurs first at the periphery of the hematoma and progresses toward the center. This pattern appears because intrahematoma oxygen tension is lowest in the periphery, where red cells are adjacent to oxygen-starved tissue, and highest in the center, because red cells do not use oxygen for their metabolism. The iron atoms of deoxy-hemoglobin have five ligands and four unpaired electrons and hence are paramagnetic. Susceptibility effect is present because the iron is compartmentalized within intact red cell membranes, resulting in hypointensity on T2-weighted images that is due to increased T2* relaxation (see Fig. 3). Magnetic dipole–dipole interactions are prevented by the three-dimensional atomic structure of deoxy-hemoglobin, which blocks access of water protons to iron atoms. T1 relaxation times are therefore not shortened, and there is iso- or slight hypointensity on T1-weighted images (see Fig. 3). Sometimes a thin rim of T1 hyperintensity can be seen in the periphery of the hematoma, caused by early oxidation of intracellular deoxy-hemoglobin to intracellular methemoglobin.

Early subacute phase

After several days, the early subacute phase begins. The production of reducing substances declines with failure of red cell metabolism, and the iron atoms are oxidized to the ferric state, Fe^{3+}, to produce met-hemoglobin. Magnetic dipole–dipole interactions can occur because the three-dimensional structure of met-hemoglobin exposes the iron atoms to water protons. This pattern leads to decreased T1 relaxation times and marked hyperintensity on T1-weighted images. Susceptibility effect is present because the red cell membranes remain intact, and hence there is continued hypointensity on T2-weighted images (see Fig. 3).

Late subacute phase

Over several days to weeks, the red cell membranes are degraded, and the late subacute phase begins. Susceptibility effect is lost because met-hemoglobin is no longer locally sequestered within red cell membranes; it freely diffuses within the hematoma cavity, resulting in a locally homogeneous magnetic field. This pattern leads to T2* lengthening, and hence to increased hyperintensity, on T2-weighted images (see Fig. 3).

Chronic phase

Over the ensuing months, the hematoma enters the chronic phase. The degree of hyperintensity on T1- and T2-weighted images lessens as the concentration of met-hemoglobin decreases with protein breakdown. The center of the hematoma may evolve into a fluid-filled cavity with signal characteristics identical to cerebrospinal fluid, or the walls of the cavity may collapse, leaving only a thin slit (see Fig. 3). As proteins are degraded, the iron atoms become liberated from the heme molecules, scavenged by macrophages, and converted into ferritin, which can be recycled. In most cases, however, the degree of iron deposition overwhelms the recycling capacity, with the excess being locally concentrated in hemosiderin molecules. The iron in hemosiderin does not have access to water protons and therefore exerts only susceptibility effect without significant dipole–dipole interactions, leading to marked hypointensity on T2-weighted images. This hypointensity is seen at the rim of the hematoma cavity and may persist indefinitely.

In practice, there is considerable variability in the orderly progression of hematoma signal change over time. The evolution of these signal characteristics may be influenced by a number of factors, including ICH size, oxygen tension, integrity of the blood–brain barrier, the presence of rebleeding, the efficiency of the patient's intrinsic repair processes, and the presence of an underlying lesion such as an arteriovenous malformation or tumor [11]. It is common to see different stages appear simultaneously. For these reasons, "dating" of bleed onset using MR imaging data alone is intrinsically imprecise.

MR imaging pulse sequences and intracerebral hemorrhage appearance

Hematoma signal characteristics are determined by the specific MR imaging pulse sequence applied. Higher magnetic field strength increases sensitivity to susceptibility effects and therefore should allow easier identification of hemorrhage. Fast spin-echo (FSE) sequences are less sensitive to magnetic susceptibility effects, owing to multiple 180° refocusing pulses, whereas echo planar imaging (EPI) and gradient recalled echo (GRE) sequences, which lack a 180° pulse, are more sensitive. Therefore, the use of FSE with relatively low-field-strength magnets, a common situation in clinical practice, is associated with a lesser degree of T2-hypointensity than is that of EPI or GRE sequences on higher-strength magnets [10,17,18].

To overcome these limitations, GRE sequences should be used whenever the identification of hemorrhage is clinically important. The GRE sequence–also known as susceptibility-weighted or T2*-weighted sequence–employs a partial flip angle without a refocusing pulse. In contrast to the use of the 180° spin-echo refocusing pulse, this method does not compensate for signal loss due to magnetic field inhomogeneities, thus producing a stronger susceptibility effect. This pattern increases sensitivity for hematoma detection in the acute and chronic stages, because the already strong susceptibility effect causes extreme hypointensity on GRE sequences (Fig. 4) [10,19]. A relative disadvantage of the GRE sequence, however, is that artifactual signal loss is generated at the boundary of tissues that normally exhibit differences in susceptibility. This signal loss is particularly prominent at the pneumatized sinuses at the skull base and may obscure underlying lesions in those areas.

Small hemosiderin deposits due to chronic, prior asymptomatic hemorrhage, sometimes referred to as "microbleeds" [20], are often only visualized on the GRE sequence. These may provide a clue to otherwise unsuspected underlying amyloid angiopathy, cavernous malformations, or hypertensive microvascular disease [21–23]. Evidence suggests that, although most hemosiderin deposits persist indefinitely, as many as 20% may become unapparent at 2 years [24]. Because most of these deposits are long lasting, the GRE sequence can be used to

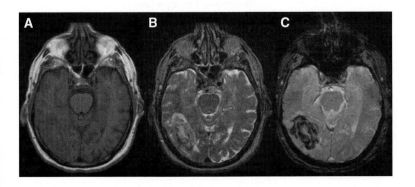

Fig. 4. GRE sequence. T1- (*A*) and T2-weighted (*B*) MR imaging sequences show acute hematoma of the right occipital lobe. Areas of hypointensity are seen on the T2-weighted sequence (*B*), caused by susceptibility effect from intracellular deoxy-hemoglobin. The susceptibility effect is far more conspicuous on the GRE sequence (*C*).

determine the cumulative hemorrhagic "history" of the patient over a prolonged period of time.

Causes of intracerebral hemorrhage

Large cohort studies have identified the following risk factors for hemorrhagic stroke: age, hypertension, African-American or Hispanic ethnicity, smoking, excessive alcohol consumption, prior ischemic stroke, low serum cholesterol, and anticoagulant medications [25]. Age and hypertension account for the greatest risk to the population. It must be recognized, however, that ICH is not a single pathologic entity and may result from a number of diseases with differing pathophysiology and risk factors. It is the responsibility of the radiologist to recognize findings that may support or refute the underlying differential diagnostic causes of ICH (Box 1). Radiologic clues to the cause of ICH may come from the topographic pattern, the signal characteristics, and the presence of other related lesions.

Box 1: Causes of intracerebral hemorrhage

Hypertension
Cerebral amyloid angiopathy
Vascular malformations

  Arteriovenous malformation
  Arteriovenous dural fistula
  Cavernous hemangioma

Hemorrhagic transformation of ischemic stroke

  Related to arterial infarction
  Related to venous infarction

Vasculitis
Moyamoya disease
Coagulopathy

  Related to anticoagulant use
  Related to thrombolytic use
  Thrombocytopenia
  Decreased synthesis of clotting factors
    (eg, hemophilia, liver disease)
  Increased consumption of clotting factors
    (eg, disseminated intravascular
    coagulation)

Brain tumor
Aneurysm

  Ruptured berry aneurysm
  Ruptured mycotic aneurysm

Related to sympathomimetic drug use

  Amphetamines
  Cocaine
  Phenylpropanolamine
  Ephedrine

Trauma

Effect of location on cause of intracerebral hemorrhage

The causes of ICH vary by location. The frequency of primary ICH at different sites, when not due to identifiable structural lesions, is shown in Table 2.

Supratentorial hemorrhages should be stratified into lobar and nonlobar ICH (Fig. 5). "Lobar ICH" is defined as hemorrhage at the superficial part of the brain, where bleeding is centered at the cortico–subcortical boundary. "Deep ICH" is defined as hemorrhage in the deeper internal supratentorial compartment, with the hemorrhage centered principally in the putamen, head of the caudate nucleus, or thalamus. The site of origin can be difficult to determine when the hemorrhage is massive; in cases where both deep and subcortical structures are involved, the site of origin is more likely to be deep.

A population-based study comparing lobar to nonlobar ICH showed that hypertension was a strong risk factor for nonlobar but not lobar ICH (relative risk = 1.0) [26]. Conversely, apolipoprotein E genotype was a strong risk factor for lobar but not nonlobar ICH. The lack of association between hypertension and lobar ICH is notable and suggests that lobar and nonlobar hemorrhage have different causes. Most cases of deep ICH in the elderly are caused by hypertensive vasculopathy [27], whereas most lobar ICH in the elderly is caused by cerebral amyloid angiopathy (CAA). Pathologic evidence of CAA was found in 74% of lobar ICH patients over 55 years of age in a North American cohort [28]. Even among the elderly with hypertension, most lobar ICH was due to CAA [28]. In younger normotensive patients, particularly those aged less than 45 years [29], prevalence

Table 2: Location of primary of intracranial hematoma

Location	No. of cases	%
Lobar	114	35
Striatum (putamen and caudate nucleus)	89	27
Thalamus	64	19
Cerebellum	34	10
Multiple	14	4
Brainstem	12	4
Intraventricular	3	1

Location of ICH in 330 consecutive patients age >18 y with primary ICH admitted to Massachusetts General Hospital between January 2001 and December 2004. Hemorrhages due to trauma, infarction, aneurysm, coagulopathy, tumor or vascular malformations were excluded. ICH in the striatum, thalamus, cerebellum and brainstem was most common (60%); these locations are typical for hypertensive hemorrhage.

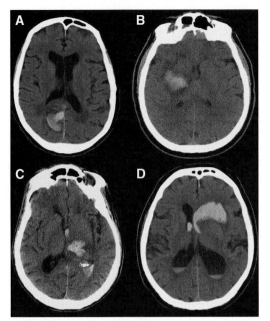

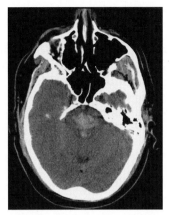

Fig. 6. Brain stem ICH. Hemorrhage is present in the central pons with extension into the aqueduct of Silvius.

hematoma resection may be life saving. Causes of cerebellar ICH include hypertension, arteriovenous malformation, and, rarely, CAA [31,32].

Fig. 5. Lobar and deep hemispheric ICH. (*A*) Lobar ICH in the medial right occipital lobe. (*B*) Putaminal ICH originating from the posterior right putamen. (*C*) Left thalamic ICH dissecting medially into the ventricular system, with hemorrhage in the third and ipsilateral lateral ventricle. (*D*) Left caudate hemorrhage extending laterally into the white matter and medially into the ventricular system.

of both hypertensive vasculopathy and CAA is reduced. Therefore, other causes of deep and lobar ICH, such as vascular malformation, underlying tumor, underlying cavernous malformation, and hypertensive crisis induced by exogenous sympathomimetic drugs, should be considered in this age group.

Brain stem hemmorhage

Brain stem hemorrhage (Fig. 6) most often occurs in the pons. Common causes include hypertensive vasculopathy, arteriovenous malformation, and cavernous malformation [30]. Mortality exceeds 60% when hypertension is the causative agent but is less for vascular malformation [30].

Cerebellar hemorrhage

Cerebellar hemorrhage (Fig. 7) is a neurosurgical emergency because the limited volume capacity of the posterior fossa leads to compression of critical brain stem structures. Typical complications of cerebellar hemorrhage include brain stem compression with cranial nerve palsy, respiratory arrest, upward and downward cerebellar herniation, and ventricular compression with acute obstructive hydrocephalus [31]. Prompt neurosurgical consultation is mandatory; suboccipital craniectomy with

Intraventricular hemorrhage

Intraventricular hemorrhage is uncommon without parenchymal involvement. Before concluding an absence of parenchymal involvement, one should carefully examine the head of the caudate and thalamus, because even minute hemorrhage in these locations may quickly rupture into the ventricular system. Primary intraventricular hemorrhage has been associated with hypertension, anterior communicating artery aneurysm, anticoagulation, vascular malformation, moyamoya disease, and intraventricular neoplasm [33,34].

Multiple simultaneous intracranial hematoma

Multiple simultaneous ICH at different locations is uncommon and has been associated with

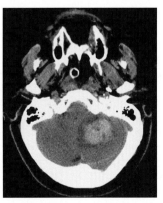

Fig. 7. Cerebellar ICH. Hemorrhage is present in the left lateral cerebellum with mild surrounding vasogenic edema.

coagulopathy, infarction, tumor, CAA, vasculitis, and hypertension [35,36].

Specific causes of intracerebral hemorrhage

ICH due to hypertensive vasculopathy, CAA, or an unknown cause is often referred to as "primary ICH" to distinguish it from ICH due to other defined causes, such as vascular malformation, tumor, trauma, and infarction. The following section describes the imaging features of primary ICH, as well as several important causes of secondary ICH.

Hypertensive hemorrhage

Even in this era of improving blood pressure control, hypertensive vasculopathy remains the most common cause of ICH, although the incidence is declining [37]. Chronic hypertension causes a degenerative cerebral microangiopathy, characterized by hyalinization of the walls of small arteries and arterioles, and ultimately fibrinoid necrosis. Small areas of red cell extravasation may be associated with vessel wall cracking or microaneurysmal dilatation of the arteriole (also referred to as Charcot-Brouchard aneurysms) [38].

ICH caused by hypertension most commonly results from rupture of the 50- to 200-μm–diameter lenticulostriate arteries that arise from the middle cerebral artery stem, leading to putaminal or caudate hemorrhage. It may also result from rupture of small perforating branches that arise from the basilar artery, leading to pontine or thalamic bleeds (see **Figs. 5 and 6**). Larger hematomas often dissect into the ventricles. Hypertensive vasculopathy is also a common cause of cerebellar ICH (see **Fig. 7**).

Cerebral amyloid angiopathy

CAA is caused by the deposition of β-amyloid in the arterial media/adventitia of the small arteries/arterioles in the meninges, cortex, and cerebellum. Affected vessels have eosinophilic walls that stain homogeneously with Congo red and demonstrate apple-green birefringence when viewed under polarized light [39]. The major risk factors for CAA-related hemorrhage are age and the presence of either the apolipoprotein E ε4 allele—which is associated with greater amyloid burden [40]—or the apolipoprotein E ε2 allele, which is associated with more severe vasculopathic change [41,42]. CAA-related hemorrhage is rare in persons aged less than 55 years, although the incidence increases exponentially in subsequent decades [43]. Recurrent hemorrhage is more frequent in CAA-related lobar ICH than in hypertensive ICH [44]. The risk of future recurrence is higher in patients with an apolipoprotein E ε2 or ε4 allele [45], moderate-to-severe white matter lesion burden [46], increased baseline number of MR imaging–detectable hemorrhages

[47], and increased rate of new MR-detectable microbleeds [47].

CAA causes lobar hemorrhage in the cortex or subcortical white matter of the cerebrum [43] or, more rarely, the cerebellum [32]. Dissection into the subarachnoid space is common, whereas ventricular extension is uncommon. Rarely, CAA may present with solely sulcal SAH, thus mimicking aneurismal SAH [48]. CAA is frequently associated with clinically silent microbleeds remote from the symptomatic ICH (**Fig. 8**) [21]. Elderly patients with lobar ICH and multiple lobar microbleeds are highly likely to have CAA; the high specificity of this radiographic syndrome has been incorporated into a rating scale for diagnostic certainty of CAA [28]. The presence of any microbleeds in deep hemispheric locations should, conversely, put the diagnosis of CAA in doubt.

Warfarin-related hemorrhage

The strongest risk factor for warfarin-related hemorrhage is intensity of anticoagulation; age and history of ischemic stroke are additional independent risk factors [49]. The superimposed presence of leukoaraiosis appears to further increase risk [50,51]. A substantial proportion of elderly patients who have warfarin-related hemorrhage have underlying CAA [52]. Most studies have found no difference in hemorrhage location between patients taking and those not taking warfarin [53], although others have found an excess of cerebellar hemorrhage [54].

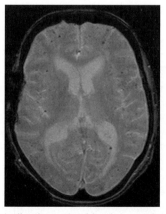

Fig. 8. Clinically silent microbleeds in amyloid angiopathy. A 72-year-old woman presented with cognitive impairment; cortical biopsy showed amyloid angiopathy. MR imaging–GRE sequence showed numerous cortical microbleeds with sparing of the deep hemispheric structures, including thalamus and basal ganglia. These lesions were not seen on the T2-weighted sequence. Sulcal vessels and calcification can also appear as small areas of hypointensity on the GRE sequence and must be distinguished from microbleeds.

Warfarin-related hematomas are more likely to expand [55] and to have fatal outcomes [56].

Vascular malformations

Vascular malformations that can bleed include arteriovenous malformations, arteriovenous dural fistulas, and cavernous malformations (also known as cavernomas). Both venous angiomas (also known as developmental venous anomalies [DVAs]) and capillary telangiectasias are generally benign lesions, which are almost never associated with hemorrhage (although as many as 25% of DVAs are associated with an underlying cavernoma). Arteriovenous malformations and arteriovenous dural fistulas can be difficult to detect without conventional catheter arteriography; suggestive but not sensitive imaging findings include dilated feeding and draining vessels on MR T2-weighted sequences, CT angiography, or MR angiography, as well as patchy enhancement (Fig. 9) [57]. Similarly, cavernous malformations are typically "silent" on all imaging modalities unless they have recently or previously bled. When recent, they may appear as "popcorn"-like lesions on T2-weighted MR images because of the presence of multiple small hemorrhages of different ages arising from the same lesion (Fig. 10). When they are chronic, the hemosiderin from prior macro- or microhemorrhage may only be detectable on MR GRE sequences. These lesions may be multiple and familial [57].

Hemorrhagic transformation of brain infarction

Infarcted brain tissue has a propensity to bleed. A common classification scheme differentiates between hemorrhagic infarction, which does not produce mass effect and is usually asymptomatic, and parenchymal hematoma, which is more extensive and may be associated with neurologic deterioration [58]. Hemorrhage due to brain infarction may be recognized by the presence of surrounding cytotoxic edema conforming to an arterial territory, but it may be difficult to diagnose when early massive hemorrhage obscures the underlying infarct [59]. Venous infarction carries a higher risk for bleeding than arterial infarction, although anticoagulation treatment is typically *indicated*—not contraindicated—in the setting of venous thrombosis [60].

Brain tumors

Brain tumors are associated with neovascularity, incompetence of the blood–brain barrier, and an increased risk for hemorrhage [61]. Tumors with a particular propensity to hemorrhage include glioblastoma multiforme, oligodendroglioma, and certain metastases such as melanoma, renal cell carcinoma, choriocarcinoma, and thyroid carcinoma (mnemonic: MR/CT). Lung cancer is also frequently hemorrhagic [61–64]. In some cases, the tumor may be asymptomatic and unrecognized until presentation with hemorrhage.

The CT and MR imaging characteristics of tumor-associated hematoma are often atypical and complex, because the blood may be of multiple ages and may be admixed with abnormal neoplastic tissue containing cysts and necrosis. Evolution of the MR signal changes is often delayed, possibly because of extremely low intratumoral partial pressure of oxygen, and hemosiderin formation may be absent [65,66]. The location may be atypical for hemorrhage caused by cerebrovascular disease, and there may be multiple simultaneous hemorrhages. The degree of vasogenic edema surrounding tumor-associated hemorrhage is greater than that in primary ICH and persists even into the chronic phase of hematoma [67]. Administration of contrast may reveal tumor enhancement (Fig. 11); the specificity of this enhancement for tumor is reduced in the subacute phase by enhancement of the hematoma capsule. In some cases, hemorrhage may completely obscure the underlying lesion; repeat imaging after hematoma resolution can allow tumor detection.

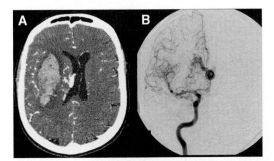

Fig. 9. ICH due to arteriovenous malformation. CT angiogram (*A*) shows a large acute hemorrhage in the right hemisphere, with multiple feeding vessels in the periventricular white matter. There is a large draining vein along the lateral wall of the right lateral ventricle. Catheter angiography (*B*, anteroposterior view of right carotid injection) confirms the presence of arteriovenous malformation.

Ruptured saccular aneurysm

Blood from a ruptured saccular aneurysm enters the subarachnoid space under great pressure and may dissect into the brain parenchyma. Parenchymal hematoma is seen in 4% to 19% of patients with SAH due to saccular aneurysm and is highly correlated with the location of the ruptured aneurysm [68]. The most common locations are the medial frontal

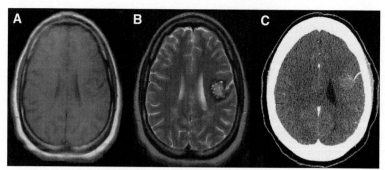

Fig. 10. Cavernous malformation. T1- (A) and T2-weighted (B) MR sequences show a large cavernous malformation in the left frontal lobe. T2-weighted sequence (B) shows a heterogenous central core of variable hyperintensity surrounded by a deeply hypointense rim, caused by hemorrhage of various ages surrounded by hemosiderin-stained tissue. CT angiogram (C) reveals this lesion to be associated with a venous angioma.

lobe adjacent to a ruptured anterior communicating artery or anterior cerebral artery aneurysm (Fig. 12) and the temporal lobe adjacent to a ruptured middle cerebral artery aneurysm. In some cases, the amount of associated subarachnoid blood may be minimal. When ICH is immediately adjacent to the subarachnoid space at the base of the brain or basal interhemispheric fissure, vascular imaging should be strongly considered to exclude saccular aneurysm.

Cerebral contusion

Brain contusion deserves mention because of the potential for misclassification as hemorrhagic stroke when a history of trauma cannot be elicited–for example, in a patient found alone and confused. Contusions frequently occur in the basal anterior frontal and temporal lobes, where the brain is adjacent to the bony floor of the anterior and middle cranial fossa [69]. They may also be seen in the cortex either on the same side as the injury or as contrecoup. Contusions may be multiple and are often associated with other evidence of

trauma, such as skull fracture, subdural hematoma, and epidural or subgaleal hematoma.

Imaging evaluation for hemorrhage in the acute stroke setting

Management decisions in the acute stroke setting rely on the differentiation of hemorrhagic from ischemic stroke. Imaging is required to make this differentiation, because there are no clinical features that reliably predict hemorrhagic stroke [1]. Demonstration of hemorrhagic absence identifies ischemic stroke patients who may be eligible for thrombolysis, whereas demonstration of hemorrhagic presence may, in the future, identify acute ICH patients eligible for medical therapies to prevent continued bleeding. One such therapy currently under investigation is recombinant activated factor VII, which has shown promising results in a phase II study [70].

CT has traditionally been preferred over MR imaging for identification of ICH. CT scanning is faster, less expensive, and more widely available; it can be safely performed in patients with contraindications

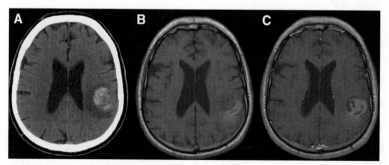

Fig. 11. ICH originating within brain tumor. CT scan (A) shows acute hemorrhage with marked surrounding edema. T1-weighted MR imaging (B) shows hyperintensity within the hematoma, consistent with met-hemoglobin (subacute hemorrhage). Following contrast administration (C), there is a marked increased central hyperintensity on the T1-weighted sequence. Biopsy showed an underlying glioblastoma multiforme.

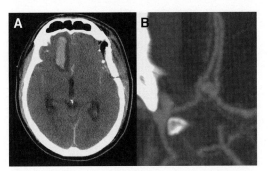

Fig. 12. ICH due to ruptured saccular aneurysm. CT scan (*A*) shows hemorrhage in the right medial basal frontal lobe. Subarachnoid hemorrhage is seen in both sylvian fissures and in the interhemispheric fissure. (A left skull defect with mild pneumocephalus is due to recent craniotomy for aneurysm clipping.) Maximum intensity projection images from the preoperative CT angiogram (*B*) reveal an anterior communicating artery aneurysm as the bleeding source.

to MR, including claustrophobia. Moreover, the sensitivity of conventional MR imaging for hyperacute hematoma detection has been questioned, because the oxy-hemoglobin stage of hemorrhage is isointense to water (see Table 1) [10]. Ample evidence indicates, however, that even in the earliest stages of hemorrhage, deoxy-hemoglobin is present in the lesion periphery, with corresponding hypointensity on T2 and GRE sequences [13–16].

MR imaging has potential advantages over CT in the evaluation of ischemic stroke, both for delineating the extent of infarction with diffusion-weighted imaging (DWI) and detecting the presence of hemorrhagic complications with GRE sequences. MR may be superior to CT for the detection of early hemorrhagic conversion of infarction [71–73], and, in patients who undergo intra-arterial thrombolysis, it may be better at distinguishing between hemorrhage and contrast extravasations (postlysis "blush") into infarcted regions [74].

MR imaging is definitely more sensitive than CT for the detection of chronic microbleeds [71], which have been linked in at least one report to a higher risk of subsequent hemorrhagic transformation of infarction [75]. Although it has been suggested [76,77]—though not proved [78]—that the presence of baseline microbleeds could be a risk factor for major hemorrhage following thrombolysis, this hypothesis has yet to affect clinical management.

Two blinded studies have compared CT and conventional MR imaging with MR GRE sequence for the detection of acute ICH in stroke patients. One study, which used acute ICH cases and selected ischemic stroke controls, found that MR imaging detected ICH with 100% sensitivity and 100% specificity [79]. The other study, which used a multicenter

prospective cohort design, found that GRE MR imaging was more sensitive than CT for both the diagnosis of hemorrhagic transformation and the detection of chronic microbleeds. As noted earlier, however, GRE MR imaging is sensitive but not specific: 3 of 29 acute ICH cases in this study were misclassified as chronic ICH. This lack of specificity may help to explain why inter-rater reliability for detection of ICH was lower for MR imaging ($\kappa = .75$ to $.82$) than for CT ($\kappa = .87$ to $.94$). Moreover, although GRE is sensitive for ICH detection, its sensitivity for SAH detection is dubious at best; the one case of SAH in the study discussed earlier was not detected by GRE [71]. The available data therefore suggest that it is feasible to use MR as the sole imaging modality for acute stroke evaluation, but that expert interpretation should be available and that caution should be exercised when excluding SAH.

The relative role of CT angiography or MR angiography in the emergent evaluation of the ICH patient has not been fully defined. Vascular imaging has the potential to identify secondary causes of ICH that might require urgent surgical treatment, such as saccular aneurysm or vascular malformation [80]. In one study, extravasation of CT angiography contrast into the hematoma, possibly representing active bleeding, was seen in 46% of patients studied at a mean of 4.5 hours and was associated with increased mortality [81].

Summary

Neuroimaging by CT or MR is necessary for the detection of hemorrhagic stroke and provides important data regarding the cause of stroke. Serial changes in the CT and MR appearance of hematoma attributable to temporal evolution must be assessed to assure accurate diagnosis. Emerging evidence suggests that the use of MR imaging alone may be adequate for identifying hemorrhage in acute stroke patients and that GRE MR imaging is superior to both CT and conventional spin-echo MR imaging sequences for the detection of chronic microbleeds and hemorrhagic conversion of infarction.

References

[1] Mohr JP, Caplan LR, Melski JW, et al. The Harvard Cooperative Stroke Registry: a prospective registry. Neurology 1978;28(8):754–62.

[2] Lasner TM, Raps EC. Clinical evaluation and management of aneurysmal subarachnoid hemorrhage. Neuroimaging Clin N Am 1997;7(4): 669–78.

[3] Bergstrom M, Ericson K, Levander B, et al. Variation with time of the attenuation values of intracranial hematomas. J Comput Assist Tomogr 1977;1(1):57–63.

[4] Kasdon DL, Scott RM, Adelman LS, et al. Cerebellar hemorrhage with decreased absorption values on computed tomography: a case report. Neuroradiology 1977;13(5):265–6.

[5] Inaji M, Tomita H, Tone O, et al. Chronological changes of perihematomal edema of human intracerebral hematoma. Acta Neurochir Suppl 2003;86:445–8.

[6] Dolinskas CA, Bilaniuk LT, Zimmerman RA, et al. Computed tomography of intracerebral hematomas. I. Transmission CT observations on hematoma resolution. AJR Am J Roentgenol 1977;129(4):681–8.

[7] Messina AV. Computed tomography: contrast enhancement in resolving intracerebral hemorrhage. AJR Am J Roentgenol 1976;127(6):1050–2.

[8] Ichikawa K, Yanagihara C. Sedimentation level in acute intracerebral hematoma in a patient receiving anticoagulation therapy: an autopsy study. Neuroradiology 1998;40(6):380–2.

[9] Pfleger MJ, Hardee EP, Contant CF Jr, et al. Sensitivity and specificity of fluid-blood levels for coagulopathy in acute intracerebral hematomas. AJNR Am J Neuroradiol 1994;15(2):217–23.

[10] Bradley WG Jr. MR appearance of hemorrhage in the brain. Radiology 1993;189(1):15–26.

[11] Atlas SW, Thulborn KR. Intracranial hemorrhage. In: Atlas SW, editor. Magnetic resonance imaging of the brain and spine. 3rd edition. Philadelphia: Lippincott Williams & Wilkins; 2002. p. 773–832.

[12] Gomori JM, Grossman RI, Goldberg HI, et al. Intracranial hematomas: imaging by high-field MR. Radiology 1985;157(1):87–93.

[13] Linfante I, Llinas RH, Caplan LR, et al. MRI features of intracerebral hemorrhage within 2 hours from symptom onset. Stroke 1999;30(11):2263–7.

[14] Patel MR, Edelman RR, Warach S. Detection of hyperacute primary intraparenchymal hemorrhage by magnetic resonance imaging. Stroke 1996;27(12):2321–4.

[15] Wiesmann M, Mayer TE, Yousry I, et al. Detection of hyperacute parenchymal hemorrhage of the brain using echo-planar T2*-weighted and diffusion-weighted MRI. Eur Radiol 2001;11(5):849–53.

[16] Wintermark M, Maeder P, Reichhart M, et al. MR pattern of hyperacute cerebral hemorrhage. J Magn Reson Imaging 2002;15(6):705–9.

[17] Allkemper T, Tombach B, Schwindt W, et al. Acute and subacute intracerebral hemorrhages: comparison of MR imaging at 1.5 and 3.0 T–initial experience. Radiology 2004;232(3):874–81.

[18] Wolansky LJ, Holodny AI, Sheth MP, et al. Double-shot magnetic resonance imaging of cerebral lesions: fast spin-echo versus echo planar sequences. J Neuroimaging 2000;10(3):131–7.

[19] Liang L, Korogi Y, Sugahara T, et al. Detection of intracranial hemorrhage with susceptibility-weighted MR sequences. AJNR Am J Neuroradiol 1999;20(8):1527–34.

[20] Fazekas F, Kleinert R, Roob G, et al. Histopathologic analysis of foci of signal loss on gradient-echo T2*-weighted MR images in patients with spontaneous intracerebral hemorrhage: evidence of microangiopathy-related microbleeds. AJNR Am J Neuroradiol 1999;20(4):637–42.

[21] Greenberg SM, Finklestein SP, Schaefer PW. Petechial hemorrhages accompanying lobar hemorrhage: detection by gradient-echo MRI. Neurology 1996;46(6):1751–4.

[22] Jeong SW, Jung KH, Chu K, et al. Clinical and radiologic differences between primary intracerebral hemorrhage with and without microbleeds on gradient-echo magnetic resonance images. Arch Neurol 2004;61(6):905–9.

[23] Kato H, Izumiyama M, Izumiyama K, et al. Silent cerebral microbleeds on T2*-weighted MRI: correlation with stroke subtype, stroke recurrence, and leukoaraiosis. Stroke 2002;33(6):1536–40.

[24] Messori A, Polonara G, Mabiglia C, et al. Is haemosiderin visible indefinitely on gradient-echo MRI following traumatic intracerebral haemorrhage? Neuroradiology 2003;45(12):881–6.

[25] Smith EE, Koroshetz WJ. Epidemiology of stroke. In: Furie KL, Kelly PJ, editors. Current clinical neurology: handbook of stroke prevention in clinical practice. Totowa (NJ): Humana Press; 2004. p. 1–17.

[26] Woo D, Sauerbeck LR, Kissela BM, et al. Genetic and environmental risk factors for intracerebral hemorrhage: preliminary results of a population-based study. Stroke 2002;33(5):1190–5.

[27] Fisher CM. Pathological observations in hypertensive cerebral hemorrhage. J Neuropathol Exp Neurol 1971;30(3):536–50.

[28] Knudsen KA, Rosand J, Karluk D, et al. Clinical diagnosis of cerebral amyloid angiopathy: validation of the Boston criteria. Neurology 2001;56(4):537–9.

[29] Zhu XL, Chan MS, Poon WS. Spontaneous intracranial hemorrhage: which patients need diagnostic cerebral angiography? A prospective study of 206 cases and review of the literature. Stroke 1997;28(7):1406–9.

[30] Rabinstein AA, Tisch SH, McClelland RL, et al. Cause is the main predictor of outcome in patients with pontine hemorrhage. Cerebrovascular Diseases 2004;17(1):66–71.

[31] Ott KH, Kase CS, Ojemann RG, et al. Cerebellar hemorrhage: diagnosis and treatment. A review of 56 cases. Arch Neurol 1974;31(3):160–7.

[32] Itoh Y, Yamada M, Hayakawa M, et al. Cerebral amyloid angiopathy: a significant cause of cerebellar as well as lobar cerebral hemorrhage in the elderly. J Neurol Sci 1993;116(2):135–41.

[33] Angelopoulos M, Gupta SR, Azat Kia B. Primary intraventricular hemorrhage in adults: clinical features, risk factors, and outcome. Surg Neurol 1995;44(5):433–6.

[34] Marti-Fabregas J, Piles S, Guardia E, et al. Spontaneous primary intraventricular hemorrhage:

clinical data, etiology and outcome. J Neurol 1999;246(4):287–91.

[35] Maurino J, Saposnik G, Lepera S, et al. Multiple simultaneous intracerebral hemorrhages: clinical features and outcome. Arch Neurol 2001;58(4):629–32.

[36] Tucker WS, Bilbao JM, Klodawsky H. Cerebral amyloid angiopathy and multiple intracerebral hematomas. Neurosurgery 1980;7(6):611–4.

[37] Furlan AJ, Whisnant JP, Elveback LR. The decreasing incidence of primary intracerebral hemorrhage: a population study. Ann Neurol 1979;5(4):367–73.

[38] Fisher CM. Cerebral miliary aneurysms in hypertension. Am J Pathol 1972;66(2):313–30.

[39] Vinters HV, Gilbert JJ. Cerebral amyloid angiopathy: incidence and complications in the aging brain. II. The distribution of amyloid vascular changes. Stroke 1983;14(6):924–8.

[40] Greenberg SM, Briggs ME, Hyman BT, et al. Apolipoprotein E epsilon 4 is associated with the presence and earlier onset of hemorrhage in cerebral amyloid angiopathy. Stroke 1996;27(8):1333–7.

[41] Greenberg SM, Vonsattel JP, Segal AZ, et al. Association of apolipoprotein E epsilon2 and vasculopathy in cerebral amyloid angiopathy. Neurology 1998;50(4):961–5.

[42] McCarron MO, Nicoll JA, Stewart J, et al. The apolipoprotein E epsilon2 allele and the pathological features in cerebral amyloid angiopathy-related hemorrhage. J Neuropathol Exp Neurol 1999;58(7):711–8.

[43] Vinters HV. Cerebral amyloid angiopathy. A critical review. Stroke 1987;18(2):311–24.

[44] Bailey RD, Hart RG, Benavente O, et al. Recurrent brain hemorrhage is more frequent than ischemic stroke after intracranial hemorrhage. Neurology 2001;56(6):773–7.

[45] O'Donnell HC, Rosand J, Knudsen KA, et al. Apolipoprotein E genotype and the risk of recurrent lobar intracerebral hemorrhage. N Engl J Med 2000;342(4):240–5.

[46] Smith EE, Gurol ME, Eng JA, et al. White matter lesions, cognition, and recurrent hemorrhage in lobar intracerebral hemorrhage. Neurology 2004;63(9):1606–12.

[47] Greenberg SM, Eng JA, Ning M, et al. Hemorrhage burden predicts recurrent intracerebral hemorrhage after lobar hemorrhage. Stroke 2004;35(6):1415–20.

[48] Ohshima T, Endo T, Nukui H, et al. Cerebral amyloid angiopathy as a cause of subarachnoid hemorrhage. Stroke 1990;21(3):480–3.

[49] Hylek EM, Singer DE. Risk factors for intracranial hemorrhage in outpatients taking warfarin. Ann Intern Med 1994;120(11):897–902.

[50] Smith EE, Rosand J, Knudsen KA, et al. Leukoaraiosis is associated with warfarin-related hemorrhage following ischemic stroke. Neurology 2002;59(2):193–7.

[51] Gorter JW. Major bleeding during anticoagulation after cerebral ischemia: patterns and risk factors. Stroke Prevention in Reversible Ischemia Trial (SPIRIT). European Atrial Fibrillation Trial (EAFT) study groups. Neurology 1999;53(6):1319–27.

[52] Rosand J, Hylek EM, O'Donnell HC, et al. Warfarin-associated hemorrhage and cerebral amyloid angiopathy: a genetic and pathologic study. Neurology 2000;55(7):947–51.

[53] Hart RG, Boop BS, Anderson DC. Oral anticoagulants and intracranial hemorrhage. Facts and hypotheses. Stroke 1995;26(8):1471–7.

[54] Kase CS, Robinson RK, Stein RW, et al. Anticoagulant-related intracerebral hemorrhage. Neurology 1985;35(7):943–8.

[55] Flibotte JJ, Hagan N, O'Donnell J, et al. Warfarin, hematoma expansion, and outcome of intracerebral hemorrhage. Neurology 2004;63(6):1059–64.

[56] Rosand J, Eckman MH, Knudsen KA, et al. The effect of warfarin and intensity of anticoagulation on outcome of intracerebral hemorrhage. Arch Intern Med 2004;164(8):880–4.

[57] Barnes B, Cawley CM, Barrow DL. Intracerebral hemorrhage secondary to vascular lesions. Neurosurg Clin N Am 2002;13(3):289–97.

[58] Fiorelli M, Bastianello S, von Kummer R, et al. Hemorrhagic transformation within 36 hours of a cerebral infarct: relationships with early clinical deterioration and 3-month outcome in the European Cooperative Acute Stroke Study I (ECASS I) cohort. Stroke 1999;30(11):2280–4.

[59] Smith EE, Fitzsimmons AL, Nogueira RG, et al. Spontaneous hyperacute postischemic hemorrhage leading to death. J Neuroimaging 2004;14(4):361–4.

[60] de Bruijn SF, de Haan RJ, Stam J. Clinical features and prognostic factors of cerebral venous sinus thrombosis in a prospective series of 59 patients. For the Cerebral Venous Sinus Thrombosis Study Group. J Neurol Neurosurg Psychiatry 2001;70(1):105–8.

[61] Little JR, Dial B, Belanger G, et al. Brain hemorrhage from intracranial tumor. Stroke 1979;10(3):283–8.

[62] Kondziolka D, Bernstein M, Resch L, et al. Significance of hemorrhage into brain tumors: clinicopathological study. J Neurosurg 1987;67(6):852–7.

[63] Wakai S, Yamakawa K, Manaka S, et al. Spontaneous intracranial hemorrhage caused by brain tumor: its incidence and clinical significance. Neurosurgery 1982;10(4):437–44.

[64] Mandybur TI. Intracranial hemorrhage caused by metastatic tumors. Neurology 1977;27(7):650–5.

[65] Destian S, Sze G, Krol G, et al. MR imaging of hemorrhagic intracranial neoplasms. AJR Am J Roentgenol 1989;152(1):137–44.

[66] Atlas SW, Grossman RI, Gomori JM, et al. Hemorrhagic intracranial malignant neoplasms: spin-echo MR imaging. Radiology 1987;164(1): 71–7.

[67] Tung GA, Julius BD, Rogg JM. MRI of intracerebral hematoma: value of vasogenic edema ratio for predicting the cause. Neuroradiology 2003; 45(6):357–62.

[68] Abbed KM, Ogilvy CS. Intracerebral hematoma from aneurysm rupture. Neurosurg Focus 2003; 15(4):E4.

[69] Adams JH, Doyle D, Graham DI, et al. The contusion index: a reappraisal in human and experimental non-missile head injury. Neuropathol Appl Neurobiol 1985;11(4):299–308.

[70] Mayer SA, Brun NC, Begtrup K, et al. Recombinant activated factor VII for acute intracerebral hemorrhage. N Engl J Med 2005;352(8):777–85.

[71] Kidwell CS, Chalela JA, Saver JL, et al. Comparison of MRI and CT for detection of acute intracerebral hemorrhage. JAMA 2004;292(15):1823–30.

[72] Nighoghossian N, Hermier M, Berthezene Y, et al. Early diagnosis of hemorrhagic transformation: diffusion/perfusion–weighted MRI versus CT scan. Cerebrovasc Dis 2001;11(3):151–6.

[73] Weingarten K, Filippi C, Zimmerman RD, et al. Detection of hemorrhage in acute cerebral infarction. Evaluation with spin-echo and gradient-echo MRI. Clin Imaging 1994;18(1):43–55.

[74] Greer DM, Koroshetz WJ, Cullen S, et al. Magnetic resonance imaging improves detection of intracerebral hemorrhage over computed tomography after intra-arterial thrombolysis. Stroke 2004;35(2):491–5.

[75] Nighoghossian N, Hermier M, Adeleine P, et al. Old microbleeds are a potential risk factor for cerebral bleeding after ischemic stroke: a gradient-echo T2*-weighted brain MRI study. Stroke 2002;33(3):735–42.

[76] Chalela JA, Kang DW, Warach S. Multiple cerebral microbleeds: MRI marker of a diffuse hemorrhage-prone state. J Neuroimaging 2004; 14(1):54–7.

[77] Kidwell CS, Saver JL, Villablanca JP, et al. Magnetic resonance imaging detection of microbleeds before thrombolysis: an emerging application. Stroke 2002;33(1):95–8.

[78] Derex L, Nighoghossian N, Hermier M, et al. Thrombolysis for ischemic stroke in patients with old microbleeds on pretreatment MRI. Cerebrovasc Dis 2004;17(2–3):238–41.

[79] Fiebach JB, Schellinger PD, Gass A, et al. Stroke magnetic resonance imaging is accurate in hyperacute intracerebral hemorrhage: a multicenter study on the validity of stroke imaging. Stroke 2004;35(2):502–6.

[80] Eshwar Chandra N, Khandelwal N, Bapuraj JR, et al. Spontaneous intracranial hematomas: role of dynamic CT and angiography. Acta Neurol Scand 1998;98(3):176–81.

[81] Becker KJ, Baxter AB, Bybee HM, et al. Extravasation of radiographic contrast is an independent predictor of death in primary intracerebral hemorrhage. Stroke 1999;30(10):2025–32.

MAGNETIC
RESONANCE
IMAGING CLINICS

Magn Reson Imaging Clin N Am 14 (2006) 141–168

Diffusion-Weighted Imaging in Acute Stroke

Pamela W. Schaefer, MD[a,b,]*, Wiliam A. Copen, MD[b], Michael H. Lev, MD[a,b], R. Gilberto Gonzalez, MD, PhD[a,b]

- Self-diffusion and the apparent diffusion coefficient
- The Stejskal-Tanner pulse sequence
- Multiple image acquisitions and measurement of apparent diffusion coefficient
- Diffusion MR imaging for acute stroke
- Ischemic stroke and water diffusion
- Time course of diffusion lesion evolution
- Reliability
- Diffusion-weighted imaging reversibility
- Diffusion tensor imaging
- Diffusion in combination with perfusion MR imaging in the evaluation of acute stroke
  - *Diffusion and perfusion MR imaging in predicting tissue viability*
  - *Diffusion and perfusion MR imaging in predicting hemorrhagic transformation of acute stroke*
  - *Correlation of diffusion and perfusion MR imaging with clinical outcome*
- Stroke mimics
  - *Nonischemic lesions with no acute abnormality on routine or diffusion-weighted images*
  - *Syndromes with reversible clinical deficits that may have decreased diffusion*
  - *Vasogenic edema syndromes*
  - *Other entities with decreased diffusion*
- Venous infarction
- Summary
- References

This review begins by explaining the pulse sequences and postprocessing techniques that are used to create diffusion-weighted images (DWI). Subsequently, the pathophysiology of ischemic stroke is discussed, with emphasis on processes that result in changes in water diffusion. Finally, the use of DWI in the care of patients who have actute stroke is discussed, including optimal integration of DWI with other imaging data to facilitate clinical decision making.

Self-diffusion and the apparent diffusion coefficient

DWI, like almost all other clinical MR imaging techniques, creates images based on signals arising from hydrogen nuclei. In the context of magnetic resonance (MR) physics, hydrogen nuclei often are called spins, because the axis of orientation of their magnetic spins is a critically defining property. Because most spins in living tissue exist as part of

This article was originally published in *Neuroimaging Clinics of North America* 2005;15(3):503–30.

[a] Massachusetts General Hospital, Boston, MA, USA

[b] Harvard Medical School, Boston, MA, USA

* Corresponding author. Division of Neuroradiology, Department of Radiology, Massachusetts General Hospital, 55 Fruit Street, Gray B285, Boston, MA 02114.

E-mail address: pschaefer@partners.org (P.W. Schaefer).

water molecules, signal intensity in MR imaging is determined largely by differences in the local magnetic environments surrounding water.

In brain tissue, or in any other environment with a temperature above absolute zero, water molecules exhibit random motion (Fig. 1) whose rate is determined by D, the diffusion coefficient (or diffusivity coefficient) as expressed in Fick's law. DWI seeks to quantify D, although it cannot do so directly. Instead, DWI pulse sequences measure the change in position of water molecules that occurs during a short time interval, Δ, which lasts only a fraction of a second. During the period Δ, the random motion of each water molecule causes it to become displaced from its initial position by a distance L. The value of L varies randomly among different water molecules, and DWI cannot measure L for any individual molecule. DWI can, however, measure $\bar{L}$, the mean displacement for all water molecules in a particular imaging voxel. $\bar{L}$ is greater when the D is greater, according to the following relationship (Eq. 1), described by Einstein:

$$\bar{L} = \sqrt{2D\Delta} \tag{1}$$

DWI pulse sequences, because they are sensitive to differences in $\bar{L}$, are capable of estimating the D of

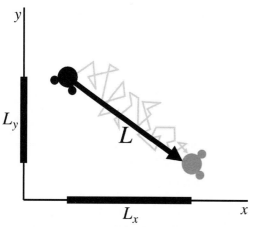

Fig. 1. Self-diffusion. During a period D lasting a fraction of a second, random motion causes each water molecule to become displaced by a path length L. DWI is capable of measuring $\bar{L}$, the average path length traversed by all water molecules within an imaging voxel. The magnitude of $\bar{L}$ is related to the magnitude of the D (see Eq. 1). Note that each individual DWI acquisition is capable of measuring only that component of each path that is parallel to the direction in which the diffusion gradients are oriented. For example, if the diffusion gradients are oriented along the X axis, only L_x, the projection of L on the X axis, can be measured. Therefore, accurate estimation of D requires image acquisition in at least three orthogonal directions.

water in each voxel of tissue. Because this estimate is only an indirect one, it is called the apparent diffusion coefficient (ADC).

The Stejskal-Tanner pulse sequence

Most DWI pulse sequences are based on the work of Stejskal and Tanner [1]. The Stejskal-Tanner pulse sequence represents a small modification to the typical spin-echo pulse sequence that is used most often for clinical imaging. For DWI, long time to repetition (TR) and time to echo (TE) values usually are used, so that DWI has T2 and diffusion weighting. Also, because DWI is sensitive to patient motion, ultrafast spin-echo, echoplanar techniques are used.

The novel aspect of the Stejskal-Tanner pulse sequence that results in images with diffusion weighting is the addition of two pulsed magnetic field gradients to the spin-echo sequence (Fig. 2) [1]. The two gradients have identical direction, steepness, and temporal duration and are separated in time by a period Δ. The 180°-radiofrequency pulse that defines the spin-echo pulse sequence occurs exactly in the middle of D.

The Stejskal-Tanner pulse sequence, like a conventional spin-echo pulse sequence, begins with a 90°-radiofrequency pulse that forces all spins to precess in the transverse plane at the same rate and in phase with one another. Subsequently, when the first of the two magnetic field gradients unique to DWI is turned on, its effect is to alter the rate of precession of each spin temporarily, to a degree that depends on its position along the axis of the field gradient. Then, when the gradient is turned off, all spins again precess at the same rate, but they have acquired differences in phase that reflect their position. In effect, their position has been "labeled" by their phase. For this reason, the first of the extra magnetic field gradients used for DWI sometimes is called the labeling gradient.

During the period Δ, the spins are free to diffuse freely within the voxel, carrying with them the differences in phase that reflect their original positions at the time of the labeling gradient. The 180°-radiofrequency pulse preserves these phase differences, but reverses their signs, so that initially "leading" spins become "lagging" ones.

The second unique aspect of the Stejskal-Tanner pulse sequence is the unlabeling gradient, which is a pulsed magnetic field gradient of the same direction, steepness, and temporal duration as the labeling gradient. The unlabeling gradient once again changes the rate of precession of each spin temporarily, to a degree reflecting its position along the axis of the gradient. Accordingly, when the gradient is turned off, each spin resumes precession at its

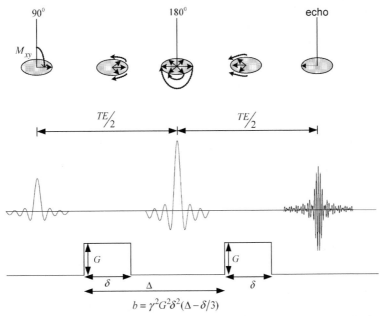

Fig. 2. Stejskal-Tanner diffusion spin-echo sequence. Spins accumulate phase shift during the first gradient pulse. The 180° pulse inverts the phase of all spins. The second gradient lobe induces another phase shift that effectively is opposite to the first gradient pulse as a result of the effect of the spin echo. The phase shifts are identical in magnitude and cancel each other out. For moving or diffusing spins, the translation of the spins to different locations in a time t results in an incomplete refocusing and, hence, the attenuation of the resulting echo. D, diffusion coefficient; γ, gyromagnetic ratio; and G, magnitude of, δ, width of, and Δ, time between the two balanced diffusion gradient pulses.

original rate but has experienced a second, location-dependent change in phase.

For a spin that has not moved since the time of the labeling gradient, the changes in phase induced by the labeling and unlabeling gradients negate one another, and the spin precesses as if the labeling and unlabeling gradients never were present. Spins that have moved along the axis of the gradients during the period Δ, however, accumulate differences in phase, relative to one another, that cause a drop in the overall signal intensity arising from the voxel. The loss of signal intensity is described by Eq. 2.

$$S_{DWI} = S_0 e^{-bD} \tag{2}$$

for which S_{DWI} is the signal intensity on DWI, S_0 is the signal intensity that would have been measured by an identical T2-weighted spin-echo pulse sequence without diffusion gradients, e is the natural logarithm base which equals approximately 2.71828, D is the ADC, and b, the gradient factor, colloquially called the b value, which describes the degree of diffusion-weighting in the image. The gradient factor is a function of the strength and duration of the diffusion gradients and of the time Δ that elapses between them. The user usually specifies the b value that is desired for the pulse

sequence rather than individually designating the strength, duration, and temporal separation of the diffusion gradients.

To summarize, a typical clinical diffusion-weighted pulse sequence is a spin-echo sequence that has been modified to produce T2-weighted images in which signal intensity in each voxel is attenuated by a degree that depends on the ADC in the voxel. Larger values of ADC result in greater degrees of signal attenuation. The degree of T2 weighting in the image is determined by the TR and TE chosen for the pulse sequence, and the degree of diffusion weighting is determined by an exponential function of the gradient factor, or b value, which is specified by the user as part of the pulse sequence.

Multiple image acquisitions and measurement of apparent diffusion coefficient

A single DWI acquired in the manner described previously is not, by itself, able to measure ADC and quantify water diffusion. There are two reasons for this. The first is that in a single DWI, the contributions to signal intensity of T2 and diffusion cannot be separated. In Eq. 2, if a particular voxel exhibits higher-than-normal signal intensity in a DWI (ie, S_{DWI} is large), it is unclear if ADC is low (ie, *D* is small) or if this voxel simply exhibits relatively long T2 and is, therefore, hyperintense on T2-weighted images (ie, S_0 is large). The latter situation often is called "T2 shine-through" and can lead to the misinterpretation of a hyperintense lesion in DWI as representing a focus of low ADC.

The simplest way to differentiate a lesion with low ADC from one that is merely T2 hyperintense is to obtain DWI with at least two different values of *b*. When this is done, Eq. 2 can be solved for *D*, and ADC can be calculated. Then, maps of ADC can be synthesized in which each pixel's brightness is assigned to represent the ADC calculated for the corresponding voxel of brain tissue. A lesion that appears dark on the ADC map is one in which ADC truly is lower than normal.

Although any two or more values of *b* can be chosen, for reasons related to noise propagation, the most accurate estimates of *D* are obtained when only two values of *b* are used: a maximum value on the order of 1000 s/mm^2 and zero. It can be seen from Eq. 2 that the second image, in which *b* = 0, is just a T2-weighted image, acquired using the same imaging parameters and voxel locations as the high–*b*-value DWI.

The second reason why a single high-*b* DWI is incapable of measuring ADC is because of the anisotropy of water diffusion. In a single DWI acquisition, the pulse sequence uses labeling and unlabeling gradients that are oriented in only one direction. Therefore, signal attenuation in DWI does not actually depend on $\bar{L}$, but rather on that component of $\bar{L}$ that lies along the direction of the labeling and unlabeling gradients. This is acceptable if imaging water molecules in a beaker, in which molecules are equally likely to diffuse in any direction and

diffusion is, therefore, isotropic. In brain tissue, however, water diffusion is anisotropic; water molecules diffuse at different rates in different directions. White matter diffusion is especially anisotropic. Because cell membranes and myelin form a significant barrier to diffusion, water molecules are more likely to diffuse in a direction parallel to axonal orientation than in a perpendicular direction. Therefore, a single DWI acquired with labeling and unlabeling gradients oriented parallel to axonal orientation measures ADC values that are relatively high, whereas an image acquired with gradients oriented perpendicular to axonal orientation measures ADC values that are relatively low. In clinical practice, acquisition of a single high–*b*-value image results in patchy areas of white matter hyperintensity that simulate low ADC and can be mistaken for acute infarctions.

The solution to this problem is to acquire at least three separate high–*b*-value images, with labeling and unlabeling gradients applied in orthogonal directions. The resulting images are combined mathematically into a single image, in which signal intensity for each voxel is assigned the geometric mean of signal intensity in the three component images. In the composite image, tissue appears hyperintense because of either decreased ADC or T2 abnormalities but not because of artifacts related to the orientation of the diffusion gradients and white matter tracts.

Diffusion MR imaging for acute stroke

For acute stroke studies, DWI, exponential images, ADC maps, and T2-weighted images should be reviewed (Fig. 3). In lesions, such as acute ischemic strokes, the T2 and diffusion effects cause increased

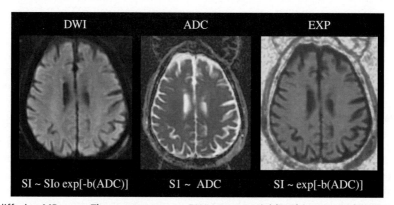

Fig. 3. Typical diffusion MR maps. The appearances on DWI, exponential (EXP) image, and ADC map and the corresponding mathematic expressions for their signal intensities are shown. Image parameters are *b* = 1,000 s/mm^2; effective gradient, 25 mT/m; repetition time, 7500 msec; minimum echo time; matrix, 128 × 128; field of view, 200 × 200 mm; section thickness, 5 mm with 1-mm gap. SI, signal intensity, SIo, signal intensity on T2-weighted image.

signal on DWI and regions of decreased diffusion are identified best on DWI. The exponential image and ADC maps are used to exclude "T2 shine-through" as the cause of the increased signal on DWI (Fig. 4). Truly decreased diffusion is hypointense on ADC and hyperintense on exponential images (Fig. 5). The exponential and ADC images also are useful for detecting areas of increased diffusion that may be masked by T2 effects on DWI. On DWI, regions with elevated diffusion may be slightly hypointense, isointense, or slightly hyperintense, depending on the strength of the diffusion and T2 components. Regions with elevated diffusion are hyperintense on ADC maps and hypointense on exponential images.

Ischemic stroke and water diffusion

Although DWI has proved useful in studying a variety of different diseases, the technique first gained widespread use because of its unparalleled sensitivity in the detection of acute stroke and its specificity in distinguishing acute infarctions from other lesions. These capabilities can be understood by reviewing the patholophysiologic changes that occur in ischemic brain tissue and by considering their effects on the ADC.

Fig. 6A depicts cellular organization in normal gray matter schematically. Approximately 80% of gray matter volume is composed of cells, with the remaining 20% composed of the interstitial space and blood vessels. The intracellular space and the interstitial space differ with respect to their concentrations of various ionic species, and energy-dependent membrane ion pumps maintain these differences. The operation of membrane ion pumps is dependent on cellular synthesis of adenosine triphosphate (ATP) and other high-energy phosphate compounds, which in turn require delivery of oxygen and metabolites.

The collective effect of energy-dependent ion pumps is to extract ions from the intracellular space and deposit them in the extracellular interstitial space. In ischemic conditions, when ATP concentrations and membrane ion pumps, such as the sodium-ATPase pump, begin to fail, there is a net migration of ions from the extracellular space to the intracellular space. Water follows by osmosis, resulting in cellular swelling (see Fig. 6B). This swelling is called cytotoxic edema, which begins within minutes after stroke onset. It results in no change in the mass, volume, or overall water content of affected tissue, because it reflects not an addition of water but a shift of water from the extracellular to the intracellular space. In an acute gray matter infarction, cytotoxic edema increases the fraction of water molecules that are in the intracellular space, from approximately 80% to approximately 95%.

Cytotoxic edema results in a characteristic decrease in ADC and, therefore, an increase in signal intensity on DWI that can be detected minutes after stroke onset. Several theories are proposed to explain this change in ADC. The predominant theory is that water movement is more restricted in the intracellular compared with the extracellular space [2–4]. In the intracellular space, cellular organelles, cytoskeletal macromolecules, and other subcellular structures serve as barriers to the random motion of water molecules. In addition, intracellular metabolite ADCs are reduced significantly in ischemic rat brain. Proposed explanations are increased intracellular viscosity as a result of microtubule dissociation and fragmentation of other cellular components as a result of collapse of the energy-dependent cytoskeleton; increased tortuosity of

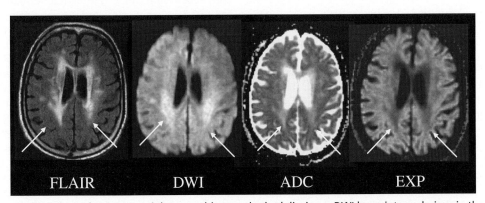

Fig. 4. "T2 shine-through." Seventy-eight-year-old man who had dizziness. DWI hyperintense lesions in the right posterior frontal subcortical white matter and bilateral posterior corona radiata are hyperintense on FLAIR images and ADC maps and hypointense on exponential images. These findings are consistent with elevated diffusion secondary to microangiopathic change rather than acute infarction suggested by DWI alone.

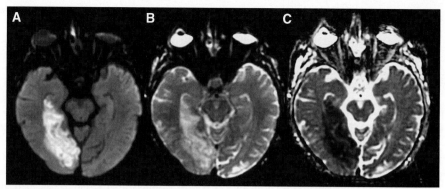

Fig. 5. Example images produced by a diffusion-weighted pulse sequence. (A) DWI, obtained by geometrically averaging the individual high–*b*-value images, demonstrates a large hyperintense lesion in the right temporal and occipital lobes. Because this image is T2 weighted and diffusion weighted, it cannot be determined if this lesion is hyperintense because of T2 prolongation or because of low ADC values or both. (B) T2-weighted image, obtained by arithmetically averaging several images acquired with the diffusion gradients turned off, demonstrates that the lesion does have prolonged T2. (C) In an ADC map, obtained by solving Eq. 2 for ADC on a pixel-by-pixel basis using the values depicted in images (A) and (B), the lesion is darker than surrounding brain tissue and, therefore, has lower ADC.

the intracellular space; and decreased cytoplasmic mobility [5–7].

Furthermore, changes in the extracellular space may contribute to the decreased diffusion associated with acute stroke. With cellular swelling, there is reduced extracellular space volume and a decrease in the diffusion of low-molecular-weight tracer molecules in animal models [8,9]. This is believed to result from a greater tortuosity of the paths that extracellular molecules must traverse to avoid contact with the relatively impermeable cell membranes. Other factors, such as temperature decrease and cell membrane permeability, play a minor role in explaining ADC decreases in ischemic brain tissue [10–12].

Time course of diffusion lesion evolution

Decreased diffusion in ischemic brain tissue is observed as early as 30 minutes after arterial occlusion and progresses through a stereotypic sequence of ADC reduction, followed by subsequent increase, pseudonormalization and, finally, permanent elevation. (Figs. 7 and 8) [13–18]. Initially, the ADC continues to decrease with maximal signal reduction at 1 to 4 days. There is marked hyperintensity on DWI (a combination of T2 and diffusion weighting), less hyperintensity on exponential images, and hypointensity on ADC images. Subsequently, release of inflammatory mediators from ischemic brain tissue leads to vasogenic edema with extravasation of water molecules from blood vessels to expand the interstitial space (see Fig. 6C), where water molecule diffusion is highly unrestricted. Consequently, after approximately 4 days, the ADC begins to rise and returns to baseline at 1 to 2 weeks. This process is called pseudonormalization to reflect the fact that the tissue is irreversibly necrotic despite normal ADC values. At this point, a stroke usually is mildly hyperintense on DWI because of the T2 component and isointense on the ADC and exponential images. Thereafter, the ADC is elevated secondary to increasing extracellular water, cell membrane breakdown and disintegration, gradual phagocytosis of necrotic debris that takes place over months to years, and gliosis. There is slight hypointensity, isointensity, or hyperintensity on DWI (depending on the strength of the T2 and diffusion components), increased signal intensity on ADC maps, and decreased signal on exponential images.

The time course is influenced by several factors. Early reperfusion can lead to pseudonormalization at 1 to 2 days in patients who receive intravenous recombinant tissue plasminogen activator (rtPA) within 3 hours after stroke onset [19]. Furthermore, there are different temporal rates of tissue evolution toward infarction within a single ischemic lesion. In one study, although the average ADC of an ischemic lesion was depressed within 10 hours, different zones within an ischemic lesion demonstrated low, pseudonormal, or elevated ADCs [20]. Stroke type also is an important factor. Minimum ADC is reached more slowly and transition from decreasing to increasing ADC is later in lacunes versus other stroke types (nonlacunes) [18]. In nonlacunes, the subsequent rate of ADC increase is more rapid in younger versus older patients. In spite of these variations, in the absence of thrombolysis, tissue with reduced ADC nearly always progresses to infarction.

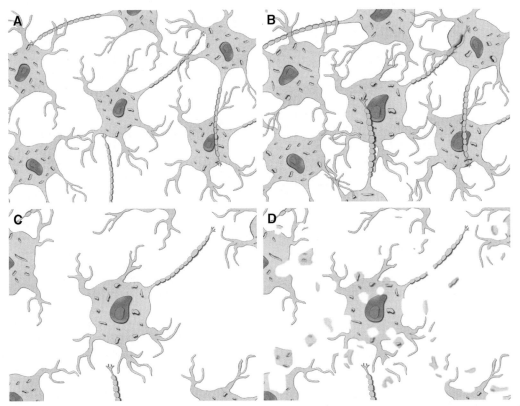

Fig. 6. Stages of ischemic damage to brain tissue. (*A*) Normal gray matter. (*B*) Cytotoxic edema. Within minutes after onset of ischemia, failure of energy-dependent membrane ion pumps causes an accumulation of ions in the intracellular space. Water follows by osmosis, resulting in cellular swelling. This process is associated with a decrease in ADC and accounts for DWI's superior sensitivity in the detection of acute infarcts. (*C*) Vasogenic edema. Release of inflammatory mediators results in efflux of new water from the vasculature, which is associated with an increase in ADC. Vasogenic edema becomes evident on MR imaging within approximately 6 hours after stroke onset and peaks approximately 3 to 5 days thereafter. (*D*) Cellular breakdown. During the ensuing weeks, months, and years, breakdown of cellular membranes and gradual phagocytosis of necrotic debris further remove restrictions on water diffusion, resulting in further increases in ADC.

Reliability

Because detection of hypoattenuation on CT and hyperintensity on T2-weighted and FLAIR MR images requires marked increases in tissue water, conventional CT and MR imaging cannot detect hyperacute infarctions (less than 6 hours) reliably. CT is 38% to 45% sensitive and conventional MR imaging sequences are 18% to 46% sensitive for the detection of hyperacute infarctions [21,22]. For infarctions imaged within 24 hours, one study reports a sensitivity of 58% for CT and 82% for MR imaging [23]. Conversely, DWI are highly sensitive and specific in the detection of hyperacute and acute infarctions [21,24–26]. They are sensitive to the detection of decreased diffusion of water molecules that occurs early in ischemia, and they have a much higher contrast-to-noise ratio compared with CT, FLAIR, and T2-weighted sequences.

Reported sensitivities range from 88% to 100% and reported specificities range from 86% to 100%.

Most false-negative DWI occur with punctate brainstem, thalamic, or basal ganglia infarctions (Fig. 9) [21,24,25,27]. Some lesions are seen on follow-up MR imaging and some lesions are not seen at follow-up but are presumed on the basis of an abnormal neurologic examination. False-negative DWI also occur in patients who have regions with increased mean transit time (MTT) or decreased relative cerebral blood flow (CBF) that demonstrate hyperintensity on follow-up DWI; that is, initially, they have brain regions with ischemic but viable tissue that eventually progresses to infarction.

False-positive DWI occurs in patients who have subacute or chronic infarctions with "T2 shine-through," specifically, a lesion is hyperintense on DWI resulting from increased T2 signal rather than decreased diffusion. Interpreting DWI with

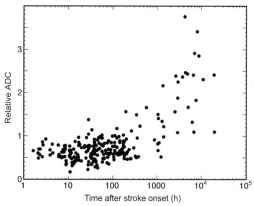

Fig. 7. Time course of ADC in stroke. In the core of an infarction, relative ADC (ADC expressed as a fraction of its normal value) begins to decrease from its normal value of 1 soon after stroke onset. It reaches its minimum within the first day and then begins to increase again, passing through normal values, and ultimately remaining permanently elevated. Note that the X axis is a logarithmic scale. (*From* Copen WA, et al. Ischemic stroke: effects of etiology and patient age on the time course of the core apparent diffusion coefficient. Radiology 2001;221:27–34; with permission.)

ADC maps or exponential images easily avoids this pitfall. In general, acute lesions demonstrate hypointense signal on ADC maps and hyperintense signal on exponential images, whereas subacute to chronic lesions demonstrate hyperintense signal on ADC maps and hypointense signal on exponential images. False-positive DWI also can be seen with other entities that demonstrate decreased diffusion. These include cerebral abscess (restricted diffusion resulting from increased viscosity), tumor (restricted diffusion resulting from dense cell packing), venous infarctions, demyelinative lesions (decreased diffusion resulting from myelin vacuolization), hemorrhage, herpes encephalitis (decreased diffusion resulting from cell necrosis), and diffuse axonal injury (decreased diffusion resulting from cytotoxic edema or axotomy). Because these lesions typically are reviewed in combination with T1, FLAIR, T2, and gadolinium-enhanced T1-weighted images, they usually can be differentiated easily from acute infarctions.

Diffusion-weighted imaging reversibility

DWI reversible tissue refers to tissue that is abnormal on initial DWI but normal on follow-up images. In the absence of thrombolysis or other intra-arterial (IA) recanalization procedures, DWI reversibility is rare. Grant and colleagues could identify only 21 out of thousands of DWI hyperintense lesions in patients who had acute focal neurologic deficits that resolved or appeared smaller on follow-up images and most had causes other than ischemic stroke [28]. The causes were acute stroke or TIA (three patients), transient global amnesia (TGA) (seven patients), status epilepticus (four patients), hemiplegic migraine (three patients), and venous sinus thrombosis (four patients). ADC ratios (ipsilateral over contralateral normal-appearing brain tissue) were similar to those observed with acute stroke (0.64–0.79 for gray matter and 0.20–0.87 for white matter).

In the setting of intravenous or IA thrombolysis, DWI reversibility is observed in up to 33% of DWI abnormal tissue (**Fig. 10**) [29]. A normal appearance on follow-up images may not reflect complete tissue recovery, however. Kidwell and coworkers demonstrate a decrease in size from the initial DWI abnormality to the follow-up DWI abnormality immediately after IA thrombolysis in 8 of 18 patients, but DWI lesion volume subsequently increased in five patients. Several studies demonstrate that ADCs are significantly higher in DWI reversible tissue compared with DWI abnormal tissue that progresses to infarction. Mean ADCs range from 663 to 732 $\times$ 10^{-6} mm^2 per second in DWI-reversible regions compared with 608 to 650 $\times$ 10^{-6} mm^2 per second in DWI-abnormal regions that infarct [29,30]. Animal models also show high correlation between threshold ADCs of 550 $\times$ 10^{-6} mm^2 per second and tissue volume with histologic infarction [31].

Other studies suggest that an ADC threshold for tissue infarction does not exist. In one study of patients who had early reperfusion, less than half of the tissue volume with an initial ADC of less than 60% of normal appeared abnormal on T2-weighted images at day 7 [32]. This is well below the threshold ADCs of approximately 80% of normal tissue (discussed previously). It is likely that duration and severity of ischemia, rather than absolute ADC value, determine whether or not tissue recovers. For example, the degree of ADC decrease correlates strongly with degree of CBF decrease, and the CBF threshold for tissue infarction increases with increasing occlusion time (discussed later) [33,34].

Diffusion tensor imaging

Acquisition of three high–*b*-value images with gradients applied in orthogonal directions plus a fourth image with a low *b*-value (ideally zero) suffice for measurement of ADC. It can be advantageous (although more time consuming), however, to acquire high–*b*-value images with gradients applied in a larger number of directions. If at least

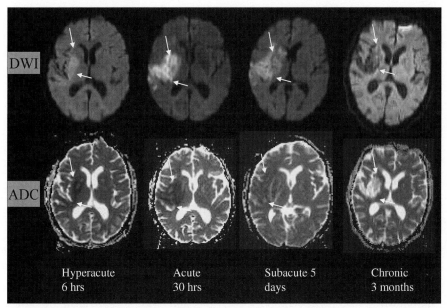

Fig. 8. DWI and ADC time course of stroke evolution. Seventy-two-year-old woman who had acute left hemiparesis. At 6 hours, the right MCA infarction is hyperintense on DWI and hypointense on ADC images secondary to early cytotoxic edema. At 30 hours, DWI hyperintensity and ADC hypointensity are more pronounced secondary to increased cytotoxic edema. At 5 days, the ADC hypointensity is mild, indicating that the ADC has nearly pseudonormalized. This is secondary to cell lysis and the development of vasogenic edema. The lesion remains markedly hyperintense on DWI because the T2 and diffusion components are combined. At 3 months, the infarction is DWI hypointense and ADC hyperintense, indicating elevation of diffusion due to gliosis and tissue cavitation.

six diffusion gradient directions are used, then not only ADC but also the entire diffusion tensor can be calculated. This technique is called diffusion tensor imaging (DTI).

The diffusion tensor is an abstract 3-D object that describes the likelihood of a water molecule to diffuse from a central point in every possible direction (Fig. 11). In a beaker of water, the diffusion tensor is spherical, reflecting the equal likelihood of a water molecule to diffuse in any direction. In white matter, the tensor is elongated and cigar-shaped, reflecting the greater likelihood of diffusion along the direction of white matter tracts. The tensor is represented mathematically by a 3×3 matrix that is axis symmetric and, therefore, has six unique elements (hence, the need for six diffusion gradient directions).

DTI allows the calculation of three parameters that all may be useful in the evaluation of acute ischemic stroke.

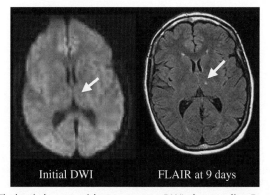

Fig. 9. False-negative DWI. Thalamic lacune without an acute DWI abnormality. Forty-five-year-old woman who had sensory syndrome. Initial DWI demonstrates no definite acute infarction. Follow-up FLAIR image at 9 days demonstrates a punctate hyperintense left thalamic lacunar infarction (*arrow*).

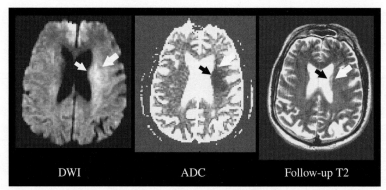

Fig. 10. Acute ischemic stroke with DWI reversibility. Sixty-nine-year-old man who had acute dysarthria and hemiparesis. MRA demonstrates MCA occlusion. He was treated with IA rtPA with complete recanalization. DWI and ADC maps demonstrate acute ischemia involving the left caudate body and corona radiata. Follow-up T2-weighted images demonstrate hyperintensity, consistent with infarction in the caudate body (*small arrow*). Most of the corona radiata (*large arrow*), however, appears normal on follow-up T2-weighted images.

1. The trace of the diffusion tensor [Tr(ADC)] or the average diffusivity, <D> (<D> = $[\lambda_1 + \lambda_2 + \lambda_3]/3$, where λ_1, λ_2, and λ_3 are the eigenvalues or three principal directions of the diffusion tensor) that measures the overall diffusion in a region, independent of direction [35].
2. Diffusion anisotropy indices, such as fractional anisotropy (FA) or the lattice index, that measure the amount of difference in diffusion in different directions [36,37].
3. Fiber orientation mapping that provides information on white matter tract structure, integrity, and connectivity [38–40].

Because of its increased signal-to-noise ratio, measurement of average diffusivity, <D>, has provided new information on differences between gray and white matter diffusion that were not appreciable with measurement of diffusion along three orthogonal directions [41,42]. For example, <D> images can identify regions of reduced white matter diffusion that appear normal on DWI. Furthermore, studies demonstrate that <D> decreases are greater in white matter versus gray matter in the acute and subacute periods, whereas <D> increases are higher in white matter versus gray matter in the chronic period. Although gray matter typically is believed to be more vulnerable to ischemia than white matter, recent animal experiments demonstrate that severe histopathologic changes can occur in white matter as early as 30 minutes after acute stroke onset. Furthermore, reduced bulk water motion from cytoskeletal collapse and disruption

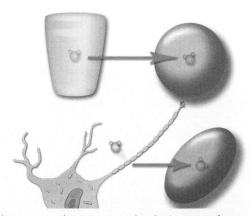

Fig. 11. The diffusion tensor. (*Upper arrow*) For water molecules in a cup of water, diffusion is isotropic, and the tensor is spherical. The graphic representation of the tensor above implies that, during a finite time period, a water molecule is equally likely to move from its original position at the center of the sphere to any point on the surface of the sphere. (*Lower arrow*) For water molecules in white matter, diffusion is anisotropic, and the tensor is cigar-shaped. Water molecules are more likely to diffuse parallel to the axis of traversing axons than perpendicular to that axis.

of fast axonal transport, which do not exist in gray matter, may occur in white matter.

Diffusion anisotropy occurs because water diffusion is different in different directions because of tissue structure [43,44]. Gray matter has relatively low diffusion anisotropy. White matter, however, as a result of highly organized tract bundles, has relatively high diffusion anisotropy, with diffusion much greater parallel, rather than perpendicular, to the fiber tracts [35,43,45,46]. Oligodendrocyte concentration and fast axonal transport also may contribute to white matter diffusion anisotropy. In addition, it is believed that the intracellular compartment is more anisotropic than the extracellular compartment because of the presence of microtubules, organelles, and intact membranes [47,48].

With acute stroke, FA correlates with time of stroke onset [49,50]. In general, FA is elevated in the hyperacute and early acute periods, becomes reduced at approximately 12 to 24 hours, and progressively decreases over time. Because strokes evolve at different rates, however, there is heterogeneity in the change in FA over time within different regions of a single ischemic lesion and between different ischemic lesions [49,50]. Furthermore, the decreases in FA associated with ischemia are significantly greater in white matter compared with gray matter, likely as a result of structural differences [42,50]. In the white matter extracellular space, there are dense arrays of parallel white matter tracts. With acute ischemia, the diffusion decrease is much greater in lambda 1, the eigenvalue that coincides with the long axis of white matter fiber tracts, compared with the other eigenvalues. In the gray matter extracellular space there is a meshwork. With acute ischemia, the diffusion decrease is more similar between eigenvalues.

Yang and colleagues describe three temporally related different phases in the relationship between FA and ADC (Fig. 12). Increased FA and reduced ADC characterize the initial phase; reduced FA and reduced ADC characterize a second, intermediate phase; and reduced FA with elevated ADC characterize a more chronic third phase [50]. In addition, FA inversely correlates with T2 signal change [51]. These changes can be explained as follows. As cytotoxic edema develops, there is a shift of water from the extracellular to the intracellular space, but cell membranes remain intact and there is not a significant overall increase in tissue water. This explains elevated FA, reduced ADC, and normal T2. As the ischemic insult continues, cells lyse, the glial reaction occurs, and there is degradation of the blood-brain barrier, an overall increase in tissue water, predominantly in the extracellular space, occurs. This explains reduced FA, elevated ADC, and elevated T2. Reduced FA, reduced ADC, and elevated T2 may occur when there is an overall increase in tissue water, but the intracellular fraction still is high enough to cause reduced ADC, and the extracellular portion is high enough to cause reduced FA. Other factors, such as loss of axonal transport, loss of cellular integrity, and decreases in interstitial fluid flow, may contribute to decreases in FA over time.

Fiber orientation mapping can provide new information on how strokes affect adjacent white matter tracts. Fiber orientation mapping can detect wallerian degeneration prior to conventional MR imaging and may be useful in predicting motor function in the long term (Fig. 13). One study demonstrates that FA is decreased significantly in the corticospinal tracts in patients who have acute stroke and who have moderate to severe hemiparesis but not in patients who have no or mild hemiparesis at long-term follow-up [52]. Another study of patients who had subacute stroke demonstrates a significant reduction in the eigenvalues parallel to the corticospinal tract at 2 to 3 weeks in eight patients who had stroke and had poor recovery but not in eight patients who had good recovery [53]. In the chronic period, DTI can distinguish between a primary stroke and a region of wallerian degeneration. A primary chronic stroke has reduced FA and elevated mean diffusivity, whereas the corticospinal tract has reduced FA but preserved or only slightly elevated mean diffusivity [54].

Diffusion in combination with perfusion MR imaging in the evaluation of acute stroke

Diffusion and perfusion MR imaging in predicting tissue viability

In the clinical setting, DWI is interpreted in combination with perfusion-weighted images. The most important clinical impact may result from defining the ischemic penumbra, a region that is ischemic but still viable and that may infarct if not treated. Therefore, most investigation is focused on strokes resulting from a proximal occlusion with a perfusion lesion larger than the diffusion lesion (Figs. 14 and 15). Operationally, the diffusion abnormality is believed to represent the ischemic core and the region characterized by normal diffusion, but abnormal perfusion is believed to represent the ischemic penumbra [16,55–60]. Definition of the penumbra is complicated because of the multiple hemodynamic parameters that may be calculated from the perfusion MR imaging data, such as cerebral blood volume (CBV), CBF, MTT, and other tissue transit time measures (time to peak [TTP], relative peak height, and so forth).

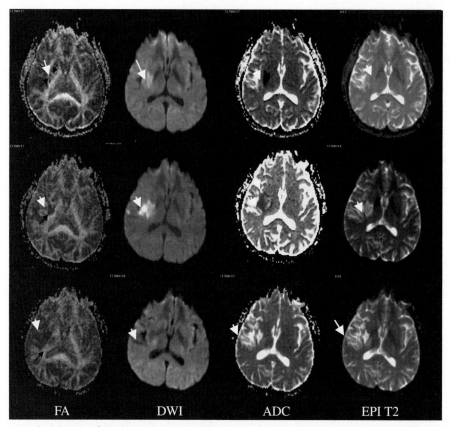

FA   DWI   ADC   EPI T2

Fig. 12. Temporal evolution of FA changes in acute ischemic stroke. An elderly man who had left hemiparesis was examined at 4 hours, 5 days, and 5 months after onset. At four hours (*row 1*), the right putamen stroke (*arrow*) is hyperintense on FA images, hyperintense on DWI, hypointense on ADC images, and not seen on echo planar T2-weighted images. These findings represent the first stage of FA changes in stroke described by Yang and colleagues. After 5 days (*row 2*), the lesion is hypointense on FA images, hyperintense on DWI, hypointense on ADC images, and hyperintense on echo planar T2-weighted images. These findings represent the second stage of FA changes in stroke described by Yang and colleagues. At 5 months (*row 3*), the lesion is hypointense on FA images, hypointense on DWI, hyperintense on ADC images and hyperintense on T2-weighted images. These findings represent the third stage of FA changes in stroke described by Yang and colleagues.

Several articles focus on diffusion and perfusion volumetric data. After arterial occlusion, brain regions with decreased diffusion and decreased perfusion are believed to represent nonviable tissue or the infarction core. The majority of strokes increase in volume on DWI with the peak volumetric measurements achieved at 2 to 3 days post ictus. The initial DWI lesion volume correlates highly with final infarction volume with reported correlation coefficients (r^2) ranging from 0.69 to 0.98 [17,30,61–63]. The initial CBV lesion volume usually is similar to DWI lesion volume and also correlates highly with final infarction volume, with r^2 ranging from 0.79 to 0.81 [30,62,64]. In one large series, predicted lesion growth from the initial DWI to the follow-up lesion size was 24% and from the initial CBV to the follow-up lesion size was 22% (Fig. 16). When there is a rare DWI-CBV mismatch, DWI lesion volume still correlates highly with final infarction volume, but the predicted lesion growth increases to approximately 60% [30]. The CBV, in this setting, also correlates highly with final infarction volume with no predicted lesion growth. In other words, when there is a DWI-CBV mismatch, DWI abnormality typically grows into the size of the CBV abnormality.

Many more strokes are characterized by a DWI-CBF or a DWI-MTT mismatch compared with a DWI-CBV mismatch. In general, initial CBF and MTT volumes correlate less well with final infarction volume than CBV and on average greatly overestimate final infarction volume. r^2 range from 0.3 to 0.67 for CBF and from 0.3 to 0.69 for MTT [30,62,64–66]. Predicted final infarction volume was 44% of the initial CBF abnormality and 32% of the initial MTT abnormality in one study [30]. Another study demonstrates that size of the

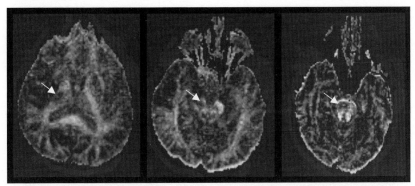

Fig. 13. Wallerian degeneration in the right corticospinal tract 3 months after an infarction in the right MCA territory. FA images demonstrate hypointensity secondary to reduced FA in the right corticospinal tract.

DWI-CBF and DWI-MTT mismatches correlate with final infarction volume. r^2 for DWI-CBF and DWI-MTT mismatch volume versus final infarction volume were 0.657 and 0.561, respectively [64].

In small vessel infarctions (perforator infarctions and distal embolic infarctions) and in whole-territory, large-vessel infarctions, the initial perfusion (CBV, CBF, and MTT) and diffusion lesion volumes usually are similar and there is little to no lesion growth (Fig. 17). A diffusion lesion larger than the perfusion lesion or a diffusion lesion without a perfusion abnormality usually occurs with early reperfusion. Similarly, in this situation, there usually is no significant lesion growth.

More recently, research has focused on defining diffusion and perfusion MR parameter lesion ratios

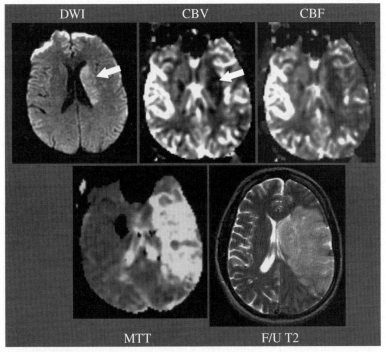

Fig. 14. Diffusion-perfusion mismatch where the infarction grows into nearly all of the tissue at risk of infarction. Fifty-year-old woman who had aphasia and right-sided weakness resulting from a left MCA stem embolus, imaged at 6 hours. DWI demonstrates hyperintensity, consistent with acute infarction, in the left corona radiata and caudate nucleus (*arrow*). The CBV map demonstrates a hypointense lesion similar in size to the DWI abnormality (*arrow*). CBF and MTT images demonstrate much larger abnormal regions (CBF hypointense and MTT hyperintense) involving the left frontal and parietal lobes. The CBF and MTT abnormal but DWI normal tissue reflect the operational ischemic penumbra. In spite of heparin and hypertensive therapy, follow-up T2-weighted image demonstrate growth of the infarction into most of the ischemic penumbra.

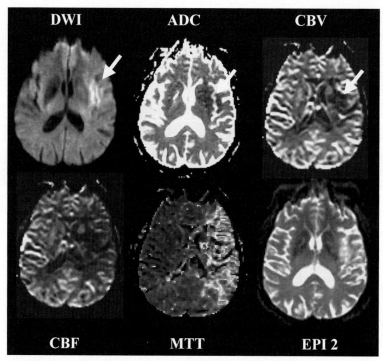

Fig. 15. Diffusion-perfusion mismatch where entire penumbra recovers. Seventy-six-year-old man who had mild right hemiparesis, right facial droop with left MCA stem embolus, imaged at 2 hours. There is hyperintensity on DWI and hypointensity on the CBV maps in the left insula, left putamen, and left inferior frontal lobe (*arrow*). This region is believed to represent the core of ischemic tissue and was abnormal on follow-up T2-weighted images. The CBF and MTT images show larger abnormalities involving most of the visualized left MCA territory. The DWI and CBV are normal but CBF and MTT abnormal tissue is believed to represent the ischemic penumbra. The patient was started on heparin and hypertensive therapy. None of the ischemic penumbra progressed to infarction.

or absolute values in infarction core, penumbra that progresses to infarction, and penumbra that remains viable. Most papers demonstrate that CBF is the most useful parameter for distinguishing hypoperfused tissue that progresses to infarction from hypoperfused tissue that remains viable in patients not treated with thrombolysis or other IA recanalization parameters (Fig. 18). Reported rCBF ratios for core range from 0.12 to 0.44, for penumbra that progresses to infarction from 0.35 to 0.56, and for penumbra that remains viable from 0.58 to 0.78 [67–71]. Assuming a normal CBF of 50 milliliters per 100 grams per minute [72], these ratios translate to 6 to 22 milliliters per 100 grams per minute for core, 17.5 to 28 per 100 grams per minute for penumbra that progresses to infarction, and 29 to 39 milliliters per 100 grams per minute for penumbra that remains viable.

Variability in CBF ratios likely results from several different factors. The data obtained represents a single time point in a dynamic process. One major factor is variability in timing of tissue reperfusion. Jones and colleagues demonstrate that severity and duration of CBF reduction up to 4 hours define

a threshold for tissue infarction in monkeys [34]. For example, the CBF threshold for tissue infarction with reperfusion at 2 to 3 hours was 10 to 12 milliliters per 100 gram per minute, whereas the threshold for tissue infarction with permanent occlusion was 17 to 18 milliliters per 100 gram per minute. Furthermore, Ueda and colleagues, in a study of patients treated with thrombolysis, demonstrate that duration of ischemia affects the CBF threshold for tissue viability for up to 5 hours [73]. Another factor is that normal average CBF in human parenchyma varies greatly, from 21.1 to 65.3 milliliters per 100 gram per minute, depending on age and location in gray matter versus white matter [72,74–77]. Other factors include variability in methodologies, variability in initial and follow-up imaging times, and variability in postischemic tissue responses.

Low CBV ratios are highly predictive of infarction. Elevated CBV is not predictive of tissue viability and CBV ratios for the two different penumbral regions may not be significantly different (Fig. 19). Lesion ratios range from 0.25 to 0.89 for lesion core, 0.69 to 1.44 for penumbra that progresses to

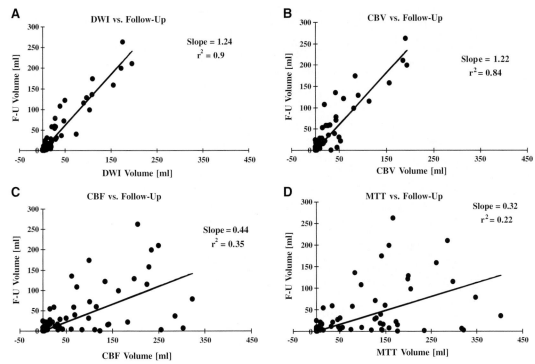

Fig. 16. Initial lesion size versus final lesion size in 81 patients. Scatter plots demonstrate (*A*) initial DWI lesion volume versus final lesion volume, r^2 = 0.9 and slope = 1.24 ± 0.08; (*B*) initial CBV lesion volume versus final lesion volume, r^2 = 0.84 and slope = 1.22 ± 0.11; (*C*) initial CBF lesion volume versus final lesion volume, r^2 = 0.35 and slope = 0.44 ± 0.09; (*D*) initial MTT versus final lesion volume (vertical axis). r^2 = 0.22 and slope = 0.32 ± 0.08. The DWI has the highest correlation to a linear fit. Of the perfusion images, the CBV has the highest correlation to a linear fit. (*From* Schaefer PW, et al. Predicting cerebral ischemic infarct volume with diffusion and perfusion MR imaging. AJNR Am J Neuroradiol 2002;23:1785–94; with permission.)

infarction, and 0.94 to 1.29 for penumbra that remains viable [67–71,78]. The finding of elevated CBV in the ischemic penumbra is in accordance with positron emission tomographic studies demonstrating that initially decreased cerebral perfusion pressure produces vasodilatation and an increase in the CBV in order to maintain constant CBF and oxygen extraction fraction [79]. With further decreases in cerebral perfusion pressure, the compensatory vasodilatation reaches a maximum and CBF begins to fall. CBV initially continues to rise and then falls as capillary beds collapse. Thus, elevated CBV appears to represent an unstable situation and is not sustainable over time.

Some studies demonstrate no statistically significant differences in MTT between infarction core and the two (viable and nonviable) penumbral regions, whereas others demonstrate differences between all three regions or between the viable and nonviable penumbral regions [67–71,78]. Reported MTT ratios for core range from 1.70 to 2.53, for penumbra that progresses to infarction range from 1.74 to 2.19, and for penumbra that remains viable range from 1.65 to 1.66. Previous

studies demonstrated that only DWI normal tissue with a TTP of greater than or equal to 6 seconds is at risk of significant lesion enlargement and that tissue with TTP of greater than 6 to 8 seconds correlates highly with final infarction volume [80,81]. One study reports that a greater proportion of severely hypoperfused (>6 seconds MTT) tissue recovered in patients who have stroke treated with IV tissue-type plasminogen activator (tPA) versus patients who have stroke treated with conventional therapies [82]. One study that evaluated the ability of CBF, MTT, TTP, and relative peak height to predict infarction growth finds that a combination of TTP and relative peak height provided the best prediction of infarction growth (peak height less than 54% and TTP greater than 5.2 seconds had a sensitivity of 71% and a specificity of 98%) [83].

In general, ADC values are significantly different between the core and the two (viable and nonviable) penumbral regions. Some reports demonstrate significant differences between the ADC values for the penumbral regions, whereas others report no statistically significant difference

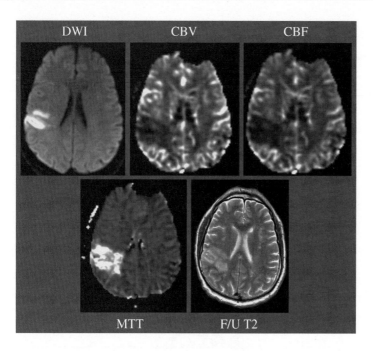

Fig. 17. Diffusion-perfusion match in branch vessel occlusion. Seventy-one-year-old man who had left arm and face weakness. DWI demonstrates an acute infarction in the right inferior parietal region. Defects similar in size are seen on the CBV, CBF, and MTT maps. There is no diffusion-perfusion mismatch. Follow-up T2-weighted image demonstrates no significant lesion growth.

between these regions. In one large study, absolute mean ADC values for infarction core, penumbra that progresses to infarction, and penumbra that remains viable were 661, 782, and 823 × 10⁻⁶ mm²/s, respectively [84]. Other investigators report ADC ratios for infarction core, penumbra that progresses to infarction, and hypoperfused tissue that remains viable of 0.62 to 0.63, 0.89 to 0.90, and 0.93 to 0.96, respectively [67,69].

The aforementioned approaches focused on regions or volumes of tissue. Because there is heterogeneity in diffusion and perfusion parameters within ischemic tissue, Wu and coworkers performed a voxel by voxel analysis of abnormalities on six maps (T2, ADC, DWI, CBV, CBF, and MTT) compared with follow-up T2-weighted images and developed thresholding and generalized linear model algorithms to predict tissue outcome [85]. They found that at their optimal operating points,

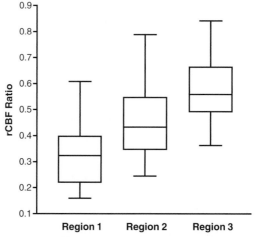

Fig. 18. rCBF ratios. Box and whiskers graph of lesion/contralateral ratio mean values for each patient. Region 1: infarction core with DWI, MTT, and follow-up abnormalities. Region 2: penumbra which infarctions representing tissue that is DWI normal but MTT abnormal and demonstrates infarction at follow-up. Region 3: viable, hypoperfused tissue that recovers representing tissue that is DWI normal but MTT abnormal and appears normal at follow-up. (*From* Schaefer PW, et al. Assessing tissue viability with MR diffusion and perfusion imaging. AJNR Am J Neuroradiol 2003;24:436–43; with permission.)

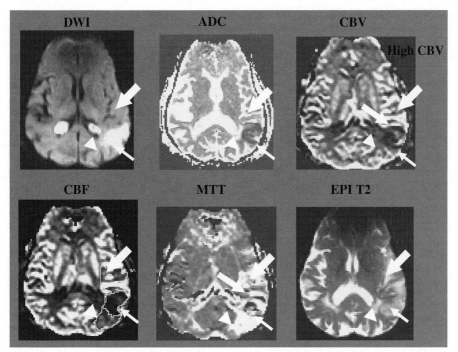

Fig. 19. Diffusion-perfusion mismatch, where a region with elevated CBV but low CBF that progresses to infarction. Eighty-three-year-old woman who had right hemiparesis and aphasia. Three regions are outlined on the CBF maps. The thin white arrow marks infarction core characterized by decreased diffusion, low CBV, low CBF, elevated MTT, and follow-up infarction. The thick white arrow marks penumbra that infarcts which in this case is a DWI normal region with elevated CBV, low CBF, elevated MTT, and follow-up infarction. The white arrowhead marks penumbra that remains viable, which is a DWI and CBV normal region with low CBF, elevated MTT, and normal follow-up.

thresholding algorithms combining DWI and PWI provided 66% sensitivity and 83% specificity and that generalized linear model algorithms combining DWI and PWI provided 66% sensitivity and 84% specificity.

Diffusion and perfusion MR imaging in predicting hemorrhagic transformation of acute stroke

Hemorrhagic transformation (HT) of cerebral infarction refers to secondary bleeding into ischemic tissue with a natural incidence of 15% to 26% during the first 2 weeks and up to 43% over the first month after cerebral infarction [86–89]. Factors that increase the risk of HT include stroke etiology (HT is more frequent with embolic strokes), reperfusion, good collateral circulation, hypertension, anticoagulant therapy, and thrombolytic therapy. Furthermore, in patients treated with IA thrombolytic therapy, higher National Institutes of Health stroke scale (NIHSS) scores, longer time to recanalization, lower platelet counts, and higher glucose levels predispose patients to HT [90].

It is commonly believed that HT results from reperfusion into severely ischemic tissue because more severe ischemia leads to greater disruption of the cerebral microvasculature and greater degradation of the blood-brain barrier. Subsequently, reperfusion into the damaged capillaries after clot lysis leads to blood extravasation and petechial hemorrhage or a hematoma. Many studies describe HT in spite of persistent arterial occlusion [86,91]. HT in this setting may result from preservation of collateral flow. Furthermore, rtPA thrombolytic therapy may aggravate ischemia-induced microvascular damage by activation of the plasminogen-plasmin system with activation of metalloproteinases that may cause degradation of the basal lamina [92–94].

Because ADC values are believed to mark the severity of ischemia, several studies have assessed the value of the ADC to predict HT (Fig. 20). One study demonstrates that the volume of the initial DWI lesion and the absolute number of voxels with an ADC value less than or equal to 550×10^{-6} mm²/s correlates with HT of infarctions treated with intravenous tPA [95]. Another study demonstrates that the mean ADC of ischemic regions with subsequent HT is significantly lower than the mean

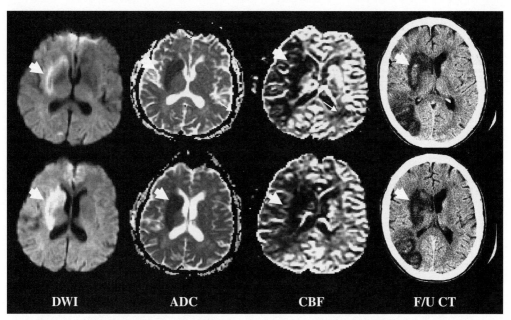

DWI   **ADC**   **CBF**   **F/U CT**

Fig. 20. Acute ischemic stroke with HT. Seventy-six-year-old man who had left hemiparesis, treated with IA rtPA. There is an acute stroke (DWI hyperintense, ADC hypointense) involving the right insula, basal ganglia, and deep white matter. There is marked reduction in ADC and CBF in the basal ganglia and deep white matter (*white arrows*) where there is HT on follow-up CT. Follow-up CT also demonstrates extension of the infarction into the right parietal portion of the ischemic penumbra.

ADC of all analyzed ischemic regions ($510 \pm 140 \times 10^{-6}$ mm^2/s versus $623 \pm 113 \times 10^{-6}$ mm^2/s) [96]. There also was a significant difference when comparing the hemorrhagic ischemic regions with the bland ischemic regions within the same ischemic lesion. A third study demonstrates 100% sensitivity and 71% specificity for predicting HT when infarctions were separated into those with a mean ADC core of less than 300×10^{-6} mm^2/s) versus those with a mean ADC core of greater than 300×10^{-6} mm^2/s) [97].

CBF may be the best perfusion parameter for identifying ischemic tissue that will undergo HT. With single photon emission CT (SPECT) imaging, Ueda and colleagues demonstrate an increased likelihood of HT in ischemic brain tissue with a cerebral blood flow (CBF) less than 35% of the normal cerebellar blood flow [98]. It also is demonstrated that CBF ratios are significantly lower in middle cerebral artery (MCA) infarctions that undergo HT versus those that do not. In one study, all ischemic tissue with a mean CBF ratio of less than 0.18 developed hemorrhage [99]. Other imaging parameters predictive of HT include: (1) hypodensity in greater than one third of the MCA territory on CT [100]; (2) early parenchymal enhancement on gadolinium-enhanced, T1-weighted images [101], and (3) prior microbleeds detected on T2* gradient-echo imaging [102].

Correlation of diffusion and perfusion MR imaging with clinical outcome

Several studies show how DWI can be used to predict clinical outcome. Some studies demonstrate statistically significant correlations between the acute anterior circulation DWI and ADC lesion volume and acute and chronic neurologic assessment tests, including the NIHSS, the Canadian neurologic scale, the Glasgow outcome score, the Barthel index, and the modified Rankin scale [16,63,103–108]. Correlations between DWI and ADC volume and clinical outcome range from $r = 0.65$ to 0.78. In general, correlations are stronger for cortical strokes than for penetrator artery strokes [16,104]. Lesion location may explain this difference. For example, a small ischemic lesion in the brainstem could produce a worse neurologic deficit than a cortical lesion of the same size. In fact, one study of posterior circulation strokes showed no correlation between initial DWI lesion volume and NIHSS [109]. A significant correlation also is reported between the acute ADC ratio (ADC of lesion/ADC of normal contralateral brain) and chronic neurologic assessment scales [16,103]. Furthermore, one study demonstrates that patients who have a mismatch between the initial NIHSS score (greater than 8) and the initial DWI lesion volume (less than 25 mL) had a higher probability of infarction growth and early neurologic deterioration [110]. Another demonstrates that for ICA and MCA strokes, a DWI volume greater than 89 cm^3 was highly predictive receiver operating characteristic (ROC) curve with 85.7% sensitivity and 95.7% specificity) of early neurologic deterioration [111].

Initial CBV, CBF, MTT, and TTP lesion volumes also correlate with NIHSS, the Canadian neurological scale, the Barthel index, the Scandinavian stroke scale, and the modified Rankin scale. Correlation coefficients range from 0.71 to 0.97 [63,66,107,112,113]. Correlations are widely variable and it is unclear which initial perfusion map best predicts clinical outcome. In one study that compares initial CBV, CBF, and MTT volumes with modified Rankin scale, initial CBF volume had the highest correlation [113]. In another study that compares initial DWI, CBV, and MTT volumes with modified NIHSS, Rankin scale, and Barthel index, initial CBV had the highest correlation [114]. In general, patients who have perfusion lesion volumes larger than diffusion MR lesion volumes (diffusion-perfusion mismatches) have worse outcomes with larger final infarction volumes compared with patients who do not have a diffusion-perfusion mismatch. Furthermore, the size of the diffusion-perfusion mismatch correlates with clinical outcome scales. In one study, patients who had a DWI-MTT mismatch larger than 100 mL had a significantly larger lesion growth and a poorer outcome than patients who had a smaller mismatch [107]. Thrombolytic therapy resulting from early recanalization with reperfusion can limit lesion growth and alter these correlations. In one study of patients treated with intravenous rtPA, initial MTT volume correlates with the initial NIHSS but does not correlate with the NIHSS measured at 2 to 3 months [82]. In another study, the best independent predictor of excellent outcome in patients treated with IV tPA is an MTT lesion volume decrease of more than 30% 2 hours after IV tPA therapy [115].

Stroke mimics

These syndromes generally fall into four categories: (1) nonischemic lesions with no acute abnormality on routine or DWI; (2) ischemic lesions with reversible clinical deficits that may have imaging abnormalities; (3) vasogenic edema syndromes that may mimic acute infarction clinically and on conventional imaging; and (4) other entities with decreased diffusion.

Nonischemic lesions with no acute abnormality on routine or diffusion-weighted images

Nonischemic syndromes that present with signs and symptoms of acute stroke but have no acute abnormality identified on DWI or routine MR imaging include peripheral vertigo, migraines, seizures, dementia, functional disorders, and metabolic disorders. The clinical deficits associated with these syndromes usually are reversible. If initial imaging is normal and a clinical deficit persists, repeat DWI should be obtained [27]. False-negative DWI and PWI images occur in patients who have small brainstem or deep gray nuclei lacunar infarctions.

Syndromes with reversible clinical deficits that may have decreased diffusion

Transient ischemic attack

An acute neurologic deficit of presumed vascular etiology that resolves within 24 hours is defined as a transient ischemic attack. Of patients who have transient ischemic attacks, 21% to 48% have DWI hyperintense lesions, consistent with small infarctions (**Fig. 21**) [116–119]. These lesions usually are less than 15 mm in size and are in the clinically appropriate vascular territory. In one study, 20% percent of the lesions were not seen at follow-up; the lesions could have been too small to see on follow-up conventional MR imaging because of atrophy or they could have been reversible [117]. The small DWI lesions most likely are not the cause of patients' symptoms but may represent markers of a more widespread reversible ischemia. Reported statistically significant independent predictors of lesions with decreased diffusion on DWI are previous nonstereotypic TIA, cortical syndrome, an identified stroke mechanism, TIA duration greater than 30 minutes, aphasia, motor deficits, and disturbance of higher brain function [116,117,119,120]. One study demonstrates an increased stroke risk in patients who have transient ischemic attacks and abnormalities on DWI [118]. In another study, the information obtained from DWI changed the suspected localization of the ischemic lesion and the suspected etiologic mechanism in more than one third of patients [117].

Transient global amnesia

TGA is a clinical syndrome characterized by sudden onset of profound memory impairment, resulting in retrograde and anterograde amnesia without other neurologic deficits. The symptoms typically resolve in 3 to 4 hours. Many patients who have TGA have no acute abnormality on conventional or DWI [121]. Other studies, however, report punctate lesions with decreased diffusion in the medial hippocampus, the parahippocampal gyrus, and the splenium of the corpus callosum [122–125]. Follow-up T2-weighted sequences in some patients show persistence of these lesions that the investigators conclude were small infarctions. One study, however, reports more diffuse and subtle DWI

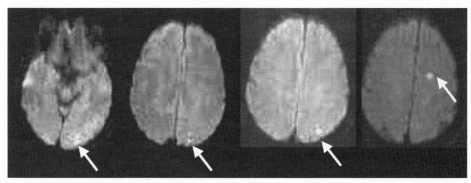

Fig. 21. Transient ischemic attack. Fity-seven-year-old man who had transient right hemiparesis. DWI demonstrate punctate infarctions (*arrows*) in the left occipital, parietal, and frontal lobes.

hyperintense lesions in the hippocampus that resolved on follow-up imaging [126]. The investigators conclude that this phenomenon might be secondary to spreading depression rather than reversible ischemia. A more recent study demonstrates that the detection of DWI changes in TGA is delayed [127]; the investigators observed DWI abnormalities in only 2 of 31 patients who had TGA in the hyperacute phase, but at 48 hours, 26 of 31 patients had DWI abnormalities in the hippocampus. Currently, it is unclear whether or not the TGA patients who have DWI abnormalities have a different prognosis, different etiologic mechanism, or whether or not they should be managed differently compared with patients who have TGA but do not have DWI abnormalities.

Vasogenic edema syndromes

Patients who have these syndromes frequently present with acute neurologic deficits, which raises the question of acute ischemic stroke. Furthermore, conventional imaging cannot reliably differentiate cytotoxic from vasogenic edema because both types of edema produce T2 hyperintensity in gray or white matter. Diffusion MR imaging, however, has become essential in differentiating these syndromes from acute stroke. Whereas cytotoxic edema is characterized by decreased diffusion, vasogenic edema is characterized by elevated diffusion resulting from a relative increase in water in the extracellular compartment [128–130]. Vasogenic edema is hypointense to slightly hyperintense on DWI, because these images have T2 and diffusion contributions. Vasogenic edema is hyperintense on ADC maps and hypointense on exponential images, whereas cytotoxic edema is hypointense in ADC maps and hyperintense on exponential images.

Posterior reversible encephalopathy syndrome
Posterior reversible encephalopathy syndrome (PRES) is a syndrome that occurs secondary to loss of cerebral autoregulation and capillary leakage

in association with a variety of clinical entities [131–143]. These include acute hypertension; treatment with immunosuppressive agents, such as cyclosporin and tacrolimus; treatment with chemotherapeutic agents, such as intrathecal methotrexate, cisplatin, and interferon-α; and hematologic disorders, such as hemolytic uremic syndrome, thrombotic thrombocytopenia purpura, acute intermittent porphyria, and cryoglobulinemia. Typical presenting features are headaches, decreased alertness, altered mental status, seizures, and visual loss, including cortical blindness. The pathophysiology is not entirely clear [130,144]. The predominant hypothesis is that markedly increased pressure or toxins damage endothelial tight junctions. This leads to extravasation of fluid and the development of vasogenic edema. Another, less likely, possibility, based on angiographic findings of narrowing in medium- and large-size vessels, is that vasospasm is the major pathophysiologic mechanism.

T2- and FLAIR-weighted sequences typically demonstrate bilateral symmetric hyperintensity and swelling in cortex and subcortical white matter in the occipital, parietal, and posterior temporal lobes and the posterior fossa. The posterior circulation predominance is believed to result from the fact that there is less sympathetic innervation (which supplies vasoconstrictive protection to the brain in the setting of acute hypertension) in the posterior compared with the anterior circulation. Anterior circulation lesions are not uncommon, however, and frequently are in a border-zone distribution. Acutely, DWI usually show elevated and less frequently normal diffusion (Fig. 22). This is helpful because posterior distribution lesions can mimic basilar tip occlusion with arterial infarctions and border-zone anterior circulation lesions can mimic watershed infarctions clinically and on T2-weighted sequences. Unlike PRES, arterial and watershed infarctions are characterized by decreased diffusion. The clinical deficits and MR abnormalities typically are reversible. Rare small areas of decreased

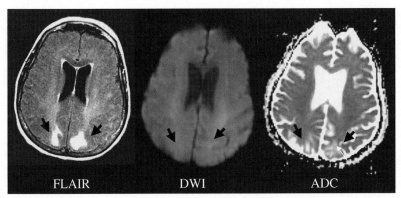

Fig. 22. PRES. Sixty-four-year-old woman who had mental status changes. FLAIR images demonstrate hyperintense lesions in the bilateral parietal occipital regions that suggest acute infarctions (*arrows*). The lesions are isointense on DWI and hyperintense on ADC images. These diffusion MR characteristics are consistent with vasogenic edema.

diffusion that progress to infarction are observed, however, and in some cases, tissue characterized initially by elevated or normal diffusion progresses to infarction [145].

Hyperperfusion syndrome after carotid endarterectomy

In rare cases after carotid endarterectomy, patients may develop a hyperperfusion syndrome [146]. Patients typically present with seizures but may have focal neurologic deficits. T2-weighted images demonstrate hyperintensity in frontal and parietal cortex and subcortical white matter that may mimic arterial infarction. Unlike acute infarctions, however, the lesions have elevated diffusion. Also, there may be increased rather than diminished flow-related enhancement in the ipsilateral MCA. It is believed that similar to PRES, increased pressure damages endothelial tight junctions, leading to a capillary leak syndrome and development of vasogenic edema.

Other syndromes

Rarely, other disease entities, such as HIV or other viral encephalopathies, tumor, and acute demyelination, can present with acute neurologic deficits and patterns of edema on conventional images suggestive of stroke. Similar to PRES and hyperperfusion syndrome after carotid endarterectomy, DWI show increased diffusion.

Other entities with decreased diffusion

Several other entities have decreased diffusion [147]. These include acute demyelinative lesions with decreased diffusion resulting from myelin vacuolization; some products of hemorrhage (oxyhemoglobin and extracellular methemoglobin); herpes encephalitis with decreased diffusion

resulting from cytotoxic edema from cell necrosis; diffuse axonal injury with decreased diffusion resulting from cytotoxic edema or axotomy with retraction ball formation; abscess with decreased diffusion resulting from the high viscosity of pus; tumors, such as lymphoma and small round cell tumors, with decreased diffusion resulting from dense cell packing; and Creutzfeldt-Jakob disease, with decreased diffusion from myelin vacuolization. When these lesions are reviewed in combination with routine T1, FLAIR, T2, and gadolinium-enhanced T1-weighted images, they usually are differentiated readily from acute infarctions. Occasionally, diffusion and conventional imaging cannot distinguish between a single demyelinative lesion or nonenhancing tumor versus an acute stroke. In these situations, spectroscopy may be helpful.

Venous infarction

Cerebral venous sinus thombosis (CVT) is a rare condition that affects fewer than 1 in 10,000 people. The most common presenting signs and symptoms are headache, seizures, vomiting, and papilledema. Visual changes, altered consciousness cranial nerve palsies, nystagmus, and focal neurologic deficits also are common. Predisposing factors are protein C and S deficiencies; malignancies; pregnancy; medications, such as oral contraceptives, steroids, and hormone replacement therapy; collagen vascular diseases; infection; trauma; surgery; and immobilization [148].

The pathophysiology of CVT is as follows [149–160]. Venous obstruction results in increased venous pressure, increased intracranial pressure, decreased perfusion pressure, and decreased CBF. Increased venous pressure may result in vasogenic edema from breakdown of the blood-brain barrier

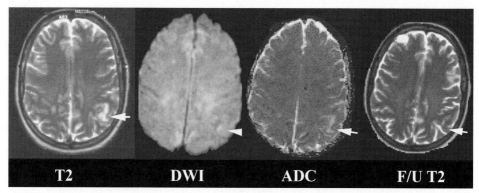

Fig. 23. Thirty-one-year-old woman who had seizures and superior sagittal sinus thrombosis. There is a T2 hyperintense lesion in the left parietal lobe (*arrow*). The lesion is characterized by elevated diffusion (isointense on DWI and hyperintense on ADC), consistent with vasogenic edema and has resolved on follow-up T2-weighted images.

and extravasation of fluid into the extracellular space. Blood also may extravasate into the extracellular space. Severely decreased blood flow also may result in cytotoxic edema associated with infarction. Increases in CSF production and resorption also are reported.

Parenchymal findings on imaging correlate with degree of venous pressure elevation [161]. With mild to moderate pressure elevations, there is parenchymal swelling with sulcal effacement but without signal abnormality. As pressure elevations become more severe, there is increasing edema and development of intraparenchymal hemorrhage in up to 40% of patients who have CVT [162,163]. Bilateral parasagittal T2 hyperintense lesions characterize superior sagittal sinus thrombosis. Transverse sinus thrombosis results in T2 hyperintense signal abnormality in the temporal lobe, and deep venous thrombosis is characterized by T2 hyperintense signal abnormalities in the bilateral thalami and basal ganglia.

DWI has proved helpful in the differentiation of venous from arterial infarction and in the prediction of tissue outcome (Figs. 23 and 24). T2 hyperintense lesions may have decreased diffusion, elevated diffusion, or a mixed pattern [164–166]. Lesions with elevated diffusion are believed to represent vasogenic edema and usually resolve. Lesions with decreased diffusion are believed to represent cytotoxic edema. Unlike arterial stroke, some of these lesions resolve and some persist. Resolution of lesions with decreased diffusion may be related to better drainage of blood through collateral pathways in some patients. In one study, lesions with decreased diffusion that resolved were seen only in patients who had seizure activity [164].

Summary

Diffusion MR imaging has improved evaluation of acute ischemic stroke vastly. It is highly sensitive and specific in the detection of infarction at early

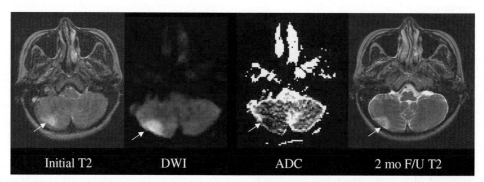

Fig. 24. Superior sagittal, right transverse, and right sigmoid sinus thrombosis. Thirty-one-year-old man who had severe headache and vomiting. MR venogram (not shown) demonstrates thrombosis of the superior sagittal, right transverse, and right sigmoid sinuses. The T2 hyperintense right cerebellar lesion has decreased diffusion (DWI hyperintense and ADC hypointense), consistent with cytotoxic edema (*short white arrow*). The lesion is present at follow-up.

time points when CT and conventional MR sequences are unreliable. The initial DWI lesion is believed to represent infarction core and usually progresses to infarction unless there is early reperfusion. The initial DWI lesion volume and ADC ratios correlate highly with final infarction volume and with acute and chronic neurologic assessment tests. ADC values may be useful in differentiating tissue destined to infarct from that potentially salvageable with reperfusion therapy. ADC values also may be useful for determining tissue at risk of HT after reperfusion therapy. DTI can quantify differences in the responses of gray versus white matter to ischemia. FA may be important in determining stroke onset time, and tractography provides early detection of wallerian degeneration that may be important in determining prognosis. Finally, DWI can determine which patients who have TIA are at risk for subsequent large vessel infarction and can differentiate stroke from stroke mimics. With improvements in MR software and hardware, diffusion MR undoubtedly will continue to improve the management of patients who have acute stroke.

References

[1] Stejskal E, Tanner J. Spin diffusion measurements: spin echos in the presence of time-dependent field gradient. J Chem Phys 1965; 42:288–92.

[2] Sevick RJ, Kanda F, Mintorovitch J, et al. Cytotoxic brain edema: assessment with diffusion-weighted MR imaging. Radiology 1992;185: 687–90.

[3] Mintorovitch J, Yang GY, Shimuzu H, et al. Diffusion-weighted magnetic resonance imaging of acute focal cerebral ischemia: comparison of signal intensity with changes in brain water and Na+, K(+)-ATPase activity. J Cereb Blood Flow Metab 1994;14:332–6.

[4] Benveniste H, Hedlund LW, Johnson GA. Mechanism of detection of acute cerebral ischemia in rats by diffusion-weighted magnetic resonance microscopy. Stroke 1992;23:746–54.

[5] Wick M, Nagatomo Y, Prielmeier F, et al. Alteration of intracellular metabolite diffusion in rat brain in vivo during ischemia and reperfusion. Stroke 1995;26:1930–3 [discussion: 1934].

[6] van der Toorn A, Dijkhuizen RM, Tulleken CA, et al. Diffusion of metabolites in normal and ischemic rat brain measured by localized 1H MRS. Magn Reson Med 1996;36:914–22.

[7] Duong TQ, Ackerman JJ, Ying HS, et al. Evaluation of extra- and intracellular apparent diffusion in normal and globally ischemic rat brain via 19F NMR. Magn Reson Med 1998;40:1–13.

[8] Niendorf T, Dijkuizen RM, Norris DG, et al. Biexponential diffusion attenuation in various states of brain tissue: implications for diffusion-weighted imaging. Magn Reson Med 1996;36: 847–57.

[9] Sykova E, Svoboda J, Polak J, et al. Extracellular volume fraction and diffusion characteristics during progressive ischemia and terminal anoxia in the spinal cord of the rat. J Cereb Blood Flow Metab 1994;14:301–11.

[10] Morikawa E, Gingsberg MD, Dietrich WD, et al. The significance of brain temperature in focal cerebral ischemia: histopathological consequences of middle cerebral artery occlusion in the rat. J Cereb Blood Flow Metab 1992;12:380–9.

[11] Le Bihan D, Delannoy J, Levin RL. Temperature mapping with MR imaging of molecular diffusion: application to hyperthermia. Radiology 1989;171:853–7.

[12] Szafer A, Zhong J, Gore JC. Theoretical model for water diffusion in tissues. Magn Reson Med 1995;33:697–712.

[13] Warach S, Gaa J, Siewert B, et al. Acute human stroke studied by whole brain echo planar diffusion-weighted magnetic resonance imaging. Ann Neurol 1995;37:231–41.

[14] Schlaug G, Siewert B, Benfield A, et al. Time course of the apparent diffusion coefficient (ADC) abnormality in human stroke. Neurology 1997;49:113–9.

[15] Lutsep HL, Albers GW, DeCrespigny A, et al. Clinical utility of diffusion-weighted magnetic resonance imaging in the assessment of ischemic stroke. Ann Neurol 1997;41:574–80.

[16] Schwamm LH, Koroshetz WJ, Sorensen AG, et al. Time course of lesion development in patients with acute stroke: serial diffusion- and hemodynamic-weighted magnetic resonance imaging. Stroke 1998;29:2268–76.

[17] Beaulieu C, DeCrispigny A, Tong DC, et al. Longitudinal magnetic resonance imaging study of perfusion and diffusion in stroke: evolution of lesion volume and correlation with clinical outcome. Ann Neurol 1999;46:568–78.

[18] Copen WA, Schwamm LH, Gonzalez RG, et al. Ischemic stroke: effects of etiology and patient age on the time course of the core apparent diffusion coefficient. Radiology 2001;221:27–34.

[19] Marks MP, Tong DC, Beaulieu C, et al. Evaluation of early reperfusion and i.v. tPA therapy using diffusion- and perfusion-weighted MRI. Neurology 1999;52:1792–8.

[20] Nagesh V, Welch KM, Windham JP, et al. Time course of ADCw changes in ischemic stroke: beyond the human eye! Stroke 1998;29: 1778–82.

[21] Gonzalez RG, Schaefer PW, Buonanno FS, et al. Diffusion-weighted MR imaging: diagnostic accuracy in patients imaged within 6 hours of stroke symptom onset. Radiology 1999;210: 155–62.

[22] Mohr J, Biller J, Hial S, et al. Magnetic resonance versus computed tomographic imaging in acute stroke. Stroke 1995;26:807–12.

[23] Bryan R, Levy L, Whitlow W, et al. Diagnosis of acute cerebral infarction: comparison of CT and MR imaging. AJNR Am J Neuroradiol 1991;12: 611–20.

[24] Lovblad KO, Laubach HJ, Baird AE, et al. Clinical experience with diffusion-weighted MR in patients with acute stroke. AJNR Am J Neuroradiol 1998;19:1061–6.

[25] Mullins ME, Schaefer PW, Sorensen AG, et al. CT and conventional and diffusion-weighted MR imaging in acute stroke: study in 691 patients at presentation to the emergency department. Radiology 2002;224:353–60.

[26] Marks MP, DeCrispigny A, Lentz D, et al. Acute and chronic stroke: navigated spin-echo diffusion-weighted MR imaging. Radiology 1996; 199:403–8.

[27] Ay H, Buonanno FS, Rordorf G, et al. Normal diffusion-weighted MRI during stroke-like deficits. Neurology 1999;52:1784–92.

[28] Grant PE, He J, Halpern EF, et al. Frequency and clinical context of decreased apparent diffusion coefficient reversal in the human brain. Radiology 2001;221:43–50.

[29] Kidwell CS, Saver JL, Starkman S, et al. Late secondary ischemic injury in patients receiving intraarterial thrombolysis. Ann Neurol 2002;52: 698–703.

[30] Schaefer PW, et al. Predicting cerebral ischemic infarct volume with diffusion and perfusion MR imaging. AJNR Am J Neuroradiol 2002; 23:1785–94.

[31] Dardzinski BJ, Sotak CH, Fisher M, et al. Apparent diffusion coefficient mapping of experimental focal cerebral ischemia using diffusion-weighted echo-planar imaging. Magn Reson Med 1993;30:318–25.

[32] Fiehler J, Foth M, Kucinski T, et al. Severe ADC decreases do not predict irreversible tissue damage in humans. Stroke 2002;33:79–86.

[33] Fiehler J, Knob R, Reichenbacher JR, et al. Apparent diffusion coefficient decreases and magnetic resonance imaging perfusion parameters are associated in ischemic tissue of acute stroke patients. J Cereb Blood Flow Metab 2001;21:577–84.

[34] Jones TH, Morawetz RB, Crowell RM, et al. Thresholds of focal cerebral ischemia in awake monkeys. J Neurosurg 1981;54:773–82.

[35] Le Bihan D, Mangin JF, Poupon C, et al. Diffusion tensor imaging: concepts and applications. J Magn Reson Imaging 2001;13:534–46.

[36] Basser PJ, Pierpaoli C. Microstructural and physiological features of tissues elucidated by quantitative-diffusion-tensor MRI. J Magn Reson B 1996;111:209–19.

[37] Shimony JS, McKinstry RC, Akbudak E, et al. Quantitative diffusion-tensor anisotropy brain MR imaging: normative human data and anatomic analysis. Radiology 1999;212:770–84.

[38] Bammer R, Acar B, Moseley ME. In vivo MR tractography using diffusion imaging. Eur J Radiol 2003;45:223–34.

[39] Conturo TE, Lori NF, Cull TS, et al. Tracking neuronal fiber pathways in the living human brain. Proc Natl Acad Sci USA 1999;96: 10422–7.

[40] Makris N, Worth AJ, Sorensen AG, et al. Morphometry of in vivo human white matter association pathways with diffusion-weighted magnetic resonance imaging. Ann Neurol 1997;42:951–62.

[41] Mukherjee P, Bahn MM, McKinstry RC, et al. Differences between gray matter and white matter water diffusion in stroke: diffusion-tensor MR imaging in 12 patients. Radiology 2000; 215:211–20.

[42] Sorensen AG, Wu O, Copen WA, et al. Human acute cerebral ischemia: detection of changes in water diffusion anisotropy by using MR imaging. Radiology 1999;212:785–92.

[43] Pierpaoli C, Jezzard P, Basser PJ, et al. Diffusion tensor MR imaging of the human brain. Radiology 1996;201:637–48.

[44] Reese TG, Weisskoff RM, Smith RN, et al. Imaging myocardial fiber architecture in vivo with magnetic resonance. Magn Reson Med 1995; 34:786–91.

[45] Moseley ME, Cohen Y, Kucharczyk J, et al. Diffusion-weighted MR imaging of anisotropic water diffusion in cat central nervous system. Radiology 1990;176:439–45.

[46] Moseley ME, Kucharczyk J, Asgari HS, et al. Anisotropy in diffusion-weighted MRI. Magn Reson Med 1991;19:321–6.

[47] Le Bihan D, van Zijl P. From the diffusion coefficient to the diffusion tensor. NMR Biomed 2002;15:431–4.

[48] Beaulieu C. The basis of anisotropic water diffusion in the nervous system—a technical review. NMR Biomed 2002;15:435–55.

[49] Zelaya F, Flood N, Chalk JB, et al. An evaluation of the time dependence of the anisotropy of the water diffusion tensor in acute human ischemia. Magn Reson Imaging 1999;17:331–48.

[50] Yang Q, Tress BM, Barber PA, et al. Serial study of apparent diffusion coefficient and anisotropy in patients with acute stroke. Stroke 1999;30: 2382–90.

[51] Ozsunar Y, Grant PE, Huisman T, et al. Evolution of water diffusion and anisotropy in hyperacute stroke: significant correlation between fractional anisotropy and T2. AJNR Am J Neuroradiol 2004;25:699–705.

[52] Higano S, Zhong J, Shrier DA, et al. Diffusion anisotropy of the internal capsule and the corona radiata in association with stroke and tumors as measured by diffusion-weighted MR imaging. AJNR Am J Neuroradiol 2001;22: 456–63.

[53] Watanabe T, Honda Y, Fujii Y, et al. Three-dimensional anisotropy contrast magnetic resonance axonography to predict the prognosis for motor function in patients suffering from stroke. J Neurosurg 2001;94:955–60.

[54] Werring DJ, Toosy AT, Clark CA, et al. Diffusion tensor imaging can detect and quantify corticospinal tract degeneration after stroke. J Neurol Neurosurg Psychiatry 2000;69:269–72.

[55] Kucharczyk J, Mintorovitch J, Asgari HS, et al. Diffusion/perfusion MR imaging of acute cerebral ischemia. Magn Reson Med 1991;19:311–5.

[56] Mintorovitch J, Moseley ME, Cohen Y, et al. Comparison of diffusion- and T2-weighted MRI for the early detection of cerebral ischemia and reperfusion in rats. Magn Reson Med 1991;18:39–50.

[57] Moseley ME, Cohen Y, Mintorovitch J, et al. Early detection of regional cerebral ischemia in cats: comparison of diffusion- and T2-weighted MRI and spectroscopy. Magn Reson Med 1990;14:330–46.

[58] Rosen BR, Belliveau JW, Vevea JM, et al. Perfusion imaging with NMR contrast agents. Magn Reson Med 1990;14:249–65.

[59] Rosen BR, Belliveau JW, Buchbinder BR, et al. Contrast agents and cerebral hemodynamics. Magn Reson Med 1991;19:285–92.

[60] Baird AE, Benfield A, Schlaug G, et al. Enlargement of human cerebral ischemic lesion volumes measured by diffusion-weighted magnetic resonance imaging. Ann Neurol 1997;41:581–9.

[61] Rordorf G, Koroshetz WJ, Copen WA, et al. Regional ischemia and ischemic injury in patients with acute middle cerebral artery stroke as defined by early diffusion-weighted and perfusion-weighted MRI. Stroke 1998;29:939–43.

[62] Sorensen AG, Copen WA, Ostergaard L, et al. Hyperacute stroke: simultaneous measurement of relative cerebral blood volume, relative cerebral blood flow, and mean tissue transit time. Radiology 1999;210:519–27.

[63] Tong DC, Yenari MA, Albers GW, et al. Correlation of perfusion- and diffusion-weighted MRI with NIHSS score in acute (<6.5 hour) ischemic stroke. Neurology 1998;50:864–70.

[64] Karonen JO, Liu Y, Vanninen RL, et al. Combined perfusion- and diffusion-weighted MR imaging in acute ischemic stroke during the 1st week: a longitudinal study. Radiology 2000;217:886–94.

[65] Karonen JO, Vanninen RL, Liu Y, et al. Combined diffusion and perfusion MRI with correlation to single-photon emission CT in acute ischemic stroke. Ischemic penumbra predicts infarct growth. Stroke 1999;30:1583–90.

[66] Barber PA, Darby DG, Desmond PM, et al. Prediction of stroke outcome with echoplanar perfusion- and diffusion-weighted MRI. Neurology 1998;51:418–26.

[67] Schaefer PW, Ozsunar Y, He J, et al. Assessing tissue viability with MR diffusion and perfusion imaging. AJNR Am J Neuroradiol 2003;24:436–43.

[68] Schlaug G, Benfield A, Baird AE, et al. The ischemic penumbra: operationally defined by diffusion and perfusion MRI. Neurology 1999;53:1528–37.

[69] Rohl L, Ostergaard L, Simonsen CZ, et al. Viability thresholds of ischemic penumbra of hyperacute stroke defined by perfusion-weighted MRI and apparent diffusion coefficient. Stroke 2001;32:1140–6.

[70] Liu Y, Karonen JO, Vanninen RL, et al. Cerebral hemodynamics in human acute ischemic stroke: a study with diffusion- and perfusion-weighted magnetic resonance imaging and SPECT. J Cereb Blood Flow Metab 2000;20:910–20.

[71] Grandin CB, Duprez JP, Smith AM, et al. Usefulness of magnetic resonance-derived quantitative measurements of cerebral blood flow and volume in prediction of infarct growth in hyperacute stroke. Stroke 2001;32:1147–53.

[72] Lassen NA. Normal average value of cerebral blood flow in younger adults is 50 ml/100 g/min. J Cereb Blood Flow Metab 1985;5:347–9.

[73] Ueda T, Sakaki S, Yuh WT, et al. Outcome in acute stroke with successful intra-arterial thrombolysis and predictive value of initial single-photon emission-computed tomography. J Cereb Blood Flow Metab 1999;19:99–108.

[74] Rempp KA, Brix G, Wenz F, et al. Quantification of regional cerebral blood flow and volume with dynamic susceptibility contrast-enhanced MR imaging. Radiology 1994;193:637–41.

[75] Frackowiak RS, Lenzi GL, Jones T, et al. Quantitative measurement of regional cerebral blood flow and oxygen metabolism in man using 15O and positron emission tomography: theory, procedure, and normal values. J Comput Assist Tomogr 1980;4:727–36.

[76] Furlan M, Marchal G, Viader F, et al. Spontaneous neurological recovery after stroke and the fate of the ischemic penumbra. Ann Neurol 1996;40:216–26.

[77] Marchal G, Beaudouin V, Rioux P, et al. Prolonged persistence of substantial volumes of potentially viable brain tissue after stroke: a correlative PET-CT study with voxel-based data analysis. Stroke 1996;27:599–606.

[78] Hatazawa J, Shimosegawa E, Toyoshima H, et al. Cerebral blood volume in acute brain infarction: A combined study with dynamic susceptibility contrast MRI and 99mTc-HMPAO-SPECT. Stroke 1999;30:800–6.

[79] Powers WJ. Cerebral hemodynamics in ischemic cerebrovascular disease. Ann Neurol 1991;29:231–40.

[80] Wittsack HJ, Ritzl A, Fink GR, et al. MR imaging in acute stroke: diffusion-weighted and perfusion imaging parameters for predicting infarct size. Radiology 2002;222:397–403.

[81] Neumann-Haefelin T, Wittsack HJ, Wenserski F, et al. Diffusion and perfusion-weighted MRI. The DWI/PWI mismatch region in acute stroke. Stroke 1999;8:1591–7.

[82] Parsons MW, Barber PA, Chalk J, et al. Diffusion- and perfusion-weighted MRI response to thrombolysis in stroke. Ann Neurol 2002;51: 28–37.

[83] Grandin CB, Duprez TP, Smith AM, et al. Which MR-derived perfusion parameters are the best predictors of infarct growth in hyperacute stroke? Comparative study between relative and quantitative measurements. Radiology 2002;223:361–70.

[84] Oppenheim C, Grandin C, Samson Y, et al. Is there an apparent diffusion coefficient threshold in predicting tissue viability in hyperacute stroke? Stroke 2001;32:2486–91.

[85] Wu O, et al. Predicting tissue outcome in acute human cerebral ischemia using combined diffusion- and perfusion-weighted MR imaging. Stroke 2001;32:933–42.

[86] Horowitz SH, Zito JL, Donnarumma R, et al. Computed tomographic-angiographic findings within the first five hours of cerebral infarction. Stroke 1991;22:1245–53.

[87] Hornig CR, Dorndorf W, Agnoli AL. Hemorrhagic cerebral infarction—a prospective study. Stroke 1986;17:179–85.

[88] Hakim AM, Ryder-Cooke A, Melanson D. Sequential computerized tomographic appearance of strokes. Stroke 1983;14:893–7.

[89] Calandre L, Ortega JF, Bermejo F. Anticoagulation and hemorrhagic infarction in cerebral embolism secondary to rheumatic heart disease. Arch Neurol 1984;41:1152–4.

[90] Kidwell CS, Saver JL, Carneado J, et al. Predictors of hemorrhagic transformation in patients receiving intra-arterial thrombolysis. Stroke 2002;33:717–24.

[91] Ogata J, Yutani C, Imakita M, et al. Hemorrhagic infarct of the brain without a reopening of the occluded arteries in cardioembolic stroke. Stroke 1989;20:876–83.

[92] Lijnen HR, Silence J, Lemmens G, et al. Regulation of gelatinase activity in mice with targeted inactivation of components of the plasminogen/plasmin system. Thromb Haemost 1998;79: 1171–6.

[93] Liotta LA, Goldfarb RH, Brundage R, et al. Effect of plasminogen activator (urokinase), plasmin, and thrombin on glycoprotein and collagenous components of basement membrane. Cancer Res 1981;41(11 Pt 1):4629–36.

[94] Carmeliet P, Moons L, Lijnen R, et al. Urokinase-generated plasmin activates matrix metalloproteinases during aneurysm formation. Nat Genet 1997;17:439–44.

[95] Selim M, Fink JN, Kumar S, et al. Predictors of hemorrhagic transformation after intravenous recombinant tissue plasminogen activator: prognostic value of the initial apparent diffusion coefficient and diffusion-weighted lesion volume. Stroke 2002;33:2047–52.

[96] Tong DC, Adami A, Moseley ME, et al. Prediction of hemorrhagic transformation following acute stroke: role of diffusion- and perfusion-weighted magnetic resonance imaging. Arch Neurol 2001;58:587–93.

[97] Oppenheim C, Samson Y, Dormont D, et al. DWI prediction of symptomatic hemorrhagic transformation in acute MCA infarct. J Neuroradiol 2002;29:6–13.

[98] Ueda T, Hatakeyama T, Kumon Y, et al. Evaluation of risk of hemorrhagic transformation in local intra-arterial thrombolysis in acute ischemic stroke by initial SPECT. Stroke 1994;25: 298–303.

[99] Schaefer PW, Roccatagliata L, Schwamm L, et al. Assessing hemorrhagic transformation with diffusion and perfusion MR imaging. In: Book of abstracts of the 41st annual meeting of the American Society of Neuroradiology, Washington, DC April 28–May 2, 2003.

[100] von Kummer R, Allen KL, Holle R, et al. Acute stroke: usefulness of early CT findings before thrombolytic therapy. Radiology 1997;205: 327–33.

[101] Vo KD, Santiago F, Lin W, et al. MR imaging enhancement patterns as predictors of hemorrhagic transformation in acute ischemic stroke. AJNR Am J Neuroradiol 2003;24:674–9.

[102] Kidwell CS, Saver JL, Villablanca JP, et al. Magnetic resonance imaging detection of microbleeds before thrombolysis: an emerging application. Stroke 2002;33:95–8.

[103] van Everdingen KJ, van der Grond, Kappelle LJ, et al. Diffusion-weighted magnetic resonance imaging in acute stroke. Stroke 1998;29: 1783–90.

[104] Lovblad KO, Baird AE, Schlaug G, et al. Ischemic lesion volumes in acute stroke by diffusion-weighted magnetic resonance imaging correlate with clinical outcome. Ann Neurol 1997;42:164–70.

[105] Engelter S, Provenzale JM, Petrella JR, et al. Infarct volume on apparent diffusion coefficient maps correlates with length of stay and outcome after middle cerebral artery stroke. Cerebrovasc Dis 2003;15:188–91.

[106] Nighoghossian N, Hermier M, Adeleine P, et al. Baseline magnetic resonance imaging parameters and stroke outcome in patients treated by intravenous tissue plasminogen activator. Stroke 2003;34:458–63.

[107] Rohl L, Geday J, Ostergaard L, et al. Correlation between diffusion- and perfusion-weighted MRI and neurological deficit measured by the Scandinavian Stroke Scale and Barthel Index in hyperacute subcortical stroke (< or = 6 hours). Cerebrovasc Dis 2001;12:203–13.

[108] Thijs V, Lausberg M, Beaulieu C, et al. Is early ischemic lesion volume on diffusion-weighted imaging an independent predictor of stroke outcome? A multivariable analysis. Stroke 2000;31:2597–602.

[109] Engelter S, Wetzel S, Radue E, et al. The clinical signifcance of diffusion-weighted MR imaging

in infratentorial strokes. Neurology 2004;62: 474–80.

[110] Davalos A, et al. The clinical-DWI mismatch: a new diagnostic approach to the brain tissue at risk of infarction. Neurology 2004;62: 2187–92.

[111] Arenillas J, Rovira A, Molina C, et al. Prediction of early neurologic deterioration using diffusion- and perfusion- weighted imaging in hyperacute middle cerebral artery stroke. Stroke 2002; 33:2197–203.

[112] Baird AE, Lovblad KO, Dashe JF, et al. Clinical correlations of diffusion and perfusion lesion volumes in acute ischemic stroke. Cerebrovasc Dis 2000;10:441–8.

[113] Parsons MW, Yang Q, Barber PA, et al. Perfusion magnetic resonance imaging maps in hyperacute stroke: relative cerebral blood flow most accurately identifies tissue destined to infarct. Stroke 2001;32:1581–7.

[114] Kluytmans M, van Everdingen KJ, Kappelle LJ, et al. Prognostic value of perfusion- and diffusion-weighted MR imaging in first 3 days of stroke. Eur Radiol 2000;10:1434–41.

[115] Chalela JA, Kang DW, Luby M, et al. Early magnetic resonance imaging findings in patients receiving tissue plasminogen activator predict outcome: insights into the pathophysiology of acute stroke in the thrombolysis era. Ann Neurol 2004;55:105–12.

[116] Ay H, Oliveira-Filho J, Buonanno FS, et al. 'Footprints' of transient ischemic attacks: a diffusion-weighted MRI study. Cerebrovasc Dis 2002;14: 177–86.

[117] Kidwell CS, Alger JR, Di Salle F, et al. Diffusion MRI in patients with transient ischemic attacks. Stroke 1999;30:1174–80.

[118] Purroy F, Montaner J, Rovira A, et al. Higher risk of further vascular events among transient ischemic attack patients with diffusion-weighted imaging acute lesions. Stroke 2004;35(10): 2313–9.

[119] Crisostomo R, Garcia M, Tong D. Detection of diffusion-weighted MRI abnormalities in patients with transient ischemic attack: correlation wsith clinical characteristics. Stroke 2003;34:932–7.

[120] Inatomi Y, Kimura K, Yonehara T, et al. DWI abnormalities and clinical characteristics in TIA patients. Neurology 2004;62:376–80.

[121] Huber R, Aschoff AJ, Ludolph AC, et al. Transient Global Amnesia. Evidence against vascular ischemic etiology from diffusion weighted imaging. J Neurol 2002;249:1520–4.

[122] Saito K, Kimura K, Minematsu K, et al. Transient global amnesia associated with an acute infarction in the retrosplenium of the corpus callosum. J Neurol Sci 2003;210:95–7.

[123] Matsui M, Imamura T, Sakamoto S, et al. Transient global amnesia: increased signal intensity in the right hippocampus on diffusion-weighted magnetic resonance imaging. Neuroradiology 2002;44:235–8.

[124] Ay H, Furie KL, Yamada K, et al. Diffusion-weighted MRI characterizes the ischemic lesion in transient global amnesia. Neurology 1998; 51:901–3.

[125] Greer DM, Schaefer PW, Schwamm LH. Unilateral temporal lobe stroke causing ischemic transient global amnesia: role for diffusion-weighted imaging in the initial evaluation. J Neuroimaging 2001;11:317–9.

[126] Woolfenden AR, O'Brien MW, Schwartzberg RE, et al. Diffusion-weighted MRI in transient global amnesia precipitated by cerebral angiography. Stroke 1997;28:2311–4.

[127] Sedlaczek O, Hirsch J, Grips E, et al. Detection of delayed focal MR changes in the lateral hippocampus in transient global amnesia. Neurology 2004;62:2165–70.

[128] Ebisu T, Naruse S, Horikawa Y, et al. Discrimination between different types of white matter edema with diffusion-weighted MR imaging. J Magn Reson Imaging 1993;3(6):863–8.

[129] Schaefer PW, Buonanno FS, Gonzalez RG, et al. Diffusion-weighted imaging discriminates between cytotoxic and vasogenic edema in a patient with eclampsia. Stroke 1997;28:1082–5.

[130] Schwartz RB, Mulkern RV, Gudbjartsson H, et al. Diffusion-weighted MR imaging in hypertensive encephalopathy: clues to pathogenesis. AJNR Am J Neuroradiol 1998;19:859–62.

[131] Hinchey J, Nagasaki A, Nakamura K, et al. A reversible posterior leukoencephalopathy syndrome. N Engl J Med 1996;334:494–500.

[132] Nakazato T, et al. Reversible posterior leukoencephalopathy syndrome associated with tacrolimus therapy. Intern Med 2003;42:624–5.

[133] Henderson RD, Rajah H, Nicol AJ, et al. Posterior leukoencephalopathy following intrathecal chemotherapy with MRA-documented vasospasm. Neurology 2003;60:326–8.

[134] Sylvester SL, Diaz LA, Port JD, et al. Reversible posterior leukoencephalopathy in an HIV-infected patient with thrombotic thrombocytopenic purpura. Scand J Infect Dis 2002;34:706–9.

[135] Utz N, Kinkel B, Hedde JP, et al. MR imaging of acute intermittent porphyria mimicking reversible posterior leukoencephalopathy syndrome. Neuroradiology 2001;43:1059–62.

[136] Edwards MJ, Walker R, Vinnicombe S, et al. Reversible posterior leukoencephalopathy syndrome following CHOP chemotherapy for diffuse large B-cell lymphoma. Ann Oncol 2001;12:1327–9.

[137] Soylu A, Kavukcu S, Turkmen M, et al. Posterior leukoencephalopathy syndrome in poststreptococcal acute glomerulonephritis. Pediatr Nephrol 2001;16:601–3.

[138] Ikeda M, Ito S, Hataya H, et al. Reversible posterior leukoencephalopathy in a patient with minimal-change nephrotic syndrome. Am J Kidney Dis 2001;37(4):E30.

[139] Kamar N, Kany M, Bories P, et al. Reversible posterior leukoencephalopathy syndrome in

hepatitis C virus-positive long-term hemodialysis patients. Am J Kidney Dis 2001;37:E29.

[140] Honkaniemi J, Kahara V, Dastidar P, et al. Reversible posterior leukoencephalopathy after combination chemotherapy. Neuroradiology 2000;42:895–9.

[141] Taylor MB, Jackson A, Weller JM. Dynamic susceptibility contrast enhanced MRI in reversible posterior leukoencephalopathy syndrome associated with haemolytic uraemic syndrome. Br J Radiol 2000;73:438–42.

[142] Lewis MB. Cyclosporin neurotoxicity after chemotherapy. Cyclosporin causes reversible posterior leukoencephalopathy syndrome. BMJ 1999;319:54–5.

[143] Ito Y, Arahata Y, Goto Y, et al. Cisplatin neurotoxicity presenting as reversible posterior leukoencephalopathy syndrome. AJNR Am J Neuroradiol 1998;19:415–7.

[144] Covarrubias DJ, Luetmer PH, Campeau NG. Posterior reversible encephalopathy syndrome: prognostic utility of quantitative diffusion-weighted MR images. AJNR Am J Neuroradiol 2002;23:1038–48.

[145] Ay H, Buonanno FS, Schaefer PW, et al. Posterior leukoencephalopathy without severe hypertension: utility of diffusion-weighted MRI. Neurology 1998;51:1369–76.

[146] Breen JC, Caplan LR, DeWitt LD, et al. Brain edema after carotid surgery. Neurology 1996; 46:175–81.

[147] Schaefer PW, Grant PE, Gonzalez RG. Diffusion-weighted MR imaging of the brain. Radiology 2000;217:331–45.

[148] Smith WS, Hauser SL, Easton DJ. Cerebrovascular disease. In: Braunwald E, Fauci AS, Kasper DL, et al, editors. Harrison's principles of internal medicine. McGraw-Hill: New York; 2001. p. 2369–91.

[149] Ameri A, Bousser MG. Cerebral venous thrombosis. Neurol Clin 1992;10:87–111.

[150] Daif A, Awada A, al-Rajeh S, et al. Cerebral venous thrombosis in adults. A study of 40 cases from Saudi Arabia. Stroke 1995;26:1193–5.

[151] Hickey WF, Garnick MB, Henderson IC, et al. Primary cerebral venous thrombosis in patients with cancer—a rarely diagnosed paraneoplastic syndrome. Report of three cases and review of the literature. Am J Med 1982;73:740–50.

[152] Crawford SC, Digre KB, Palmer CA, et al. Thrombosis of the deep venous drainage of the brain in adults. Analysis of seven cases with review of the literature. Arch Neurol 1995;52:1101–8.

[153] Villringer A, Einhaupl KM. Dural sinus and cerebral venous thrombosis. New Horiz 1997;5: 332–41.

[154] Lefebvre P, Lierneux B, Lenaerts L, et al. Cerebral venous thrombosis and procoagulant factors—a case study. Angiology 1998;49: 563–71.

[155] Ito K, Tsugane R, Ikeda A, et al. Cerebral hemodynamics and histological changes following acute cerebral venous occlusion in cats. Tokai J Exp Clin Med 1997;22:83–93.

[156] Nagai S, Horie Y, Akai T, et al. Superior sagittal sinus thrombosis associated with primary antiphospholipid syndrome–case report. Neurol Med Chir (Tokyo) 1998;38:34–9.

[157] Vielhaber H, Ehrenforth S, Koch HG, et al. Cerebral venous sinus thrombosis in infancy and childhood: role of genetic and acquired risk factors of thrombophilia. Eur J Pediatr 1998; 157:555–60.

[158] van den Berg JS, Boerman RH, vd Stolpe A, et al. Cerebral venous thrombosis: recurrence with fatal course. J Neurol 1999;246:144–6.

[159] Forbes KP, Pipe JG, Heiserman JE. Evidence for cytotoxic edema in the pathogenesis of cerebral venous infarction. AJNR Am J Neuroradiol 2001;22:450–5.

[160] Allroggen H, Abbott RJ. Cerebral venous sinus thrombosis. Postgrad Med J 2000;76:12–5.

[161] Tsai FY, Wang AM, Matovich VB, et al. MR staging of acute dural sinus thrombosis: correlation with venous pressure measurements and implications for treatment and prognosis. AJNR Am J Neuroradiol 1995;16:1021–9.

[162] Yuh WT, Simonson TM, Wang AM, et al. Venous sinus occlusive disease: MR findings. AJNR Am J Neuroradiol 1994;15:309–16.

[163] Dormont D, Anxionnat R, Evrad S, et al. MRI in cerebral venous thrombosis. J Neuroradiol 1994;21:81–99.

[164] Mullins ME, Grant PE, Wang B, et al. Parencyhymal abnormalities associated with cerebral venous thrombosis: assessment with diffusion weighted imaging. AJNR Am J Neuroradiol 2004;25:1666–75.

[165] Ducreux D, Oppenheim C, Vandamme X, et al. Diffusion-weighted imaging patterns of brain damage associated with cerebral venous thrombosis. AJNR Am J Neuroradiol 2001;22: 261–8.

[166] Chu K, Kang DW, Yoon BW, et al. Diffusion-weighted magnetic resonance in cerebral venous thrombosis. Arch Neurol 2001;58: 1569–76.

MAGNETIC
RESONANCE
IMAGING CLINICS

Magn Reson Imaging Clin N Am 14 (2006) 169–182

The Role of Conventional MR and CT in the Work-Up of Dementia Patients

Harold Keyserling, MD[a], Srinivasan Mukundan, Jr, MD, PhD[b,c],*

- Alzheimer's disease
- Vascular dementia
  - *Multi-infarction dementia*
  - *Cerebral autosomal dominant arteriopathy with subcortical infarctions and leukoencephalopathy*
  - *Amyloid angiopathy*
- Infectious dementias
  - *HIV dementia*
  - *Progressive multifocal leukoencephalopathy*
- *Creutzfeldt-Jakob disease*
- *Neurosyphilis*
- Normal-pressure hydrocephalus
- Frontotemporal degeneration
- Lewy body dementia
- Parkinson's disease with dementia
- Progressive supranuclear palsy
- Corticobasal degeneration
- Huntington's disease
- Summary
- References

Dementia is a clinical entity with myriad etiologies that generally is characterized by a progressive deterioration of higher cortical brain functions. This classically is described as a global loss of memory, personality, and language. Although some forms of dementia may affect children and young adults, dementia is most prevalent in the elderly population. As the population of this country and other developed nations ages, dementia, like other diseases associated with aging, will become an increasing burden on the health care system.

Any pathologic process that results in sufficient neuronal destruction or dysfunction may produce dementia (Box 1). Until recently, distinguishing one type of dementia from another could be difficult and was done chiefly on a clinical basis. The role of neuroimaging primarily was to exclude acute intracranial pathology, such as stroke or active infectious processes. Often, however, the designation of a specific cause of a patient's dementia was purely of academic interest, as treatment and prevention strategies were limited. Recent advances in pharmaceutical, behavioral, and cognitive therapies to treat and prevent dementia, however, have increased the importance of distinguishing the various causal entities of dementia from one another in order to tailor such therapies.

As treatment and prevention strategies have advanced, so has understanding of the imaging manifestations of the various types of dementia. Imaging now plays an important role in the work-up of patients who have dementia, providing not only structural but also functional evaluation of the brain. Advanced imaging techniques, including positron emission tomography, functional MR imaging, MR spectroscopy, and perfusion MR imaging,

This article was originally published in *Neuroimaging Clinics of North America* 2005;15(4):789–802.
[a] Department of Radiology, Emory University School of Medicine, Atlanta, GA, USA
[b] Department of Radiology, Duke University Medical Center, Durham, NC, USA
[c] Department of Biomedical Engineering, Pratt School of Engineering, Duke University, Durham, NC, USA
* Corresponding author. Department of Radiology, DUMC, Box 3808, Durham, NC 27710.
E-mail address: mukun001@mc.duke.edu (S. Mukundan, Jr).

Box 1: Gamut of dementia

Cortical dementia

  Alzheimer's disease (AD)[a]
  Pick's disease[a]

Vascular dementia

  Multi-infarct dementia[a]
  Lacunar dementia
  Binswanger's disease
  Amyloid angiopathy[a]
  Cerebral autosomal dominant
  arteriopathy with subcortical
  infarctions
  and leukoencephalopathy
  (CADASIL)[a]

Lewy body dementia (LBD)

  Parkinson's disease (PD)[a]
  Progressive supranuclear palsy (PSP)[a]
  Diffuse LBD[a]

Infectious dementia

  HIV/AIDS dementia[a]
  Progressive multifocal
  leukoencephalopathy
  (PML)[a]
  Creutzfeldt-Jakob disease (CJD)[a]
  Neurosyphilis[a]
  Lyme disease

Toxic dementia

  Alcohol (Wernicke-
  Korsakoff syndrome)[a]
  Heavy metal
  Organic poisons

Structural/space occupying

  Normal-pressure hydrocephalus
  (NPH)[a]
  Chronic subdural hematoma
  Neoplasia

Traumatic dementia

Other dementias

  Huntington's disease[a]
  Amyotropic lateral sclerosis
  Multiple sclerosis

  [a] Discussed in text.

considerations of some, but not all, of the various common and uncommon types of dementia and their appearance on conventional CT and MRI studies.

Although no definitive scheme exists for the classification of dementias, the terms cortical, subcortical, and progressive dementia frequently are used to describe general classes of dementing disorders. These classifications can overlap somewhat. Cortical dementias, resulting from damage to the neocortex, manifest as impairment of higher functions, including thought, language, social behavior, and memory. Subcortical dementias affect more primitive regions and result in emotional changes, and movement difficulties in addition to memory disturbances. Progressive dementias worsen over time, often slowly, resulting in deterioration of cognitive ability. Dementing disorders also are subdivided into primary disorders that occur primarily in the brain without other coexistent disease and secondary disorders that result from preexisting comorbid conditions, such as vascular disease.

Alzheimer's disease

The prototypical dementing disease is AD, which is a primary, cortical dementia. Usually, AD progresses slowly over the remaining duration of a patient's life after diagnosis, which on average is 8 to 10 years. AD is the most common dementia and affects between 2 and 4 million individuals in the United States alone. Nearly 1 of 10 people older than 65 have the disease and almost half of those over 85 have AD [3]. The dementia was described first in the early 1900s by the German physician, Alois Alzheimer, who wrote of his experiences with a patient, Auguste D. After the patient's death, a postmortem examination demonstrated a vastly atrophic brain containing what have become the two characteristic pathologic hallmarks of AD: senile plaques and neurofibrillary tangles [4,5]. Today, brain biopsy or postmortem examination remains the only definitive means of diagnosing AD [6]. As brain biopsy in living patients usually is deferred, presumptive diagnosis of AD usually is made on a clinical basis. Many guidelines and consensus statements are available in the literature [7–10]. Although a full discussion is beyond the scope of this work, presumptive clinical diagnostic criteria in general focus on memory impairment accompanied by cognitive decline in language, orientation, or executive functioning. Diagnostic accuracy rates higher the 90% are reported in dedicated AD centers for patients in moderate to late stages of dementia [11,12].

More therapeutic options for AD now are available, and modern treatment regimens exploit this

provide a functional assessment of brain activation and metabolism in patients who have dementia [1,2]. Currently, most radiologists are not likely to encounter functional studies in their daily practices. Conversely, structural studies, such as conventional CT and MR imaging, still play an important role in the evaluation of patients who have dementia. This article reviews the clinical manifestations and

by frequently using combination drug therapies [13]. Cholinesterase inhibitors are the mainstay of therapy to combat the cholinergic deficient state of patients. Currently, three cholinesterase inhibitors, donepezil, rivastigmine, and galantamine, are available in the United States. Recently, memantine, an N-methyl-D-aspartate (NMDA)-receptor antagonist has been approved for use in the United States. It is postulated that chronic low-level excitation of NMDA receptors by abnormal glutamate activity may result in neuronal damage or loss. In addition, antioxidant therapy, psychotropic drugs, and herbal treatments frequently are used by patients.

The current role of conventional CT and MR imaging in the work-up of patients who have dementing disorders is to characterize the gross structure of the brain and surroundings. Typical MRI evaluation consists of T1-weighted imaging to assess gross brain anatomy and to exclude the presence of subdural hematoma, mass effect, hydrocephalus, or other anomalies. In addition, cortical atrophy in atypical patterns for AD, such as frontotemporal, can implicate other dementias (ie, Pick's disease). Conventional T2 spin-echo or fluid attenuation inversion recovery (FLAIR) sequences are helpful to assess for signal abnormality. The presence of high T2 signal involving cortical and subcortical regions suggests vascular territory infarction of thromboembolic origin or watershed infarction. Punctate high T2 signal in the deep gray-matter nuclei or white-matter tracts (frequently hypointense centrally on FLAIR imaging) suggests lacunar infarction. The presence of posterior thalamic or periaqueductal hyperintense T2 signal is seen in Wernicke-Korsakoff syndrome (Fig. 1). Ventricular

atrophy out of proportion to sulcal atrophy, especially if periventricular T2 hyperintense signal is present (transependymal flow of cerebrospinal fluid), is characteristic of NPH. Confluent periventricular T2 and FLAIR hyperintensity frequently involving the pons is consistent with microvascular ischemic change, known as leukoariosis, and can suggest a vascular dementia, or in extreme cases, amyloid angiopathy. To this end, gradient-echo T2* imaging may be helpful to evaluate for the presence of iron (hemosiderin) deposition from prior focal hemorrhages that are seen in amyloid angiopathy. Finally, contrast-enhanced, T1-weighted imaging can reveal the presence of enhancing masses, cerebritis, and other unexpected infectious or inflammatory processes, including viral and granulomatous disease.

Characteristic imaging findings in AD are not easily discernable in early disease states, in which generalized cortical volume loss, demonstrated by thinning of the gyri and prominence of the intervening sulci, may be present. As the disease progresses, focal accelerated volume loss within the medial temporal lobes, in particular the hippocampus, parahippocampal gyrus, entorhinal cortex, and amygdala, is demonstrated (Fig. 2) [14,15]. In some centers, volumetric MR imaging is obtained so that quantitative volumetric assays can be performed on medical temporal lobe [16]. It is shown that the rate of change of the hippocampal volumes on serial MRI studies is the most specific volumetric marker for identification of an early AD [17]. Earlier volumetric assays made use of CT as the imaging modality but were found less reliable predominantly because of the poorer gray-white–matter

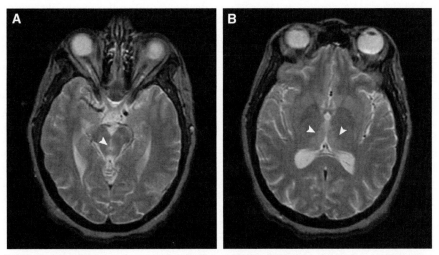

Fig. 1. Axial T2-weighted MR images of a patient who has Wernicke-Korsakoff syndrome demonstrates (*A*) periaqueductal gray matter hyperintense signal (*arrowhead*) within midbrain and (*B*) bilateral hyperintense hockey stick signal within the thalami (*arrowheads*).

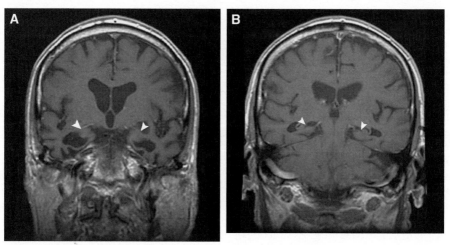

Fig. 2. Coronal T1-weighted MR images of a patient who has Alzheimer's disease demonstrates (*A*) marked bilateral atrophy of the amygdala (*arrowheads*) and (*B*) marked bilateral atrophy of the hippocampal formations (*arrowheads*).

discrimination and scan angle [18], as the affected structures are discerned best in the coronal plane. Given that many elderly patients have comorbid conditions or medical devices, such as cardiac pacemakers, that are contraindications to MRI evaluation, CT evaluation still is extremely valuable.

Vascular dementia

Vascular dementia currently is the second most common type of dementia in the elderly population; however, with the increasing prevalence of coronary artery and cerebrovascular disease in an aging population, it is believed that vascular dementia soon may be the most frequent cause of dementia [19]. According to guidelines set forth by the National Institute for Neurological Disorders and Stroke, with support from the Association Internationale pour la Recherche et l'Enseignement en Neurosciences, a probable diagnosis of vascular dementia is suggested by a temporal relationship between the development of dementia, focal neurologic deficits on physical examination, and brain imaging findings of relevant cerebrovascular disease [20]. These same criteria suggest the diagnosis of vascular dementia is unlikely in the absence of focal neurologic deficits or cerebrovascular lesions on cross-sectional brain imaging, thereby establishing the importance of neuroimaging in the diagnostic work-up of patients who have suspected vascular dementia. The most important risk factors for vascular dementia are advanced age, hypertension, diabetes mellitus, hyperlipidemia, recurrent stroke, coronary artery disease, smoking, and sleep apnea [19]. Although the presence of cerebrovascular disease on CT or MRI is not diagnostic of vascular

dementia [21], its absence may exclude the diagnosis. The causes of vascular dementia are many and include common causes of acute stroke, such as atheroembolic disease and small vessel/arteriolar occlusive disease, and less common entities, such as CADASIL and amyloid angiopathy [22]. Current treatment strategies include addressing the underlying risk factors for cerebrovascular disease, anticoagulation, and sometimes the addition of acetylcholinesterase inhibitors to patients' medication regimens [19,23].

Multi-infarction dementia

Multi-infarction dementia may be the most common form of vascular dementia. As expected, the salient imaging findings in this form of vascular dementia consist of evidence of cerebrovascular ischemic disease in the brain, usually the result of thromboembolic vascular disease. This includes evidence of multiple areas of prior cortical infarction, which may correspond to specific vascular distributions or watershed areas. On MRI and CT, these manifest as areas of focal encephalomalacia, hypodense on CT and relatively hyperintense on T2-weighted MRI. Alternately, lacunar infarctions in the basal ganglia, thalami, pons, or deep white matter may be seen in multi-infarction dementia. Related either to cortical infarction or small vessel disease, the acuity of infarctions contributing to vascular dementia can be assessed using MRI with diffusion-weighted sequences.

Confluent areas of T2 hyperintensity in the periventricular white matter extending into the white-matter regions also are described associated with many types vascular dementia (Fig. 3) [24]. Also, the presence of subcortical white-matter lesions is

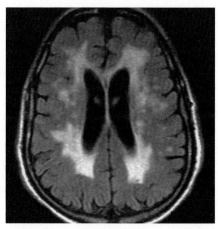

Fig. 3. Axial T2-weighted FLAIR image of a patient who has vascular dementia demonstrates nonspecific confluent hyperintense signal within the periventricular and deep white-matter tracts.

believed more suggestive of vascular types of dementia than of degenerative causes of dementia, such as AD [25], although the picture may be mixed. These lesions are found more often in the subcortical white matter at or above the level of the lateral ventricles than below this level, a phenomenon attributed to the fact that the medullary branches of the intracranial circulation reach their smallest size at these levels, making them more prone to ischemic injury [25].

Cerebral autosomal dominant arteriopathy with subcortical infarctions and leukoencephalopathy

CADASIL, as the name suggests, is a hereditary arteriopathy that may present with migraine-type headaches with aura, early-onset of multiple strokes (in patients younger than 60 years of age), resulting in stepwise progression of neurologic deficits, or dementia [26,27]. The disorder is attributed to a missense mutation on chromosome 19 [27]. In patients who have the proper clinical history and risk factors, MRI may demonstrate two predominating and often coexisting patterns of disease. One involves small, focal T2 hyperintense lesions in the basal ganglia, thalami, pons, or periventricular white matter. The second manifests as confluent T2 hyperintense areas in the subcortical white matter of the cerebral hemispheres, often symmetric in appearance and involving the temporal lobes [28]. Small T2 hyperintensities in the subcortical and periventricular white matter also may be seen in young, asymptomatic individuals who have the genetic mutation responsible for CADASIL, suggesting that MRI may be helpful in evaluating subclinical disease in young patients [29].

Amyloid angiopathy

Cerebral amyloid angiopathy is the result of accumulation of β-amyloid peptide in the media and adventitia of the vessels of the leptomeninges and the cortex of the brain. Although these pathologic findings are seen in patients who have AD, who also typically demonstrate deposition of β-amyloid peptide in the extracellular space of the brain parenchyma, isolated involvement of the vessels is suggestive of pure cerebral amyloid angiopathy [30]. These patients often suffer from multiple lobar hemorrhages, believed to be caused by rupture of weakened subcortical blood vessels and not necessarily related to hypertension [23]. Approximately 40% of patients who have cerebral amyloid angiopathy suffer from dementia [31]. Not surprisingly, hemosiderin staining reflecting remote hemorrhage in affected areas of the brain can be seen on conventional MRI [30]. Periventricular and subcortical white-matter lesions also can be seen in patients who have cerebral amyloid angiopathy, and the extent of white-matter involvement usually correlates with the number of lobar hemorrhages and degree of cognitive dysfunction [32]. Gradient-echo T2*-weighted sequences also may elicit evidence of areas of remote microhemorrhage in the subcortical white matter and in the distributions of the deep perforating arteries associated not only with amyloid angiopathy (Fig. 4) but also with other forms of small vessel disease, including lipohyalinosis [33,34].

Infectious dementias

HIV dementia

HIV dementia, also known as AIDS dementia complex, is believed to be caused by direct infection of the macrophages and microglia of the central nervous system by the HIV retrovirus [35]. Although the retrovirus does not infect neurons directly, neuronal death associated with HIV dementia is believed to be mediated by the release of neurotoxic substances from HIV-infected macrophages and microglia [35–37]. Before the advent of highly active antiretroviral therapy (HAART), up to 20% of HIV-infected individuals develop HIV dementia, and HIV dementia is the AIDS-defining illness in approximately 5% of HIV infected patients [38]. The most common imaging feature of HIV dementia is generalized cortical atrophy [39]. White-matter abnormalities on MRI also are a feature of HIV dementia. These are seen most commonly in the peritrigonal and subinsular white matter, although they can progress to a more confluent and diffuse pattern of leukoencephalopathy [40]. Although the overall incidence of HIV dementia has

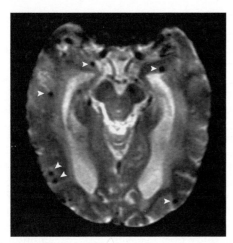

Fig. 4. Axial T2-weighted gradient-echo image of a patient who has amyloid angiopathy demonstrates numerous punctuate foci of signal loss (*arrowheads*) secondary to microhemorrhages.

decreased since the introduction of HAART, in patients failing HAART, a severe form of HIV-related leukoencephalopathy may develop. Pathologically, this is characterized by pronounced infiltration of the perivascular spaces by HIV-infected monocytes and macrophages, believed a consequence of antiretroviral-associated immune restoration. Radiologically, this manifests as severe, diffuse, white-matter abnormalities on MRI, typically involving the periventricular white matter, corpus callosum, and optic radiations [41].

Progressive multifocal leukoencephalopathy

Although the incidence of HIV dementia has declined with the advent of HAART, it is unclear if the incidence of PML has experienced a similar drop-off [38]. Most commonly seen in HIV-infected patients, PML also can be seen in individuals on immunosuppressive therapy or in patients who have hematologic malignancies. PML is caused by reactivation of the Jamestown Canyon virus, a common pathogen found in up to 75% of the population [38]. Clinically, PML may present with focal neurologic deficits, including hemiparesis and dysarthria, seizures, or dementia [42]. The prognosis for patients developing PML is grim, with a mean survival of approximately 2 to 12 months after diagnosis, although survival may be enhanced with HAART [43,44]. In addition to HAART, treatment of PML can be enhanced by the addition of one of several other therapeutic agents, including α-interferon and cidofovir.

The primary imaging feature of PML is that of a leukoencephalopathy, most commonly involving the white matter of the parietal lobes, followed in frequency by the frontal, occipital, and temporal lobes. Lesions often are multiple, and involvement may be unilateral and almost always is asymmetric [45]. On CT, lesions are seen as confluent areas of hypodensity, typically in the subcortical white matter of the cerebral hemispheres (Fig. 5). MRI recapitulates the CT features (Fig. 6), demonstrating confluent areas of hyperintense T2 and hypointense T1 signal that may scallop the gray-white junction, involving the subcortical U fibers and causing mild mass effect in a significant minority (approximately one third) of patients [45]. Lesions also may affect the periventricular white matter, the posterior fossa, the basal ganglia and thalami, and the corpus callosum [45,46]. Rarely, a central cystic area of near fluid attenuation on CT and hyperintense T2 signal on MRI may be seen in some lesions, suggesting central necrosis in advanced cases [45]. Contrast enhancement is extremely rare.

Creutzfeldt-Jakob disease

The causative agent of CJD is a protease-resistant prion protein. The disease is characterized histopathologically by neuronal destruction, gemistocytic astrocytosis, spongiform changes, and prion deposition. CJD presents in the majority of patients who have a characteristic triad of myoclonus, progressive dementia, and periodic sharp-wave patterns on electroencephalography. The clinical course typically is rapidly progressive and invariable fatal. Various forms of CJD include the sporadic form, which is the most common; familial CJD, which is associated with protein gene mutations; iatrogenic CJD, caused by prion-infected tissue transplants, hormone administration, or prion-infected surgical instruments; and variant

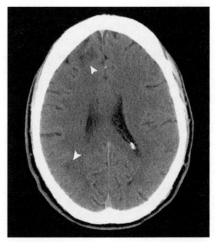

Fig. 5. Axial CT image of a patient. PML who has demonstrates patchy subcortical hypodensity (*arrowheads*).

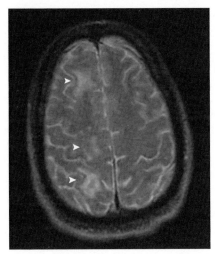

Fig. 6. Axial T2-weighted image of a patient who has PML demonstrates patchy subcortical hyperintensity (*arrowheads*).

CJD, which has been associated with the ingestion of prion-infected beef products [47].

MRI with diffusion-weighted imaging (DWI) has become an important tool in the diagnostic work-up of patients who have suspected CJD. Signal abnormalities are seen most commonly in the gray-matter structures of the brain, including the cerebral cortex, basal ganglia, and thalami. The variant form of CJD has a characteristic appearance on conventional MRI sequences (called the pulvinar sign), symmetric high-signal on T2-weighted images, and FLAIR sequences in the posterior thalami [47]. Other abnormalities described on conventional MRI sequences include high signal in the dorsal/medial thalami (the "hockey stick sign"), in the

periaqueductal gray matter, and in the caudate heads (Fig. 7). Less commonly, abnormalities on MRI may include diffuse atrophy or atrophy localized to the cerebellum, asymmetric high signal in the posterior thalami, and hyperintense T2 signal in the parieto-occipital white matter [47]. Although signal changes affecting white matter are postulated to represent secondary degeneration as a result of primary involvement of the cortical gray matter by CJD, recent autopsy series show that primary white-matter involvement, although uncommon, may be seen [48]. Diffuse signal abnormality in the white matter of the cerebral hemispheres can be seen in this case and is termed the panencephalopathic type of CJD.

It is suggested that spongiform degeneration of neurons may cause alteration of the movement of water molecules, thereby producing abnormalities seen on DWI [49]. The patterns of signal abnormalities seen on DWI in patients who have CJD include ribbon-like hyperintensities in the cortical gray matter and focal hyperintensities in the basal ganglia. These changes often are seen in the absence of signal abnormalities on routine MRI sequences early in the course of CJD [50]. DWI may be helpful particularly in the early detection of CJD, as changes can be seen within 1 month of the onset of symptoms [50–52]. It is suggested that areas of restricted diffusion on DWI that are confined to gray-matter structures may be more sensitive in the detection of CJD than the presence of protein 14-3-3 in the cerebrospinal fluid [53].

Neurosyphilis

Involvement of the central nervous system by the spirochete *Treponema pallidum* has myriad clinical

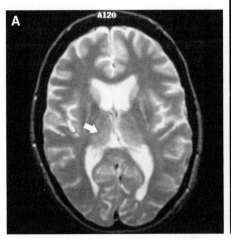

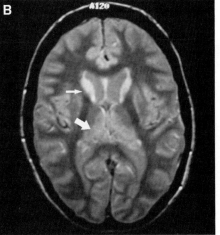

Fig. 7. Axial MR images of patient who has CJD demonstrates (*A*) bilateral hyperintense hockey stick signal within the thalami (*large arrow*) on T2-weighted images and (*B*) bilateral hyperintense signal in the heads of the caudate nuclei (*small arrow*) more apparent on proton-density image.

and radiologic manifestations. Clinically, the meningovascular form of syphilis typically is characterized by a progressive subacute encephalitic syndrome with multiple strokes that may or may not result in dementia [54]. Radiologically, meningovascular syphilis is characterized by findings stemming from the vasculitis seen in this early form of syphilis infection. This can manifest on MRI and CT as multiple areas of acute or subacute infarction in the setting of active disease, areas of encephalomalacia from remote infarction in the setting of chronic or senescent disease, and areas of narrowing, irregularity, and ectasia of the major intracranial arterial structures [55]. Areas of infarction may involve predominantly the deep white matter of the cerebral hemispheres in a pattern compatible with small-vessel ischemic disease. Alternately, large-vessel territory infarctions also may be present. Although these findings are nonspecific and can be seen in almost any vasculitis affecting the intracranial arterial circulation, the diagnosis of meningovascular syphilis should be posited in patients who have the proper clinical scenario.

CNS involvement by tertiary syphilis also may result in what is called dementia paralytica or general paresis. In these patients, the predominant radiologic finding is generalized cerebral atrophy. Occasionally, this may be more pronounced in the medial temporal lobes. It is suggested that the subset of patients who have tertiary syphilis manifesting with preferential volume loss in the medial temporal lobes may not respond as well to therapy [56]. Findings suggestive of subcortical gliosis also may be present [57]. Confluent areas of T2 hyperintensity occasionally may be seen in the white matter of the cerebral hemispheres and may regress with the initiation of antitreponemal therapy [58]. Reversible dilation of the ventricular system also is described [59].

Normal-pressure hydrocephalus

NPH is an important cause of dementia in elderly patients and classically manifests with the clinical triad of dementia, recent-onset gait apraxia, and urinary incontinence. NPH may be primary (idiopathic) or secondary (resulting from abnormalities of the arachnoid caused by history of subarachnoid hemorrhage, inflammation, or surgery). Ventricular shunting may lead to improvement of symptoms in patients who have NPH, which makes it important for clinicians and radiologists to distinguish this form of dementia from neurodegenerative forms of dementia that do not improve with shunting.

The radiologic hallmark of NPH is dilation of the ventricular system, in particular the temporal horns of the lateral ventricles, out of proportion to the appearance of the cortical sulci (Fig. 8). Dilation of the ventricles along with additional findings of dilation of the sylvian fissures, basal cisterns, or isolated sulci over the convexities or medial hemispheric surfaces also may be present in NPH. This pattern may been seen in patients whose NPH is more likely to respond favorably to ventricular shunting than in patients who have isolated ventricular enlargement [60].

In patients who have diffuse atrophy, however, preferential ventricular enlargement can be difficult to determine, making NPH difficult to distinguish from AD. Although hippocampal atrophy is associated with NPH, some studies suggest that hippocampal volumes, as measured on thin section coronal MRI in patients who have AD, are markedly diminished when compared with patients who have NPH [61,62]. Also, dilation of the perihippocampal fissures is seen much more commonly in patients who have AD than in patients who have NPH [63]. Recently, reports suggest that increased flow velocities are present within the cerebral

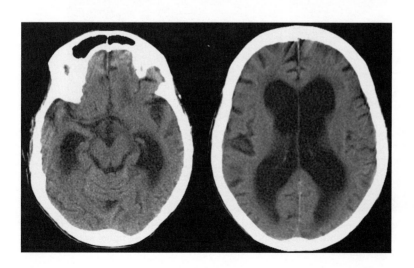

Fig. 8. Axial CT images of a patient who has NPH demonstrates marked ventricular prominence that is out of proportion to sulcal atrophy.

aqueduct that manifest as a prominent aqueductal flow-void on conventional MRI or elevated flow rates on cine phase-contrast MR imaging studies [64].

Frontotemporal degeneration

Frontotemporal degeneration (FTD) is a nonspecific term applied to various forms of dementia that result in preferential atrophy of the frontal and anterior temporal lobes. For all forms of this entity, preferential atrophy of the frontal and anterior temporal lobes helps distinguish them from AD [65]. FTD is characterized pathologically by neuronal loss, gliosis, spongiosis, and sometimes argyrophilic intraneuronal inclusion bodies (Pick bodies). There are three predominant variants of FTD, each with distinctive clinical or radiologic manifestations. Frontal variant FTD is characterized clinically by behavioral disturbances, typically resulting in antisocial behavior and disinhibition resulting from primary involvement of the frontal lobes. This may progress to the Kluver–Bucy syndrome late in the disease as involvement of the temporal lobes becomes more pronounced. Radiologically, atrophy primarily affecting the frontal lobes and anterior portions of the temporal lobes usually is not seen until late in the disease.

The second type of FTD is known as semantic dementia and typically manifests with progressive anomia resulting from loss of long-term memory of language comprehension and object recognition. Unlike in patients who have AD, short-term memory usually is intact. Radiologically, atrophy of the frontal and temporal lobes is seen, more pronounced in the temporal lobes and often asymmetric, affecting the left temporal lobe more severely than the right.

Nonfluent progressive aphasia is the third subtype of FTD. As the name implies, this form of dementia is characterized clinically by preservation of verbal comprehension with severe disruption of conversational speech, speech dysfluency, and phonologic errors. The disease may progress to mutism. Behavioral changes, as seen with frontal variant FTD, typically are not seen. Radiologically, atrophy predominates in the perisylvian regions of the frontal and temporal lobes (Fig. 9). Knife-blade atrophy, caused by marked thinning of the cortical gyri, can be seen, particularly in the anterior portion the superior temporal gyrus.

There is continued debate as to whether or not Pick's disease represents a distinct clinical entity from FTD or if it is a subtype of FTD that shares clinicoradiologic features with all three of the aforementioned subtypes of FTD with the additional finding of intraneuronal argyrophilic inclusions

(Pick bodies) at histology. The discussion of this distinction is beyond the scope of this article. It is suggested, however, that the term, Pick's complex, may be used to describe all forms of FTD and Pick's disease [66].

Lewy body dementia

DLB is a neurodegenerative disease that has many of the clinical features of PD and AD. Its histopathologic hallmark is the intraneuronal aggregation of α-synuclein protein inclusions (Lewy bodies). Clinically, patients who have DLB present with fluctuations in cognition; alterations in perception, such as visual hallucinations; depression; and nighttime agitation [67]. Distinguishing DLB from other neurodegenerative forms of dementia is important because of the potential for patients who have DLB to develop irreversible extrapyramidal symptoms when placed on conventional antidopaminergic and anticholinergic neuroleptic therapies used to treat dementia-associated psychosis. Also, patients who have DLB may develop neuroleptic sensitivity on these medications, a potentially life-threatening complication believed to be mediated by acute D2 receptor blockade. These adverse reactions to neuroleptic therapy may occur in up to one half of patients who have DLB [68].

The conventional CT and MRI appearance of DLB generally is nonspecific, most commonly manifesting as diffuse cerebral atrophy and usually not as pronounced as is seen in AD. Volumetric data suggest, however, that gray-matter structures may be more affected than white-matter structures [69]. Indeed, atrophy of the putamen is a feature of DLB and may help distinguish it from AD [70]. Preferential atrophy in the medial temporal lobes is not as pronounced as in AD [71].

Parkinson's disease with dementia

Approximately 30% to 80% of patients who have PD may develop dementia [72,73]. The dementia in patients who have PD is characterized predominantly by attention deficits and impairment in executive functions, whereas memory impairment may be a secondary effect [72]. Depression, agitation, and visual hallucinations also may be present. Overall, the dementia profile in patients who have PD is similar to that seen in patients who have DLB, which is not surprising, as the causative agent for both processes involves intraneuronal aggregations of Lewy bodies. It is suggested that PD and DLB should be considered different manifestations of Lewy body disease rather than distinct disorders unto themselves [74,75]. In PD, the distribution of Lewy bodies may not be as diffuse as in DLB.

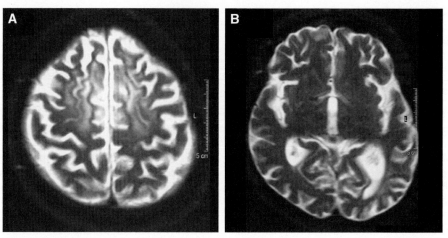

Fig. 9. Axial T2-weighted images of a patient who has Pick's disease demonstrates bilateral frontal (*A*) and temporal (*B*) volume loss.

Predominating early involvement of the substantia nigra is believed to cause the motor features of PD, which are characteristic of the disorder, distinguish it clinically from DLB, and almost always precede dementia. Patients who have PD with dementia tend to have higher concentrations of Lewy bodies in the transrhinal and entorhinal cortices, the hippocampi, and the amygdala than patients who have PD without dementia [76]. The motor and cognitive disturbances in patients who have PD may respond favorably to dopamine replacement therapy.

Conventional MRI may not demonstrate significant signal or morphologic differences between patients who have PD with dementia and those who have PD without dementia [77,78]. Patterns of volume loss are similar to those seen in DLB and are nonspecific. Narrowing of the pars compacta of the substantia nigra may be seen in patients who have longstanding PD, whereas right/left asymmetry of the pars compacta may be a feature early in the course of the disease [79].

Progressive supranuclear palsy

PSP is a neurodegenerative disorder characterized by postural instability and vertical supranuclear gaze palsy that typically presents in late adulthood. Axial rigidity and a propensity to fall are common clinical features, as are dysphagia and drooling. Dementia in these patients usually is mild until late in the disease. Pathologically, PSP is characterized by the abnormal accumulation of tau protein in neurofibrillary tangles in the basal ganglia and brainstem, and it is suggested that there may be a genetic component to this disease [80]. These patients typically do not respond well to dopamine replacement therapy.

Symmetric progressive atrophy in the midbrain, superior cerebellar peduncles, thalami, and caudate nuclei are the most characteristic imaging findings of PSP [81,82]. When viewed on sagittal imaging, the superior contour of the midbrain may have a flattened or concave profile, a finding believed highly specific for PSP [83]. Also, hyperintense T2 signal in the tegmentum on MRI, although not commonly seen in PSP, is believed a highly specific finding in this disease [83]. Atrophy of the frontal lobes, in particular the orbitofrontal and medial cortex, also may be present. Preferential volume loss in these areas may distinguish PSP from PD. The degree of atrophy seen in the frontal lobes correlates well with the level of behavioral disturbance seen clinically, as does the degree of atrophy in the caudate nuclei and brainstem with the severity of motor function impairment [81,84].

Corticobasal degeneration

The characteristic symptoms of corticobasal degeneration (CBD) involve asymmetric limb apraxia, rigidity, or akinesia. This may be accompanied by dystonia and alien limb phenomenon. Severe depression and cognitive decline, leading to dementia, also are features of the disease, and there is significant overlap in symptomatology with patients who have FTD and PSP [85,86].

Neuroimaging findings in CBD may involve progressive atrophy of the frontal lobes and caudate nuclei [87]. Often, asymmetric atrophy of the cerebral hemisphere contralateral to the clinically affected side is seen. The overall degree of cerebral atrophy is believed more severe in CBD than in AD, and the asymmetric cerebral atrophy seen in CBD is believed to distinguish it from AD [88,89].

Atrophy of the corpus callosum and hyperintense T2 signal in the putamina and globus pallidi also are described.

Huntington's disease

Huntington's disease is an autosomal dominantly inherited neurodegenerative disorder that typically presents in midadulthood, although a juvenile form of the disease presenting in patients before 21 years of age is described. Chorea and dementia are the clinical hallmarks of this disease. Psychiatric disturbances, such as depression or psychosis, may precede the development of chorea, and frank dementia usually develops after the chorea.

The characteristic imaging finding in Huntington's disease is marked atrophy of the caudate nuclei and corpus striatum [90]. Diffuse cerebral volume loss also may be seen and can be more pronounced in the frontal lobes than elsewhere [91]. Preferential gray-matter atrophy also is described in the opercular cortex, hypothalamus, and right paracentral lobule [92]. Patients who have the juvenile form of Huntington's disease also may demonstrate hyperintense T2 signal in the caudate nuclei and putamina [93].

Summary

Dementia is a clinical syndrome with many causes. There often is overlap in the clinical manifestations of various forms of dementia, making them difficult to categorize. Neuroimaging can play an important role in distinguishing one form of dementia from another. Advanced imaging techniques continue to provide greater insight into the underlying pathologic processes in patients who have dementia. Conventional MRI and CT, however, still can contribute useful information when interpreting radiologists are familiar with the patterns of volume loss and signal or density changes that are characteristic of various forms of dementia.

References

[1] Hsu YY, Du AT, Schuff N, et al. Magnetic resonance imaging and magnetic resonance spectroscopy in dementias. J Geriatr Psychiatry Neurol 2001;14:145–66.

[2] Bozzao A, Floris R, Baviera ME, et al. Diffusion and perfusion MR imaging in cases of Alzheimer's disease: correlations with cortical atrophy and lesion load. AJNR Am J Neuroradiol 2001;22:1030–6.

[3] National Institute of Neurological Disorders and Stroke. The dementias: hope through research. Available at: http://www.ninds.nih.gov/disorders/alzheimersdisease/detail_alzheimersdisease.htm. Accessed November 2005.

[4] Maurer K, Volk S, et al. and Alzheimer's disease. Lancet 1997;349:1546–9.

[5] Alzheimer A. Über eigenartige Krankheitsfälle des späteren Alters. Z Gesamte Neurol Psychiatrie 1911;4:356–85.

[6] Jellinger K. Morphology of Alzheimer disease and related disorders. In: Maurer K, Riederer P, Beckmann H, editors. Alzheimer disease: epidemiology, neuropathology and clinics. New York: Springer-Verlag; 1990. p. 61–77.

[7] Hyman BT, Trojanowski JQ. Consensus recommendations for the postmortem diagnosis of Alzheimer disease from the National Institute on Aging and the Reagan Institute Working Group on diagnostic criteria for the neuropathological assessment of Alzheimer disease. J Neuropathol Exp Neurol 1997;56:1095–7.

[8] Mirra SS, Heyman A, McKeel DW, et al. Standardization of the neuropathologic assessment of Alzheimer's disease. Neurology 1991;41:479–86.

[9] McKhann G, Drachman D, Folstein M, et al. Clinical diagnosis of Alzheimer's disease: report of the NINCDS-ADRDA Work Group under the auspices of Department of Health and Human Services Task Force on Alzheimer's Disease. Neurology 1984;34:939–44.

[10] Diagnostic and statistical manual of mental disorders. 4th ed. Washington, DC: American Psychiatric Association; 1994.

[11] Larson EB, Edwards JK, O'Meara E, et al. Neuropathologic diagnostic outcomes from a cohort of outpatients with suspected dementia. J Gerontol A Biol Sci Med Sci 1996;51(Suppl 6): M313–8.

[12] Rasmusson DX, Brandt J, Steele C, et al. Accuracy of clinical diagnosis of Alzheimer disease and clinical features of patients with non-Alzheimer disease neuropathology. Alzheimer Dis Assoc Disord 1996;10:180–8.

[13] Xiong G, Doraiswamy PM. Combination drug therapy for Alzheimer's disease: what is evidence-based, and what is not? Geriatrics 2005; 60:22–6.

[14] Seab JP, Jagust WJ, Wong ST, et al. Quantitative NMR measurements of hippocampal atrophy in Alzheimer's disease. Magn Reson Med 1988; 8:200–8.

[15] Kesslak JP, Nalcioglu O, Cotman CW. Quantification of magnetic resonance scans for hippocampal and parahippocampal atrophy in Alzheimer's disease. Neurology 1991;41:51–4.

[16] Jack CR. Structural imaging approaches to Alzheimer's disease. In: Daffner S, editor. Early diagnosis of Alzheimer's disease. Totowa (NJ): Humana; 2000. p. 127–48.

[17] Jack CR Jr, Petersen RC, Xu Y, et al. Rates of hippocampal atrophy correlate with change in clinical status in aging and AD. Neurology 2000;55:484–9.

[18] de Leon MJ, George AE, Stylopoulos LA, et al. Early marker for Alzheimer's disease: the atrophic hippocampus. Lancet 1989;2:672–3.

[19] Roman GC. Facts, myths, and controversies in vascular dementia. J Neurol Sci 2004;226: 49–52.

[20] Roman GC, Tatemichi TK, Erkinjuntti T, et al. Vascular dementia: diagnostic criteria for research studies. Report of the NINDS-AIREN International Workshop. Neurology 1993;43: 250–60.

[21] Ballard CG, Burton EJ, Barber R, et al. NINDS AIREN neuroimaging criteria do not distinguish stroke patients with and without dementia. Neurology 2004;63:983–8.

[22] Roman GC, Erkinjuntti T, Wallin A, et al. Subcortical ischaemic vascular dementia. Lancet Neurol 2002;1:426–36.

[23] Ringelstein EB, Nabavi DG. Cerebral small vessel diseases: cerebral microangiopathies. Curr Opin Neurol 2005;18:179–88.

[24] Fazekas F, Chawluk JB, Alavi A, et al. MR signal abnormalities at 1.5 T in Alzheimer's dementia and normal aging. AJR Am J Roentgenol 1987; 149:351–6.

[25] Bowen BC, Barker WW, Loewenstein DA, et al. MR signal abnormalities in memory disorder and dementia. AJR Am J Roentgenol 1990;154: 1285–92.

[26] Gladstone JP, Dodick DW. Migraine and cerebral white matter lesions: when to suspect cerebral autosomal dominant arteriopathy with subcortical infarcts and leukoencephalopathy (CADASIL). Neurologist 2005;11:19–29.

[27] Dichgans M. Cerebral autosomal dominant arteriopathy with subcortical infarcts and leukoencephalopathy: phenotypic and mutational spectrum. J Neurol Sci 2002;203–204:77–80.

[28] Skehan SJ, Hutchinson M, MacErlaine DP. Cerebral autosomal dominant arteriopathy with subcortical infarcts and leukoencephalopathy: MR findings. AJNR Am J Neuroradiol 1995;16: 2115–9.

[29] Fattapposta F, Restuccia R, Pirro C, et al. Early diagnosis in cerebral autosomal dominant arteriopathy with subcortical infarcts and leukoencephalopathy (CADASIL): the role of MRI. Funct Neurol 2004;19:239–42.

[30] Remes AM, Finnila S, Mononen H, et al. Hereditary dementia with intracerebral hemorrhages and cerebral amyloid angiopathy. Neurology 2004;63:234–40.

[31] van Straaten EC, Scheltens P, Barkhof F. MRI and CT in the diagnosis of vascular dementia. J Neurol Sci 2004;226:9–12.

[32] Smith EE, Gurol ME, Eng JA, et al. White matter lesions, cognition, and recurrent hemorrhage in lobar intracerebral hemorrhage. Neurology 2004;63:1606–12.

[33] Walker DA, Broderick DF, Kotsenas AL, et al. Routine use of gradient-echo MRI to screen for cerebral amyloid angiopathy in elderly patients. AJR Am J Roentgenol 2004;182:1547–50.

[34] Imaizumi T, Horita Y, Chiba M, et al. Dot-like hemosiderin spots on gradient echo T2*-weighted magnetic resonance imaging are associated with past history of small vessel disease in patients with intracerebral hemorrhage. J Neuroimaging 2004;14:251–7.

[35] Patel SH, Kolson DL, Glosser G, et al. Correlation between percentage of brain parenchymal volume and neurocognitive performance in HIV-infected patients. AJNR Am J Neuroradiol 2002;23:543–9.

[36] Gonzalez RG. Imaging neuroAIDS. AJNR Am J Neuroradiol 2004;25:167–8.

[37] Avison MJ, Nath A, Berger JR. Understanding pathogenesis and treatment of HIV dementia: a role for magnetic resonance? Trends Neurosci 2002;25:468–73.

[38] Manji H, Miller R. The neurology of HIV infection. J Neurol Neurosurg Psychiatry 2004; 75(Suppl 1):i29–35.

[39] Tucker KA, Robertson KR, Lin W, et al. Neuroimaging in human immunodeficiency virus infection. J Neuroimmunol 2004;157: 153–62.

[40] Tien RD, Felsberg GJ, Ferris NJ, et al. The dementias: correlation of clinical features, pathophysiology, and neuroradiology. AJR Am J Roentgenol 1993;161:245–55.

[41] Langford TD, Letendre SL, Marcotte TD, et al. Severe, demyelinating leukoencephalopathy in AIDS patients on antiretroviral therapy. AIDS 2002;16:1019–29.

[42] von Einsiedel RW, Fife TD, Aksamit AJ, et al. Progressive multifocal leukoencephalopathy in AIDS: a clinicopathologic study and review of the literature. J Neurol 1993;240:391–406.

[43] Fong IW, Toma E. The natural history of progressive multifocal leukoencephalopathy in patients with AIDS. Canadian PML Study Group. Clin Infect Dis 1995;20:1305–10.

[44] Albrecht H, Hoffmann C, Degen O, et al. Highly active antiretroviral therapy significantly improves the prognosis of patients with HIV-associated progressive multifocal leukoencephalopathy. AIDS 1998;12:1149–54.

[45] Thurnher MM, Thurnher SA, Muhlbauer B, et al. Progressive multifocal leukoencephalopathy in AIDS: initial and follow-up CT and MRI. Neuroradiology 1997;39:611–8.

[46] Whiteman ML, Post MJ, Berger JR, et al. Progressive multifocal leukoencephalopathy in 47 HIV-seropositive patients: neuroimaging with clinical and pathologic correlation. Radiology 1993;187: 233–40.

[47] Collie DA, Summers DM, Sellar RJ, et al. Diagnosing variant Creutzfeldt-Jakob disease with the pulvinar sign: MR imaging findings in 86 neuropathologically confirmed cases. AJNR Am J Neuroradiol 2003;24:1560–9.

[48] Matsusue E, Kinoshita T, Sugihara S, et al. White matter lesions in panencephalopathic type of Creutzfeldt-Jakob disease: MR imaging and pathologic correlations. AJNR Am J Neuroradiol 2004;25:910–8.

[49] Schaefer PW, Grant PE, Gonzalez RG. Diffusion-weighted MR imaging of the brain. Radiology 2000;217:331–45.

[50] Mao-Draayer Y, Braff SP, Nagle KJ, et al. Emerging patterns of diffusion-weighted MR imaging in Creutzfeldt-Jakob disease: case report and review of the literature. AJNR Am J Neuroradiol 2002;23:550–6.

[51] Shiga Y, Miyazawa K, Sato S, et al. Diffusion-weighted MRI abnormalities as an early diagnostic marker for Creutzfeldt-Jakob disease. Neurology 2004;63:443–9.

[52] Stadnik TW, Demaerel P, Luypaert RR, et al. Imaging tutorial: differential diagnosis of bright lesions on diffusion-weighted MR images. Radiographics 2003;23:e7.

[53] Mendez OE, Shang J, Jungreis CA, et al. Diffusion-weighted MRI in Creutzfeldt-Jakob disease: a better diagnostic marker than CSF protein 14-3-3? J Neuroimaging 2003;13:147–51.

[54] Fox PA, Hawkins DA, Dawson S. Dementia following an acute presentation of meningovascular neurosyphilis in an HIV-1 positive patient. AIDS 2000;14:2062–3.

[55] Holland BA, Perrett LV, Mills CM. Meningovascular syphilis: CT and MR findings. Radiology 1986;158:439–42.

[56] Kodama K, Okada S, Komatsu N, et al. Relationship between MRI findings and prognosis for patients with general paresis. J Neuropsychiatry Clin Neurosci 2000;12:246–50.

[57] Zifko U, Wimberger D, Lindner K, et al. MRI in patients with general paresis. Neuroradiology 1996;38:120–3.

[58] Berbel-Garcia A, Porta-Etessam J, Martinez-Salio A, et al. Magnetic resonance image-reversible findings in a patient with general paresis. Sex Transm Dis 2004;31:350–2.

[59] Cosottini M, Mascalchi M, Zaccara G, et al. Reversal of syphilitic hydrocephalus with intravenous penicillin. Can J Neurol Sci 1997;24:343–4.

[60] Kitagaki H, Mori E, Ishii K, et al. CSF spaces in idiopathic normal pressure hydrocephalus: morphology and volumetry. AJNR Am J Neuroradiol 1998;19:1277–84.

[61] Golomb J, de Leon MJ, George AE, et al. Hippocampal atrophy correlates with severe cognitive impairment in elderly patients with suspected normal pressure hydrocephalus. J Neurol Neurosurg Psychiatry 1994;57:590–3.

[62] Savolainen S, Laakso MP, Paljarvi L, et al. MR imaging of the hippocampus in normal pressure hydrocephalus: correlations with cortical Alzheimer's disease confirmed by pathologic analysis. AJNR Am J Neuroradiol 2000;21:409–14.

[63] Holodny AI, Waxman R, George AE, et al. MR differential diagnosis of normal-pressure hydrocephalus and Alzheimer disease: significance of perihippocampal fissures. AJNR Am J Neuroradiol 1998;19:813–9.

[64] Bradley WG. Normal pressure hydrocephalus: new concepts on etiology and diagnosis. AJNR Am J Neuroradiol 2000;21:1586–90.

[65] Kitagaki H, Mori E, Yamaji S, et al. Frontotemporal dementia and Alzheimer disease: evaluation of cortical atrophy with automated hemispheric surface display generated with MR images. Radiology 1998;208:431–9.

[66] Kertesz A, Munoz D. Pick's disease, frontotemporal dementia, and Pick complex: emerging concepts. Arch Neurol 1998;55:302–4.

[67] Baskys A. Lewy body dementia: the litmus test for neuroleptic sensitivity and extrapyramidal symptoms. J Clin Psychiatry 2004;65(Suppl 11):16–22.

[68] McKeith IG. Dementia with Lewy bodies. Br J Psychiatry 2002;180:144–7.

[69] Bozzali M, Falini A, Cercignani M, et al. Brain tissue damage in dementia with Lewy bodies: an in vivo diffusion tensor MRI study. Brain 2005;. in press.

[70] Cousins DA, Burton EJ, Burn D, et al. Atrophy of the putamen in dementia with Lewy bodies but not Alzheimer's disease: an MRI study. Neurology 2003;61:1191–5.

[71] Tam CW, Burton EJ, McKeith IG, et al. Temporal lobe atrophy on MRI in Parkinson disease with dementia: a comparison with Alzheimer disease and dementia with Lewy bodies. Neurology 2005;64:861–5.

[72] Emre M. Dementia in Parkinson's disease: cause and treatment. Curr Opin Neurol 2004;17:399–404.

[73] Lieberman A, Dziatolowski M, Kupersmith M, et al. Dementia in Parkinson disease. Ann Neurol 1979;6:355–9.

[74] McKeith IG, Mosimann UP. Dementia with Lewy bodies and Parkinson's disease. Parkinsonism Relat Disord 2004;10(Suppl 1):S15–8.

[75] Tsuboi Y, Dickson DW. Dementia with Lewy bodies and Parkinson's disease with dementia: are they different? Parkinsonism Relat Disord 2005;11(Suppl 1):S47–51.

[76] Bertrand E, Lechowicz W, Szpak GM, et al. Limbic neuropathology in idiopathic Parkinson's disease with concomitant dementia. Folia Neuropathol 2004;42:141–50.

[77] Huber SJ, Shuttleworth EC, Christy JA, et al. Magnetic resonance imaging in dementia of Parkinson's disease. J Neurol Neurosurg Psychiatry 1989;52:1221–7.

[78] Braffman BH, Grossman RI, Goldberg HI, et al. MR imaging of Parkinson disease with spin-echo and gradient-echo sequences. AJR Am J Roentgenol 1989;152:159–65.

[79] Huber SJ, Chakeres DW, Paulson GW, et al. Magnetic resonance imaging in Parkinson's disease. Arch Neurol 1990;47:735–7.

[80] Litvan I. Update on epidemiological aspects of progressive supranuclear palsy. Mov Disord 2003;18(Suppl 6):S43–50.

[81] Cordato NJ, Duggins AJ, Halliday GM, et al. Clinical deficits correlate with regional cerebral atrophy in progressive supranuclear palsy. Brain 2005;128:1595–604.

[82] Paviour DC, Price SL, Stevens JM, et al. Quantitative MRI measurement of superior cerebellar peduncle in progressive supranuclear palsy. Neurology 2005;64:675–9.

[83] Righini A, Antonini A, De Notaris R, et al. MR imaging of the superior profile of the midbrain: differential diagnosis between progressive supranuclear palsy and Parkinson disease. AJNR Am J Neuroradiol 2004;25:927–32.

[84] Paviour DC, Schott JM, Stevens JM, et al. Pathological substrate for regional distribution of increased atrophy rates in progressive supranuclear palsy. J Neurol Neurosurg Psychiatry 2004;75:1772–5.

[85] Kertesz A, Martinez-Lage P, Davidson W, et al. The corticobasal degeneration syndrome overlaps progressive aphasia and frontotemporal dementia. Neurology 2000;55:1368–75.

[86] Stover NP, Watts RL. Corticobasal degeneration. Semin Neurol 2001;21:49–58.

[87] Tsuchiya K, Miyazaki H, Ikeda K, et al. Serial brain CT in corticobasal degeneration: radiological and pathological correlation of two autopsy cases. J Neurol Sci 1997;152:23–9.

[88] Kitagaki H, Hirono N, Ishii K, et al. Corticobasal degeneration: evaluation of cortical atrophy by means of hemispheric surface display generated with MR images. Radiology 2000;216:31–8.

[89] Soliveri P, Monza D, Paridi D, et al. Cognitive and magnetic resonance imaging aspects of corticobasal degeneration and progressive supranuclear palsy. Neurology 1999;53:502–7.

[90] Aylward EH, Schwartz J, Machlin S, et al. Bicaudate ratio as a measure of caudate volume on MR images. AJNR Am J Neuroradiol 1991;12:1217–22.

[91] Aylward EH, Anderson NB, Bylsma FW, et al. Frontal lobe volume in patients with Huntington's disease. Neurology 1998;50:252–8.

[92] Kassubek J, Juengling FD, Kioschies T, et al. Topography of cerebral atrophy in early Huntington's disease: a voxel based morphometric MRI study. J Neurol Neurosurg Psychiatry 2004;75:213–20.

[93] Ho VB, Chuang HS, Rovira MJ, et al. Juvenile Huntington disease: CT and MR features. AJNR Am J Neuroradiol 1995;16:1405–12.

MAGNETIC RESONANCE IMAGING CLINICS

Magn Reson Imaging Clin N Am 14 (2006) 183–202

Diffusion Tensor Magnetic Resonance Imaging of Brain Tumors

L. Celso Hygino Cruz, Jr, MD[a], A. Gregory Sorensen, MD[b],*

Primary neoplasms of the central nervous system (CNS) have a prevalence between 15,000 and 17,000 new cases annually in the United States, and when metastatic lesions are included, brain tumors are estimated to cause the deaths of 90,000 patients every year [1,2]. Gliomas remain the most common primary CNS tumor, accounting for 40% to 50% of cases [3] and 2% to 3% of all cancers [4]. Despite new techniques of treatment, patient survival still remains low, varying between 16 and 53 weeks [5].

For more than 40 years [6], nuclear magnetic resonance has been used to analyze and assess brain tumors. It is generally accepted that conventional MRI, typically T1- and T2-weighted imaging, tends to underestimate the extent of the tumor, which can, in turn, lead to suboptimal treatment [7]. New functional MRI (fMRI) sequences, such as

diffusion imaging, perfusion imaging, and spectroscopic imaging, have been widely used to evaluate such tumors. In this review, diffusion tensor imaging (DTI), one of the newer methods, is described, particularly the ability of DTI to aid in differentiating a tumor from surrounding edema and infiltrating tumor [8] and, to some extent, to grade brain tumors [9].

Diffusion MRI

Physical basis

The random or Brownian movement of water molecules is the basis of diffusion. In the brain, the presence of tissue structures restricts free water motion [10–12], for example, rendering the diffusion of water molecules higher in the ventricles than in

This article was originally published in *Neurosurgery Clinics of North America* 2005;16(1):115–34.

[a] Clínica de Diagnóstico por Imagem, Multi-Imagem Ressonância Magnética, Av. das Américas 4666, Centro Médico Barrashopping, Rio de Janeiro, Brazil

[b] Department of Radiology, Massachusetts General Hospital, Athinoula A. Martinos Center for Biomedical Imaging, Division of Health Sciences and Technology, Haravrd-MIT, Building 149m 13th Street, Boston, MA 02421, USA

* Corresponding author.

E-mail address: sorensen@nmr.mgh.harvard.edu (A.G. Sorensen).

doi:10.1016/j.mric.2006.06.003

the parenchyma. MRI makes it possible to estimate the diffusivity of water molecules.

Because some pathologic processes seem to change the characteristic of the brain diffusion [13], diffusion-weighted imaging (DWI) has become increasingly popular over the past few years. In typical clinical practice, diffusion imaging is used to assess acute cerebral ischemia [14–17], where the water mobility acutely decreases after the onset of ischemia. The mechanisms to explain the decrease in diffusion coefficients are still controversial. Failure of the Na^+/K^+ adenosine triphosphatase pump is believed to play an important role in this process, however, leading many to term this state as *cytotoxic edema* [17,18]. Diffusion imaging has also been successfully applied to the evaluation of other neurologic conditions, such as multiple sclerosis [19–22], encephalitis [23], and Creutzfeldt-Jakob disease [24].

Most diffusion measurements today are made using a variant of the diffusion-weighted sequence first described by Stejskal and Tanner [25]. Their initial approach described a spin echo (SE) sequence together with two equal and opposite extra gradient pulses [25]; the amount of signal loss can be related to the magnitude of diffusion. For practical purposes, an echo planar imaging (EPI), SE, T2-weighted sequence is used, causing reduction of motion artifacts and speeding the time of acquisition [26]. Stejskjal and Tanner's [25] approach uses two magnetic pulses or gradients to label the spins: the application of the first diffusion gradient causes a dephasing of water protons; because they move randomly, not all water protons are in place for rephrasing from the application of the second diffusion gradient. Thus, there is a signal decrease that depends on how far the water molecules move [13]. The net signal on the final diffusion-weighted image is therefore influenced by the T2 tissue effect and by the tissue diffusion characteristics. By acquiring an image with little diffusion weighting and another image with substantial diffusion weighting, the apparent diffusion coefficient (ADC) can be calculated on a voxel-by-voxel basis, allowing the generation of a map that reflects solely the diffusion influence, excluding the T2 effects, which prevents misinterpretation from the so-called "T2 shine-through" effect [13,26].

Diffusion-weighted MRI in brain tumors

Although most of this review focuses on DTI, a few words about the more common, nontensor (or "trace-weighted") DWI approaches are appropriate. DWI has been used to assess brain tumors, and although it has had limited success as a definitive prognostic tool, its proponents suggest that in certain settings, it can increase the sensitivity and specificity of MRI in the evaluation of brain tumors by providing information about tumor cellularity, which may, in turn, improve prediction of tumor grade. Some also suggest that DWI can provide information about peritumoral neoplastic cell infiltration [8,9,27–31].

One example of a specific helpful arena in which DWI may be helpful is the distinction between brain abscesses and necrotic and cystic neoplasms on MRI. DWI can provide a sensitive and specific method for differentiating tumor from abscess in certain settings [32–35]. The abscesses have a high signal on DWI and a reduced ADC within the cavity. This restricted diffusion is thought to be related to the characteristic of the pus in the cavity. Because pus is a viscous fluid that consists of inflammatory cells, debris, and macromolecules like fibrinogen [36], this may, in turn, lead to reduced water mobility, lower ADC, and bright signal on DWI. Conversely, necrotic and cystic tumors display a low signal on DWI (similar to the cerebrospinal fluid [CSF] in the ventricles), with an increased ADC as well as isointense or hypointense DWI signal intensity in the lesion margins [34]. Although these findings can be helpful, they are, of course, not absolute; under certain conditions, restricted diffusion has been documented in hemorrhagic metastases, radiation necrosis, and cystic astrocytoma [37].

DWI is also an effective way of differentiating an arachnoid cyst from epidermoid tumors [38]. Both lesions present the same T1 and T2 signal intensity characteristic of CSF. On DWI, epidermoid tumors are hyperintense, because they are solidly composed, whereas arachnoid cysts are hypointense, demonstrating high diffusivity [38]. The ADC values of epidermoid tumors are similar to those of the brain parenchyma, whereas the ADC values of arachnoid cysts are similar to those of CSF [39]. As a result, DWI can be used to assess follow-up of surgically resected epidermoid tumors, proving efficacious in the detection of residual lesions [40].

Another use for DWI has been to attempt to assist in determination of the margins of tumors in the brain. High-grade tumors tend to spread diffusely across the brain, moving along the fiber tracts [41,42]. Some studies have demonstrated the capability of DWI to discriminate the tumor, the infiltrating tumor, the peritumoral edema, and the normal brain parenchyma [8,9,14,43]. Other studies did not find any advantages of this method with regard to the evaluation of tumor extensions [44–46], however, likely because of the difficulty of finding any border even on histopathologic examination of some tumors.

Perhaps most helpfully, DWI has been shown to assist in assessing the cellularity of tumors [44]. In some studies, high-grade tumors have been found to have low ADC values (Fig. 1). This suggests a correlation between the ADC values and tumor cellularity [46,47], with lower ADC values suggesting high-grade lesions [46,48]. In some studies, however, ADC values found in high- and low-grade gliomas have overlapped somewhat [46]. Lymphoma, a highly cellular tumor, has hyperintensity on DWI and reduced ADC values [49], and it may be in differentiating lymphoma from other CNS lesions that DWI has its greatest value. Although meningiomas also have a restricted diffusion, displaying low ADC values (Fig. 2) [46], they rarely present difficulty in diagnosis. Metastases with perilesional edema have higher ADC values than a primary brain tumor with peritumoral edema, and some have suggested that this may allow better differentiation [28].

Finally, DWI may be useful for posttreatment assessment, demonstrating acute postoperative procedure–induced changes [50] but, more importantly, possibly providing an early surrogate marker for the efficacy of the chemotherapeutic treatment [51,52], because such treatments may cause cytotoxic or vasogenic edema that DWI can differentiate and monitor. DWI also has been suggested as a tool for monitoring the effectiveness of radiation therapy [2] In summary, DWI has a limited prognostic role but may become an important tool in assessing the response to radiation therapy and chemotherapy [2] as well as the complications related to each type of therapy [53,54].

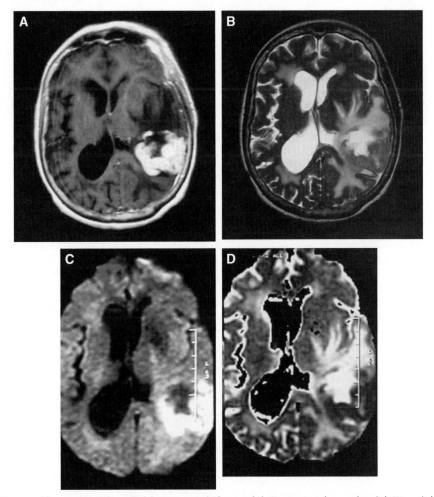

Fig. 1. A 75-year-old woman with a glioblastoma multiforme. (*A*) Contrast-enhanced, axial, T1-weighted image shows an enhancing necrotic mass surrounded by an abnormal hyperintense area on the axial T2-weighted image (T2WI). (*B*) These abnormal hyperintense T2WI areas can represent peritumoral edema or infiltrating tumor. The tumor is isohypointense on the T2WI, indicating high cellularity; this is also demonstrated as restricted diffusion on the diffusion-weighted image (*C*) and apparent diffusion coefficient map (*D*).

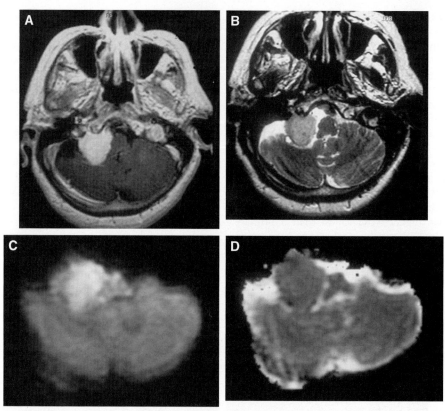

Fig. 2. An 84-year-old woman with a meningioma. An axial, postcontrast-enhanced, T1-weighted image (*A*) and an axial T2-weighted image (*B*) show an extra-axial enhancing lesion in the right cerebellopontomedullary angle cistern. Axial diffusion-weighted imaging (*C*) shows "T2-shine through," whereas the apparent diffusion coefficient map (*D*) demonstrates isointense signal intensity suggesting cellularity similar to that of brain tissue.

Diffusion tensor MRI

Physical basis

The movement of water occurs in all three directions and is assumed to behave in a manner that physicists can describe using a Gaussian approximation. When water molecules diffuse equally in all directions, this is termed *isotropic diffusion*. This phenomenon is typical in the ventricles, and at the resolution of standard MRI, also seems to be the case in the gray matter. In the white matter, however, free water molecules diffuse anisotropically, that is, the water diffusion is not equal in all three orthogonal directions [55,56,61]. This is likely because tissue structures cause impediment of the water motion; these structures likely include the cell membranes but, more importantly, the myelin sheath surrounding myelinated white matter [57]. Put another way, isotropic diffusion can be graphically represented as a sphere [58], whereas anisotropic diffusion can be graphically expressed as an ellipsoid [58], with water molecules moving farther along the long axis of a fiber bundle and less movement perpendicularly [59].

To estimate the nine tensor matrix elements required for a Gaussian description of water mobility, the diffusion gradient must be applied to at least six noncollinear directions (only six of the nine elements are unique under this assumption) [60]. The eigenvalues represent the three principal diffusion coefficients measured along the three coordinate directions of the ellipsoid [59]. The eigenvectors represent the directions of the tensor [60]. Because interpreting a tensor representation can be difficult, scalar metrics have been proposed to simplify DTI data [57]. For example, fractional anisotropy (FA) measures the fraction of the total magnitude of diffusion anisotropy. FA values vary from complete isotropic diffusion (graded as 0) up to complete anisotropic diffusion (graded as 1) [57,58].

In addition to assessment of the diffusion in a single voxel, DTI has been used to attempt to map the white matter fiber tracts. This is typically done by connecting a given voxel to the appropriately adjacent voxel in accordance with the direction that the voxel's principal eigenvector is oriented [62,63]. A color-coded map of fiber orientation can also be determined by DTI [64]. A different color has been attributed to represent a different fiber orientation along the three orthogonal spatial axes: in the standard convention, red stands for the left-to-right direction of x-oriented fibers, blue stands for the superior-to-inferior direction of y-oriented fibers, and green stands for the anterior-to-posterior direction of z-oriented fibers (**Fig. 3**) [64,65].

Diffusion tensor MRI in brain tumors

Often, a primary aim of surgical brain tumor treatment is complete lesion resection without harming vital brain functions [66,67]. Because it is generally accepted that conventional MRI underestimates the real extent of the brain tumor, given its ability to verify neoplastic cells that infiltrate peritumoral areas of abnormal T2-weighted signal intensity [68], many practitioners are uncomfortable using only conventional MRI approaches. By examining the microscopic tissue environment, DTI may be able to delineate the tumor versus the infiltrating tumor between the peritumoral edema and normal brain parenchyma more accurately, which, in turn, may help to optimize the treatment of patients [69]. Although this remains to be proven, it does appear

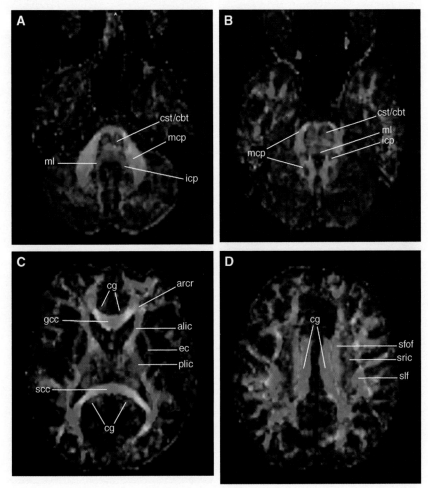

Fig. 3. Diffusion tensor imaging color-coded map of a healthy volunteer. Locations of white matter tracts are assigned on color maps. The direction of the main fiber tracts is represented by red (right-left), green-yellow (anterior-posterior), and blue (superior-inferior). Several main fiber tracts visible on color maps are annotated on the basis of anatomic knowledge. (*A–D*) Axial fractional anisotropic (FA) color maps. (*E–H*) Coronal FA color maps. (*I, J*) Sagittal FA color maps. Mcp, middle cerebral peduncle; cst, corticospinal tract; cbt, corticobulbar tract; ml, medial lemniscus; icp, inferior cerebellar peduncle; cg, cingulum; cc, corpus callosum; gcc, genu of corpus callosum; scc, splenium of corpus callosum; arcr, anterior region of corona radiata; alic, anterior limb of internal capsule; plic, posterior limb of internal capsule; ec, external capsule; sric, superior region of internal capsule; sfof, superior fronto-occipital fasciculus; ifof, inferior fronto-occipital fasciculus; slf, superior longitudinal fasciculus; ilf, inferior longitudinal fasciculus.

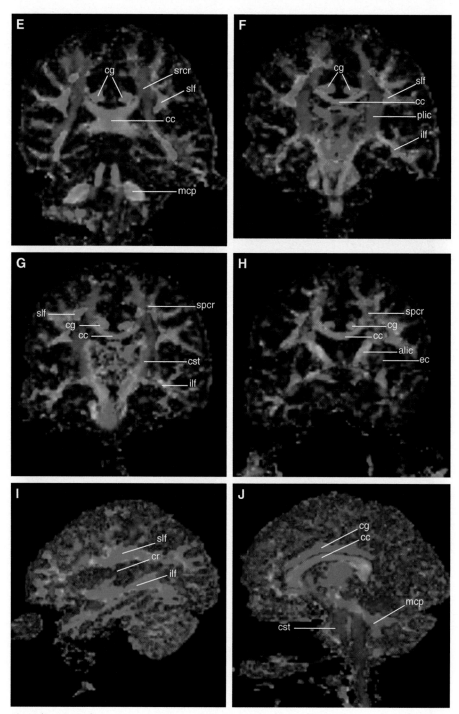

Fig. 3 (continued)

from straightforward inspection that DTI seems to be able to illustrate the relation of a tumor to the nearby main fiber tracts (Fig. 4). Because of this, many have begun to suggest that DTI might be used to aid in surgical planning [70] as well as radiotherapy planning [71] and to monitor tumor recurrence and the response to the treatment [72]. Examples of these applications are given below.

Tumor grading

As mentioned previously, DWI (nontensor diffusion) seems to provide some utility in tumor

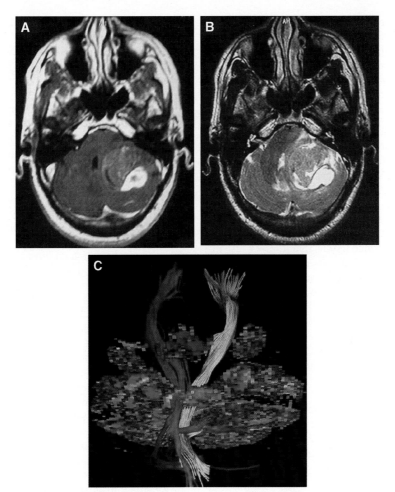

Fig. 4. A 47-year-old man with medulloblastoma. A heterogeneous mass with intratumoral hemorrhage (*A*) surrounded by peritumoral vasogenic edema (*B*) is located in the right cerebellum hemisphere. This mass causes compression and distortion of the fourth ventricle. (*C*) Tractography demonstrates contralateral displacement of the corticospinal tract without clear evidence of invasion or disruption of these fibers.

grading by assessment of tumor cellularity. To date, the additional information provided by DTI has not been shown to correlate with tumor cellularity [73], although in one series that evaluated epidermoid tumors with DTI, FA values were high, probably because of the high packing density of the cells and their solid-state cholesterol [74].

Presurgical planning

Much more enthusiasm has been shown for using DTI to illustrate the relation of a tumor to neighboring white matter tracts, with initial reports suggesting that this may be feasible [74]. DTI seems to be the only noninvasive method of obtaining information about the fiber tracts and is able to suggest them three dimensionally, although the validity of these suggestions remains to be studied carefully. Many practitioners accept an underlying assumption that

the chief cause of anisotropy is related to the white matter bundles; with this assumption, the involvement of the white matter tracts can often be clearly identified in brain tumor patients by using anisotropic maps (the FA maps are the most widely used) and so-called "diffusion tractography," where images of the mathematically described connections between voxels are generated.

White matter involvement by a tumor can be arranged into five different categories as follows:

1. Displaced: maintained normal anisotropy relative to the contralateral tract in the corresponding location but situated in an abnormal T2-weighted signal intensity area or presenting in an abnormal orientation
2. Invaded: slightly reduced anisotropy without displacement of white matter architecture, remaining identifiable on orientation maps

3. Infiltrated: reduced anisotropy but remaining identifiable on orientation maps
4. Disrupted: marked reduced anisotropy and unidentifiable on orientation maps
5. Edematous: maintained normal anisotropy and normally oriented but located in an abnormal T2-weighted signal intensity area [75]

The neoplastic cells and the peritumoral edema cause changes in the brain structure; typically, measurement of diffusion anisotropy from the normal brain parenchyma up to near the tumor demonstrates a decrease in FA values [1].

Displacement rather than destruction of white matter fibers around low-grade gliomas has been described [71,76]. Low-grade neoplasms (Fig. 5) are well-circumscribed lesions that do not cause invasion or destruction of fiber tracts. These lesions tend to produce a deviation of surrounding white matter fibers. A study described a case in which the corticospinal tract (CST) had been infiltrated by an oligodendroglioma, although it spared the motor strip and the posterior limb of the internal capsule [77]. Displacement rather than infiltration of the adjacent white matter tracts has also been described in cerebral metastases [71] and meningiomas [78].

The main fiber tracts are invaded in cases of gliomatosis cerebri (Fig. 6), which has a specific histopathologic behavior. The neoplastic cells form parallel rows among nerve fibers, preserving them; however, there is destruction of myelin sheaths. Thus, the anisotropy is slightly reduced when compared with normal subjects but greater than it is when compared with high-grade gliomas. The main fiber tracts remain identifiable on orientation maps and on the tractography.

The anisotropy in the T2-weighted hyperintense area that surrounds the tumor is reduced because of infiltration of neoplastic cells. Compared with the contralateral hemisphere in patients with high-grade gliomas (but not with low-grade gliomas or cerebral metastases) (Fig. 7), the anisotropy is also low in the white matter areas adjacent to tumors that look normal on T2-weighted images [71]. The same situation can be observed in lymphoma (Fig. 8). When compared with the abnormal white matter adjacent to metastases, Jellison et al [79] demonstrated decreased anisotropy of the abnormal white matter that surrounds the gliomas (Fig. 9). FA values decrease in the abnormal area that surrounds high-grade tumors on T2-weighted imaging. This presumably happens because of increased water content and tumor infiltration. A major brain structural disorganization then occurs [72]. Further study is necessary in this arena, because conflicting results have been described, with no difference found in FA value analyses of abnormal white matter adjacent to high-grade gliomas and metastases [72] in some studies.

The tract disruption mostly found in high-grade tumors (Fig. 10) may be caused by peritumoral edema, tumor mass effect, and tumor infiltration effect [71,78]. The anisotropic maps and tractography show destruction or discontinuation of the fiber tracts because of local tumor cell invasion (Fig. 11).

Metastatic lesions are surrounded by abnormal T2-weighted imaging that may consist of vasogenic edema. The edematous areas have reduced FA

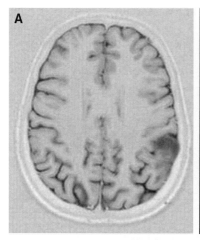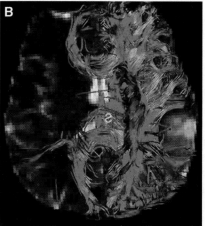

Fig. 5. A 42-year-old man with a diagnosis of a low-grade astrocytoma presented with early onset of focal seizures. (*A*) The MRI examination demonstrates an expansive lesion in the perirolandic area, which does not have hyperperfusion. (*B*) The mass lesion causes displacement of the main fiber tracts adjacent to the tumor, which is well demonstrated on tractography. There seems to be no invasion or disruption of these tracts.

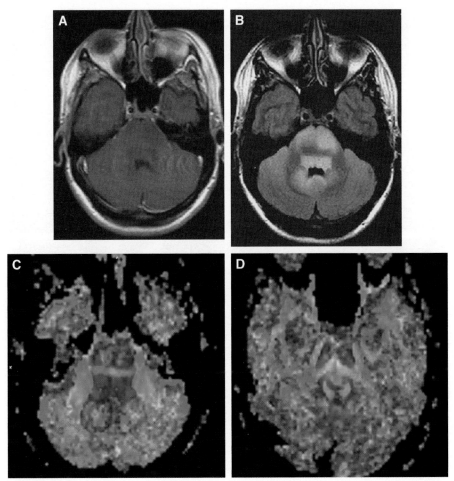

Fig. 6. An invading brain stem lesion that extends to the right cerebellum hemisphere though the middle cerebellar peduncle in a 40-year-old man who presented with left sixth cranial nerve palsy. The diagnosis of gliomatosis cerebri was made after a biopsy. The lesion does not enhance on the postcontrast T1-weighted image (*A*), has hyperintense signal on the T2-weighted image (*B*), and causes minimum expansion of the brain stem. Magnetic resonance spectroscopy shows a high myoinositol peak, a moderately high choline peak, and a subtle reduction on the *N*-acetylaspartate peak (not shown). The diffusion tensor imaging–fractional anisotropy maps (*C–F*) and tractography (*G, H*) demonstrate that the main brain stem fiber tracts are preserved. This is probably explained by the fact that gliomatosis cerebri is a diffusely invading lesion that preserves the normal underlying cytoarchitectural pattern because it does not destroy the nerve fibers.

values. This fact can be explained by the increase in water content rather than by destruction or infiltration of nerve fibers. DTI did not help to differentiate apparently normal white matter from edematous brain and enhancing peritumoral margins [69]. The drop in FA values of the area infiltrated by cell tumors is lower than in the peritumoral edema [1,70,75]. DTI can distinguish the edematous areas with intact fibers mostly found in metastases (Fig. 12) from the disrupted fibers mostly found in high-grade gliomas [80].

In short, DTI is gaining support as a preoperative MRI method of evaluating brain tumors closely related to eloquent regions [75]. DTI seems to be particularly advantageous for certain types of surgical planning, optimizing the surgical evaluation of brain tumors near white matter tracts. Formal studies demonstrating that DTI can successfully prevent postoperative complications have yet to be performed, but preliminary data look promising [80].

Combination of diffusion tensor imaging with functional MRI

Intracranial neoplasms may involve the functional cortex and the corresponding white matter tracts. The preoperative identification of eloquent areas through noninvasive methods, such as blood oxygen level dependent (BOLD) fMRI and DTI

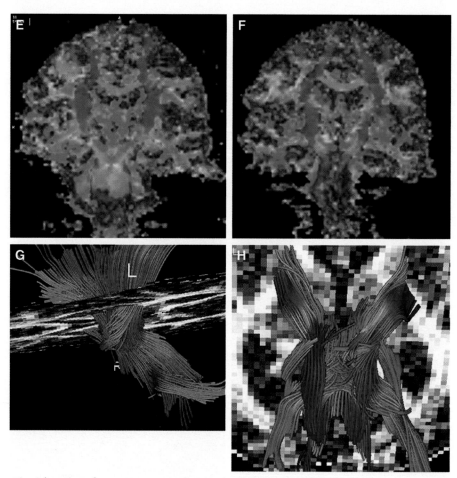

Fig. 6 (continued)

tractography, offers some advantages; not only can it reduce the time of surgery in some instances, but it may minimize some intraoperative cortical stimulation methods, such as identification of the language cortex [80].

Until recently, preoperative and perioperative methods to evaluate brain function of patients with brain tumors were restricted to cortex activation. Increasingly, investigators are beginning to combine fMRI with DTI. The attraction is that fMRI can be an accurate and noninvasive method for mapping functional cerebral cortex, identifying eloquent areas in the cortex and displaying their relation to the lesion [81], whereas DTI may be able to identify the main fiber tracts to be avoided during surgery so as to safely guide a tumor resection [1]. Consequently, the combination of DTI tractography and fMRI might allow us to map an entire functional circuit precisely [82]. Even though fMRI locates eloquent cortical areas, determination of the course and integrity of the fiber tracts remains essential to the surgical planning [80,83].

This identification of the fiber tracts can facilitate the decision-making process regarding the likelihood of an operation [1]. As a result, neurosurgeons may have more information to inform the choice of surgical approach to be taken. This better evaluation of risks by neurosurgeons is possible if they can know the spatial relation between the tumor and major fiber tracts [63] and thereby avoid postoperative neurologic deficit [2,83]. This remains to be proven in randomized trials, however.

Many investigators hope that the combined use of fMRI and DTI tractography might define the structural basis of functional connectivity in normal and pathologic brains [84]. As a consequence of the mass effect and changes in the structure of the brain caused by tumor, the identification of eloquent areas through conventional MRI results is, so to speak, impossible. Because fMRI is able to depict the exact location of the motor cortex in many instances, it should be possible to delineate the CST by DTI tractography. In one previous report [78], the authors used the motor cortex identified by

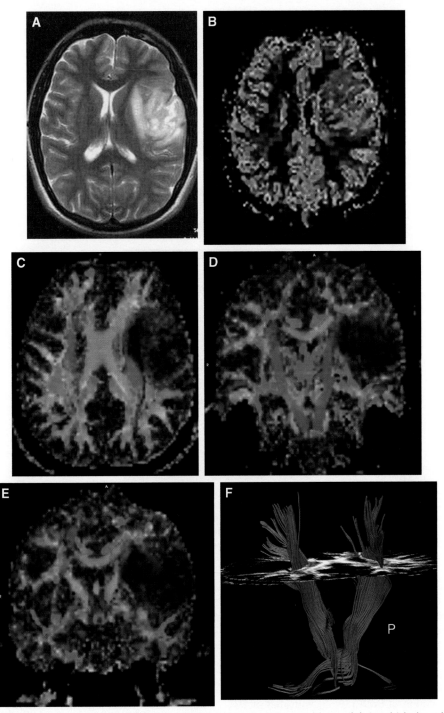

Fig. 7. A nonenhancing insular anaplastic astrocytoma lesion in a 56-year-old man (*A*), in which the relative cerebral blood volume map (*B*) demonstrates some areas of hyperperfusion within the lesion. There is infiltration of the corticospinal tract and corona radiata as well as of the superior longitudinal fasciculus on the axial (*C*) and coronal (*D, E*) diffusion tensor imaging (DTI)–fractional anisotropy maps and of the left corticospinal fibers tracts on tractography (*F*). DTI shows reduced anisotropy, but the main tracts remain identifiable on tractography.

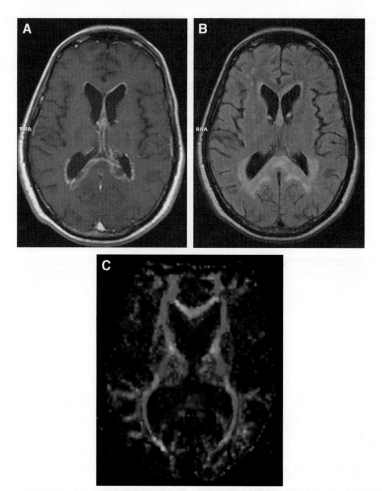

Fig. 8. A 50-year-old man with a histopathologic diagnosis of lymphoma complained of mental disturbance, cognitive impairment, and seizures. A contrast-enhanced, axial, T1-weighted image (*A*) demonstrates an enhancing lesion that involves the corpus callosum, surrounded by peritumoral edema/infiltrating lesion (*B*) associated with subependymal enhancement caused by cerebrospinal fluid dissemination. The axial fractional anisotropy color-coded map (*C*) demonstrates the infiltrating aspect of the lesion. The anisotropy in the splenium of the corpus callosum is markedly reduced.

fMRI as a starting point to trace the CST by DTI tractography. This approach could eventually be extended to other tracts as well.

The neurosurgical navigation system is a real-time device that provides a probe-guided intraoperative MRI (iMRI) display of the brain [85]. This system has already been widely used and is able to combine the information of fMRI [80,85] with that of DTI tractography [82,86], or even of both together [78,81].

Intraoperative utility of diffusion tensor imaging

iMRI has been used to guide a brain tumor resection. Such image-guidance systems can help to determine the optimal placement for the craniotomy.

Because surgical manipulations and maneuvers alter the anatomic position of brain structures and the tumor [87], morphologic changes of the brain may also occur between the time of the preoperative MRI examinations and the time of the surgery [88]. For this reason, the exact location of brain tumors based on preoperative examinations may not be the same. Because of this, iMRI has been proposed as a possible way to enable neurosurgeons to optimize their surgical approaches by avoiding critical structures and the adjacent normal brain parenchyma [87]. Some reports suggest that in 65% to 92% of the cases in which neurosurgeons believed they have performed a complete and thorough tumor resection, iMRI still depicts a lesion to be resected [89,90]. This is particularly relevant in low-grade gliomas, because studies suggest that total

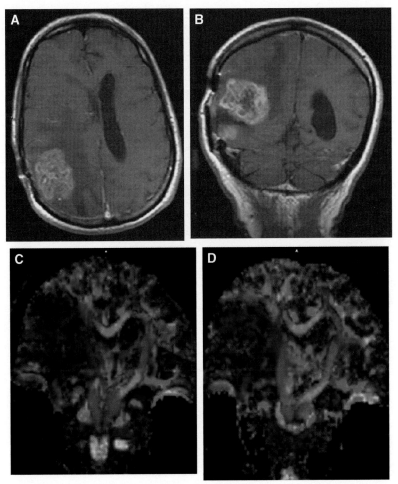

Fig. 9. (*A, B*) An expansive and infiltrating lesion in a 73-year-old man with left hemiparesis and seizures, with the diagnosis of glioblastoma multiforme. The lesion has hyperperfusion, markedly elevated choline and lactate/lipid peaks, and a low of *N*-acetylaspartate peak. (*C, D*) Coronal diffusion tensor imaging–fractional anisotropy maps show that the lesion dislocates and infiltrates the corticospinal tract and the superior longitudinal fasciculus. There is also distortion of the corpus callosum.

resection leads to a higher probability of cure. During surgery, however, such lesions can be difficult to differentiate from the normal brain parenchyma.

iMRI can be performed together with some functional sequences, such as fMRI [85] and diffusion imaging [82]. In one study, intraoperative diffusion imaging was performed during neurosurgery for the resection of a tumor using an interventional MRI system [82].

Intraoperative development of hyperacute cerebral ischemia had been previously detected in two patients, and this was confirmed later by a follow-up MRI examination. DTI, together with a neuronavigation system, was performed in a third patient as an integral part of an image-guided tumor resection. After processing the DTI data, DTI tractography was performed. The relation of the tumor to the anatomy of the white matter fiber tracts adjacent

to it was clearly and plainly demonstrated in a case of oligodendroglioma. The fiber tracts were displaced, without being infiltrated or disrupted by the tumor. The complete tumor resection was performed without any postoperative neurologic deficit. Although anecdotal, such reports suggest that intraoperative diffusion imaging may provide important clinical information, adding substantially to the intraoperative information available about the pathologic state of the brain parenchyma and the structure of white matter.

Diffusion tensor imaging in brain tumor therapy

DTI may play a role in the management of patients undergoing radiation therapy and chemotherapy. By adding information about the location of white matter tracts, DTI tractography might be used

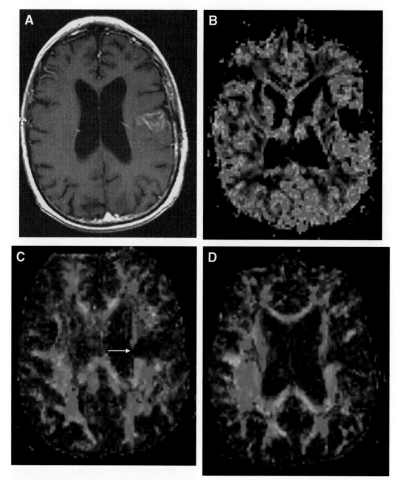

Fig. 10. A 56-year-old man with an anaplastic astrocytoma presented with right hemiparesis. The contrast-enhanced T1-weighted image (*A*) shows a left frontal lesion that has hyperperfusion on the relative cerebral blood volume map (*B*) (note the black signal caused by excessive enhancement with resulting T1 effect). (*C, D*) The axial diffusion-tensor imaging–fractional anisotropy maps demonstrate disruption of the left corona radiata (*arrow*).

successfully alongside fMRI for radiosurgery planning. In theory, this should allow a reduction of the dose applied as well as a reduction in the volume of normal brain irradiated with a high dose, hopefully reducing necrosis [71].

DTI may also help in the early detection of white matter injuries caused by chemotherapy and radiation therapy. A report showed a correlation between the reduction of FA values, young age at treatment, an increased interval since the beginning of treatment, and the poor intellectual outcome in patients with medulloblastoma [91]. The possibility of using FA or other DTI changes as a biomarker for neurotoxicity is enticing.

Limitations

Although initial reports suggest advantages of DTI in the evaluation of patients with brain tumors,

these reports are largely single-center, uncontrolled, preliminary findings. Therefore, these results must be cautiously interpreted. Furthermore, there remain substantial technical hurdles, with the rapid evolution of MRI systems making ever more powerful approaches possible. Such improvements are particularly welcome, given the limited signal-to-noise ratio of diffusion overall. For example, the limited spatial resolution of EPI approaches may lead to reduced sensitivity. The method herein assessed is only capable of depicting the prominent fiber tracts [70,92], and more advanced approaches (eg, diffusion spectrum imaging) may be much more useful in the future. Susceptibility artifacts can cause image distortion that prevents DTI data from being accurately analyzed [70], and numerous other technical challenges remain. Nevertheless, these initial data are promising.

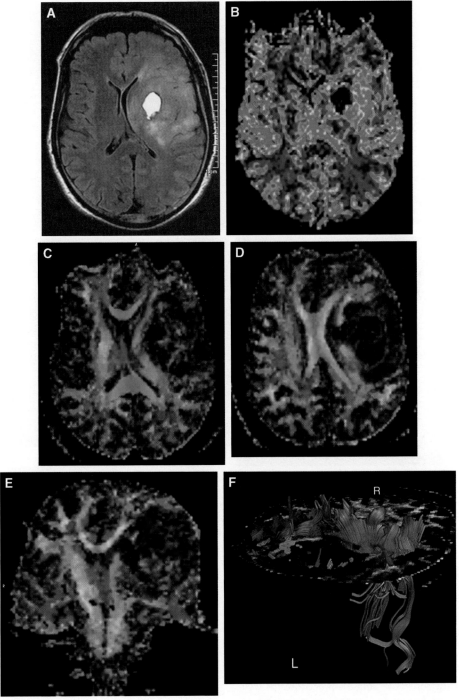

Fig. 11. A 57-year-old man with glioblastoma multiforme presented with right hemiparesis and seizures. An expansive, infiltrating, and enhancing left insular lesion with intratumoral hemorrhage (*A*) and hyperperfusion (*B*) is demonstrated. Axial (*C, D*) and coronal (*E*) diffusion tensor imaging–fractional anisotropy maps and tractography (*F*) show dislocation and disruption of the main fiber tracts, such as the anterior and posterior portions of the internal capsule and the superior longitudinal fasciculus.

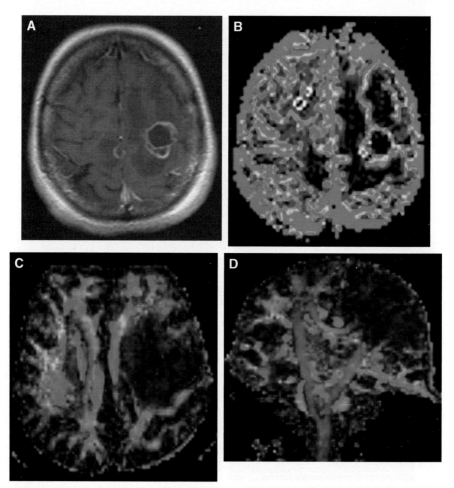

Fig. 12. A 50-year-old woman with new onset of seizures and a history of breast cancer. A round rim-enhancing lesion with a necrotic center (*A*) and hyperperfusion (*B*) is surrounded by peritumoral edema consisting of breast cancer metastasis. Axial (*C*) and coronal (*D*) diffusion tensor imaging–fractional anisotropy (FA) maps show the edematous changes in the FA values. Thus, it is difficult to identify the main fiber tracts within the vasogenic edema. This does not necessarily mean that these fibers are infiltrated with tumor or disrupted, however.

Summary

DTI seems to offer the possibility of adding important information to presurgical planning. Although experience is limited, DTI seems to provide useful local information about the structures near the tumor, and this seems to be useful in planning. In the future, DTI may provide an improved way to monitor intraoperative surgical procedures as well as their complications. Furthermore, evaluation of the response to treatment with chemotherapy and radiation therapy might also be possible. Although DTI has some limitations, its active investigation and further study are clearly warranted.

References

[1] Landis SH, Murray T, Bolden S. Cancer statistics, 1998. CA Cancer J Clin 1998;48:6–29.

[2] Berens ME, Rutka JT, Rosenblum ML. Brain tumor epidemiology, growth, and invasion. Neurosurg Clin N Am 1990;1:1–18.

[3] Koeller KK, Henry JM. Superficial gliomas: radiologic-pathologic correlation. Radiographics 2001;21:1533–56.

[4] Hunt D, Treasure P. Year of life lost due to cancer in East Anglia 1990–1994. Cambridge: East Anglian Cancer Intelligence Unit, Institute of Public Health; 1998.

[5] Brain MRC Tumor Working Party. Prognostic factor for high-grade malignant glioma: development of a prognostic index. A report of the Medical Research Council Brain Tumor Working Party. J Neurooncol 1990;9:47–55.

[6] Damadian R. Tumor detection by nuclear magnetic resonance. Science 1971;171:1151–3.

[7] Tovi M. MR imaging in cerebral gliomas analysis of tumor tissue components. Acta Radiol Suppl 1993;384:1–24.

[8] Brunberg JA, Chenevert TL, McKeever PE, Ross DA, Junck LR, Muraszko KM, et al. In vivo MR determination of water diffusion coefficients and diffusion anisotropy: correlation with structural alteration in gliomas of the cerebral hemispheres. AJNR Am J Neuroradiol 1995;16: 361–71.

[9] Tien RD, Felsberg GJ, Friedman H, Brown M, MacFall J. MR imaging of high-grade cerebral gliomas: value of diffusion-weighted echo-planar pulse sequence. AJR Am J Roentgenol 1994; 162:671–7.

[10] Holodny AI, Ollenschlager M. Diffusion imaging in brain tumor. Neuroimaging Clin N Am 2002; 12:107–24.

[11] Le Bihan D, Breton E, Lallemand D, Aubin MI, Vignaud J, Laval-Jeantet M. Diffusion and perfusion in intravoxel incoherent motion MR imaging. Radiology 1988;168:497–505.

[12] Turner R, Le Bihan D, Maier J, Vavrek R, Hedges LK, Pekar J. Echo-planar imaging of intravoxel incoherent motion. Radiology 1990; 177:407–14.

[13] Barboriak DP. Imaging of brain tumors with diffusion-weighted and diffusion tensor MR imaging. Magn Reson Imaging Clin N Am 2003;11: 379–401.

[14] Maier SE, Gudbjartsson H, Patz SL, Hsu L, Lovblad KO, Edelman RR, et al. Line scan diffusion imaging: characterization in healthy subjects and stroke patients. AJR Am J Roentgenol 1998;171:85–93.

[15] Warach S, Chien D, Li W, Ronthal M, Edelman RR. Fast magnetic resonance diffusion-weighted imaging of acute human stroke. Neurology 1992;42:1717–23.

[16] Sunshine JL, Tarr RW, Lanzieri CF, Landis DM, Selman WR, Lewin JS. Hyperacute stroke: ultrafast MR imaging to triage patients prior to therapy. Radiology 1999;212:325–32.

[17] Beauchamp NJ, Uluğ AM, Passe TJ, van Zijl PC. MR diffusion imaging in stoke: review and controversies. Radiographics 1998;18:1269–83.

[18] Schaefer PW. Applications of DWI in clinical neurology. J Neurol Sci 2001;186(Suppl 1): S25–35.

[19] Larsson HB, Thomsen C, Frederiksen J, Stubgaard M, Henriksen O. In vivo magnetic resonance measurement in the brain of patients with multiple sclerosis. Magn Reson Imaging 1993;10:7–12.

[20] Horsfield MA, Lai M, Webb SL, Barker GJ, Tofts PS, Turner R, et al. Apparent diffusion coefficients in benign and secondary progressive multiple sclerosis by nuclear magnetic resonance. Magn Reson Med 1996;36:393–400.

[21] Castriota-Scanderberg A, Tomaiuolo F, Sabatini U, Nocentini U, Grasso MG, Caltagirone C. Demyelinating plaques in relapsing-remitting and secondary progressive multiple sclerosis: assessment with diffusion MR imaging. AJNR Am J Neuroradiol 2000;21:862–8.

[22] Tsuchiya K, Hachiya J, Maehara T. Diffusion-weighted MR imaging in multiple sclerosis: comparison with contrast-enhanced study. Eur J Radiol 1999;10:7–12.

[23] Tsuchiya K, Katase S, Yoshino A, Hachiya J. Diffusion-weighted MR imaging of encephalitis. AJR Am J Roentgenol 1999;173:1097–9.

[24] Na DL, Suh CK, Choi SH, Moon HS, Seo DW, Kim SE, et al. Diffusion-weighted magnetic resonance imaging in probable Creutzfeldt-Jakob disease. Arch Neurol 1999;56:951–7.

[25] Stejskal E, Tanner J. Spin diffusion measurements: spin echos in the presence of time-dependent field gradient. J Chem Phys 1965;42: 288–92.

[26] Romero JM, Schaefer PW, Grant PE, Becerra L, Gonzáles RG. Diffusion MR imaging of acute ischemic stroke. Neuroimaging Clin N Am 2002; 12:35–53.

[27] Eis M, Els T, Hoehn-Berlage M, Hossman KA. Quantitative diffusion MR imaging of cerebral tumor and edema. Acta Neurochir Suppl (Wien) 1994;60:344–6.

[28] Krabbe K, Gideon P, Wang P, Hansen U, Thomsen C, Madsen F. MR diffusion imaging of human intracranial tumours. Neuroradiology 1997;39:483–9.

[29] Le Bihan D, Douek P, Argyropoulou M, Turner R, Patronas N, Fulham M. Diffusion and perfusion magnetic resonance imaging in brain tumors. Top Magn Reson Imaging 1993; 5:25–31.

[30] Tsuruda JS, Chew WM, Moseley ME, Norman D. Diffusion-weighted MR imaging of extraaxial tumors. Magn Reson Med 1991;19:316–20.

[31] Yanaka K, Shirai S, Kimura H, Kamezaki T, Matsumura A, Nose T. Clinical application of diffusion-weighted magnetic resonance imaging to intracranial disorders. Neurol Med Chir 1995; 16:361–71.

[32] Guo AC, Provenzale JM, Cruz LCH Jr, Petrella JR. Cerebral abscesses: investigation using apparent diffusion coefficient maps. Neuroradiology 2001;43:370–4.

[33] Bergui M, Zhong J, Bradac GB, Sales S. Diffusion-weighted images of intracranial cyst-like lesions. Neuroradiology 2001;439(10):824–9.

[34] Chang SC, Lai PH, Chen WL, Weng HH, Ho JT, Wang JS. Diffusion-weighted MRI features of brain abscess and cystic or necrotic brain tumors: comparison with conventional MRI. Clin Imaging 2002;26(4):227–36.

[35] Chan JH, Tsui EY, Chau LF, Chow KY, Chan MS, Yuen MK, et al. Discrimination of an infected brain tumor from a cerebral abscess by combined MR perfusion and diffusion imaging. Comput Med Imaging Graph 2002;26(1):19–23.

[36] Ebisu T, Tanaka C, Umeda M, Kitamura M, Naruse S, Higuichi T, et al. Discrimination of brain abscess from necrotic or cystic tumors by diffusion-weighted echo planar imaging. Magn Reson Imaging 1996;14(9):1113–6.

[37] Hartmann M, Jansen O, Heiland S, Sommer C, Munkel K, Sartor K. Restricted diffusion within ring enhancement is not pathognomonic for brain abscess. AJNR Am J Neuroradiol 2001; 22(9):1738–42.

[38] Tsuruda JS, Chew WM, Moseley ME, Norman D. Diffusion-weighted MR imaging of the brain: value of differentiating between extra-axial cysts and epidermoid tumors. AJNR Am J Neuroradiol 1990;155:1049–65.

[39] Chen S, Ikawa F, Kurisu K, Arita K, Takaba J, Kanou Y. Quantitative MR evaluation of intracranial epidermoid tumors by fast fluid-attenuated inversion recovery imaging and echo-planar diffusion-weighted imaging. AJNR Am J Neuroradiol 2001;22(6):1089–96.

[40] Laing AD, Mitchell PJ, Wallace D. Diffusion-weighted magnetic resonance imaging of intracranial epidermoid tumors. Aust Radiol 1999; 43:16–9.

[41] Burger PC, Heinz ER, Shibata T, Kleihues P. Topographic anatomy and CT correlations in the untreated glioblastoma multiforme. J Neurosurg 1988;68:698–704.

[42] Johnson PC, Hunt SJ, Drayer BP. Human cerebral gliomas: correlation of postmortem MR imaging and neuropathologic findings. Radiology 1989;170:211–7.

[43] Yoshiura T, Wu O, Zaheer A, Reese TG, Sorensen AG. Highly diffusion-sensitized MRI of brain: dissociation of gray and white matter. Magn Reson Med 2001;45:734–40.

[44] Stadnik TW, Chaskis C, Michotte A, Shabana WM, van Rompaey K, Luypaert R, et al. Diffusion-weighted MR imaging of intracerebral masses: comparison with conventional MR imaging and histologic findings. AJNR Am J Neuroradiol 2001;22:969–76.

[45] Castillo M, Smith JK, Kwock L, Wilber K. Apparent diffusion coefficients in the evaluation of high-grade cerebral gliomas. AJNR J Neuroradiol 2001;22(1):60–4.

[46] Kono K, Inoue Y, Nakayama K, Shakudo M, Morino M, Ohata K, et al. The role of diffusion-weighted imaging in patients with brain tumors. AJNR Am J Neuroradiol 2001;22:1081–8.

[47] Sugahara T, Korogi Y, Kochi M, Ikushima I, Shigematu Y, Hirai T, et al. Usefulness of diffusion-weighted MRI with echo-planar technique in the evaluation of cellularity in gliomas. J Magn Reson Imaging 1999;9:53–60.

[48] Noguchi K, Watanabe N, Nagayoshi T, Kanazawa T, Toyoshima S, Shimizu M, et al. Role of diffusion-weighted echo-planar MRI in distinguishing between brain abscess and tumor: a preliminary report. Neuroradiology 1999;41: 171–4.

[49] Guo AC, Cummings TJ, Dash RC, Provenzale JM. Lymphomas and high-grade astrocytomas: comparison of water diffusibility and histologic characteristics. Radiology 2002;224(1):177–83.

[50] Singh S, Leeds N. Postoperative diffusion imaging in the setting of craniotomies for brain masses: incidence of ischemia. Presented at the American Society of Neuroradiology 40th Annual Meeting. Vancouver, May 10–12, 2002.

[51] Kauppienen RA. Monitoring cytotoxic tumour treatment response by diffusion magnetic resonance imaging and proton spectroscopy. NMR Biomed 2002;15(1):6–17.

[52] Chenevert TL, Stegman LD, Taylor JM, Robertson PL, Greenberg HS, Rehemtulla A, et al. Diffusion magnetic resonance imaging: an early surrogate marker of therapeutic efficacy in brain tumors. J Natl Cancer Inst 2000;92(24): 2029–36.

[53] Valk PE, Dillon WP. Radiation injury of the brain. AJNR Am J Neuroradiol 1991;12(1): 45–62.

[54] Fujikawa A, Tsuchiya K, Katase S, Kurosaki Y, Hachiya J. Diffusion-weighted MR imaging of carmofur-induced leukoencephalopathy. Eur Radiol 2001;11(12):2602–6.

[55] Chenevert TL, Brunberg JA, Pipe JG. Anisotropic diffusion in human white matter: demonstration with MR techniques in vivo. Radiology 1990; 177:401–5.

[56] Moseley ME, Cohen Y, Kucharczyk J, Mintorovitch J, Asgari HS, Wendland, Diffusion-weighted MF. MR imaging of anisotropic water diffusion in cat central nervous system. Radiology 1990;176:439–45.

[57] Melhem ER, Mori S, Mukundan G, Kraut MA, Pomper MG, Van Zijl PCM. Diffusion tensor MR imaging of the brain and white matter tractography. AJR Am J Roentgenol 2002;178(1): 3–16.

[58] Ito R, Mori S, Melhem ER. Diffusion tensor MR imaging and tractography. Neuroimaging Clin N Am 2002;12(1):1–19.

[59] Pierpaoli C, Jezzard P, Basser P, Barnett A, Di Chiro G. Diffusion tensor MR imaging of the human brain. Radiology 1996;201:637–48.

[60] Basser PJ, Mattiello J, LeBihan D. Estimation of the effective self-diffusion tensor from the NMR spin echo. J Magn Reson B 1994;103: 247–54.

[61] Shimony JS, McKinstry RC, Akbudak E, Aranovitz JA, Snyder AZ, Lori NF, et al. Quantitative diffusion-tensor anisotropy brain MR imaging: normative human data and anatomic analysis. Radiology 1999;212:770–84.

[62] Basser PJ, Pajevic S, Pierpaoli C, Duda J, Aldroubi A. In vivo fiber tractography using DT-MRI data. Magn Reson Med 2000;44:625–32.

[63] Mamata H, Mamata Y, Westin CF, Shenton ME, Kikinis R, Jolesz FA, et al. High-resolution line scan diffusion tensor MR imaging of white matter fiber tract anatomy. AJNR Am J Neuroradiol 2002;23:67–75.

[64] Douek P, Turner R, Pekar J, Patronas N, Le Bihan D. MR color mapping of myelin fiber

orientation. J Comput Assist Tomogr 1991; 15(6):923–9.

[65] Pajevic S, Pierpaoli C. Color schemes to represent the orientation of anisotropic tissues from diffusion tensor data: application to white matter fiber tract mapping in the human brain. Magn Reson Med 1999;42:526–40.

[66] Maldjian JA, Schulder M, Liu WC, Mun IK, Hirschorn D, Murthy R, et al. Intraoperative functional MRI using a real-time neurosurgical navigation system. J Comput Assist Tomogr 1997;21:910–2.

[67] Schulder M, Maldjian JA, Liu WC, Holodny AI, Kalnin AT, Mun IK, et al. Functional image-guided surgery of intracranial tumors located in or near the sensorimotor cortex. J Neurosurg 1998;89:412–8.

[68] Tovi M. MR imaging in cerebral gliomas analysis of tumor tissue components. Acta Radiol Suppl 1993;384:1–24.

[69] Sha S, Bastin ME, Whittle IR, Wardlaw JM. Diffusion tensor MR imaging of high-grade cerebral gliomas. AJNR Am J Neuroradiol 2002;23:520–7.

[70] Mori S, Frederiksen K, Van Zijl PCM, Stieltjes B, Kraut MA, Slaiyappan M, et al. Brain white matter anatomy of tumor patients evaluated with diffusion tensor imaging. Ann Neurol 2002;51: 377–80.

[71] Price SJ, Burnet NG, Donovan T, Green HAL, Pena A, Antoun NM, et al. Diffusion tensor imaging of brain tumors at 3T: a potential tool for assessing white matter tract invasion. Clin Radiol 2003;58:455–62.

[72] Lu S, Ahn D, Johnson G, Cha S. Peritumoral diffusion tensor imaging of high-grade gliomas and metastatic brain tumors. AJNR Am J Neuroradiol 2003;24:937–41.

[73] Gauvain KM, McKinstry RC, Mukherjee P, Perry A, Neil JJ, Kaufman BA, et al. Evaluating pediatric brain tumor cellularity with diffusion-tensor imaging. AJR Am J Roentgenol 2001; 177:449–54.

[74] Koot RW, Jagtab AP, Akkerman EM, Heeten GJD, Majoie CBLM. Epidermoid of the lateral ventricle: evaluation with diffusion-weighted and diffusion tensor imaging. Clin Neurol Neurosurg 2003;105:270–3.

[75] Witwer BP, Moftakhar R, Hasan KM, Deshmukh P, Haughton V, Field A, et al. Diffusion-tensor imaging of white matter tracts in patients with cerebral neoplasm. J Neurosurg 2002; 97:568–75.

[76] Weishmann UC, Symms MR, Parker GJM, Clark CA, Lemieux L, Barker GJ, et al. Diffusion tensor imaging demonstrates deviation of fibers in normal appearing white matter adjacent to a brain tumour. J Neurol Neurosurg Psychiatry 2000;68:501–3.

[77] Holodny AI, Schwartz TH, Ollenschleger M, Liu WC, Schulder M. Tumor involvement of the corticospinal tract: diffusion magnetic resonance tractography with intraoperative correlation. J Neurosurg 2001;95(6):1082.

[78] Holodny AI, Ollenschleger M, Liu WC, Schulder M, Kalnin AJ. Identification of the corticospinal tracts achieved using blood-oxygen-level-dependent and diffusion functional MR imaging in patients with brain tumors. Am J Neuroradiol 2001;22:83–8.

[79] Jellison NJ, Wu Y, Field AS, Hasan KM, Alexander AL, Badie B. Diffusion tensor imaging metrics for tissue characterization: discriminating vasogenic edema from infiltrating tumor. Presented at the American Society of Neuroradiology 41st Annual Meeting. Washington, DC, April 27–May 1, 2003.

[80] Tummala RP, Chu RM, Liu H, Truwit C, Hall WA. Application of diffusion-tensor imaging to magnetic-resonance-guided brain tumor resection. Pediatr Neurosurg 2003;39:39–43.

[81] Schulder M, Maldjian JA, Liu W-C, Holodny AI, Kalnin AT, Mun IK, et al. Functional image-guided survey of intracranial tumors located in or near the sensorimotor cortex. J Neurosurg 1998;89:412–8.

[82] Krings T, Reiges MH, Thiex R, Gilsbach JM, Thron A. Functional and diffusion-weighted magnetic resonance images of space-occupying lesions affecting the motor system: imaging the motor cortex and pyramidal tracts. J Neurosurg 2001;95(5):816–24.

[83] Mamata Y, Mamata H, Nabavi A, Kacher DF, Pegolizzi RS Jr, Schwartz RB, et al. Intraoperative diffusion imaging on a 0.5 Tesla interventional scanner. J Magn Reson Imaging 2001;13:115–9.

[84] Guye M, Parker GJM, Symms M, Boulby P, Wheeler-Kingshott CAM, Salek-Haddadi A, et al. Combined functional MRI and tractography to demonstrate the connectivity of the human primary motor cortex in vivo. Neuroimage 2003;19:1349–60.

[85] Maldjian JA, Schulder M, Liu W-C, Mun I-K, Hirschorn D, Murthy R, et al. Intraoperative functional MRI using a real-time neurosurgical navigation system. J Comput Assist Tomogr 1997;21(6):910–2.

[86] Krings T, Coenen VA, Axer H, Reinges MHT, Holler M, von Keyserlingk DG, et al. In vivo 3D visualization of normal pyramidal tracts in human subjects using diffusion weighted magnetic resonance imaging and a neuronavigator system. Neurosci Lett 2001;307:192–6.

[87] Jolesz FA, Talos I-F, Schwartz RB, Mamat H, Kacher DF, Hynynen K, et al. Intraoperative magnetic resonance imaging and magnetic resonance imaging-guided therapy of brain tumors. Neuroimaging Clin N Am 2002;12:665–83.

[88] Martin AJ, Hall WA, Liu H, Pozza CH, Michel E, Casey SO, et al. Brain tumor resection: intraoperative monitoring with high-field-strength MR imaging—initial results. Radiology 2000;215: 221–8.

[89] Bradley WG. Achieving gross total resection of brain tumors: intraoperative MR imaging can make a big difference. AJNR Am J Neuroradiol 2002;23:348–9.

[90] Albert FK, Forsting M, Sartor K, Adams HP, Kunze S. Early post-operative magnetic resonance imaging after resection of malignant glioma: objective evaluation of residual tumor growth and its influence on regrowth and prognosis. Neurosurgery 1994;34:45–61.

[91] Khong P-L, Kwong DL, Chan GCF, Sham JST, Cham F-L, Ooi G-C. Diffusion-tensor imaging for the detection and qualification of treatment-induced white matter injury in children with medulloblastoma: a pilot study. AJNR Am J Neuroradiol 2003;24:734–40.

[92] Yamada K, Kizu O, Mori S, Ito H, Nakamura H, Yuen S, et al. Brain fibertracking with clinically feasible diffusion-tensor MR imaging: initial experience. Radiology 2003;227:295–301.

MAGNETIC RESONANCE IMAGING CLINICS

Magn Reson Imaging Clin N Am 14 (2006) 203–224

Update on Multiple Sclerosis

Jack H. Simon, MD, PhD*

- Clinical multiple sclerosis overview
- The focal and diffuse multiple sclerosis pathology by MR imaging
  Enhancing lesions, the blood-brain barrier, and inflammation
  Cellular imaging
  The T2 hyperintense lesion
  Chronic T1 hypointense lesions (T1 black holes)
  Multiple sclerosis lesion heterogeneity by neuropathology
- Distribution of focal lesions in the brain and spinal cord
  Characteristics and distribution of lesions in the brain
  Characteristics and distribution of lesions in the spinal cord
- The normal-appearing white and gray matter
- Axonal injury and neuronal tract degeneration
- Functional MR imaging, plasticity, and adaptive mechanisms
- Disease course by MR imaging
- Primary progressive multiple sclerosis
- The clinical significance of the MR imaging pathology
- MR imaging in the diagnosis of multiple sclerosis
  Monitoring patients by MR imaging
- Clinical imaging technique
- References

Immediately after the first descriptions of the application of MR imaging to multiple sclerosis (MS) in the early 1980s, MR imaging assumed an important role beyond that of CT in increasing confidence in the diagnosis, and in excluding clinical presentations mimicking MS but caused by other pathology. In large part because MR imaging could provide multiple important outcome measures in MS clinical trials, a great deal of information was collected from these and related studies relevant to the natural history of MS lesions, the underlying pathology, the sensitivity of MR imaging to pathology in the normal-appearing tissues, and its value as a predictor of clinical MS. Recently, MR imaging has provided new tools that can be used to understand the relationship between the focal and diffuse

pathology, including the quantitative MR imaging techniques (magnetization transfer, T1 and T2 relaxation based methods, diffusion tensor MR imaging and tractography, MR spectroscopy, perfusion), and the functional consequences and early compensatory mechanisms that the central nervous system (CNS) uses to minimize disability based on functional MR imaging studies.

In this update on MS, the basic features of the focal MR imaging lesions and the underlying pathology are first reviewed, including new insights into MS as a disease with early axonal pathology. Next, the diffuse pathology in the normal-appearing white matter (NAWM) and normal-appearing gray matter (NAGM) as revealed by conventional and quantitative MR imaging techniques is discussed,

This article was originally published in *Radiologic Clinics of North America* 2006;44(1):79–100.
Department of Radiology, University of Colorado Health Sciences Center, Denver, CO, USA
* Department of Radiology, University of Colorado Health Sciences Center, 4200 East Ninth Avenue, Box A-034, Denver, CO 80262.
E-mail address: jack.simon@uchsc.edu

including reference to how the focal and diffuse pathology may be in part linked through axonal-neuronal degeneration. MR imaging findings have been shown to be predictive of MS, and the MR imaging criteria incorporated for the first time into formal clinical diagnostic criteria for MS are next discussed. Finally, a discussion is provided as to how MR imaging is used in monitoring subclinical disease either before or subsequent to initiation of treatment, in identifying aggressive subclinical disease, and treatment of nonresponders.

Clinical multiple sclerosis overview

MS is a chronic, inflammatory, demyelinating disease of the CNS that has been estimated to affect about 250,000 to 350,000 individuals in the United States and more than 2.5 million worldwide. The etiology remains unknown, although environmental (viral) and immune-mediated factors in genetically susceptible individuals are thought to be responsible. Typically beginning in early adulthood, the prognosis is highly variable, but left untreated 50% of patients require assistance in walking within 15 years of onset, and more than 50% have cognitive deficits detected by formal neuropsychologic testing, many in the early relapsing stages of disease [1,2].

Approximately 80% to 85% of patients present with a relapsing-remitting course, with symptoms and signs evolving over days, and typically improving over weeks. The female/male ratio is about 2:1 for relapsing MS. A secondary progressive course develops after about 10 years in as many as 50% of patients, with disease progression occurring between relapses, and relapses less frequent over time. In about 15% of patients, the disease is progressive from onset (primary progressive MS), with males and females more equally affected. Rarely, patients show an initially progressive course with subsequent superimposed relapses (progressive-relapsing MS) [3]. About 10% to 20% of MS patients do well for 20 years, and are considered to have "benign" MS, a diagnosis that can at this time only be made in retrospect [4], and included in this group may be individuals with unrecognized cognitive deficits.

Presenting signs and symptoms of MS frequently include those associated with a clinically isolated syndrome (CIS) affecting one optic nerve (optic neuritis); brainstem or cerebellum (diplopia-internuclear ophthalmoplegia, ataxia, trigeminal neuralgia); or a spinal cord syndrome with partial transverse myelitis (weakness, numbness). Bladder-bowel symptoms are common. Fatigue is described by many patients as especially debilitating [1,2].

Relapsing MS is a treatable disease [1,2]. Therapy for MS is based on immunomodulatory agents including interferon beta-1a, interferon beta-1b, and glatiramer acetate. In late 2004 the Food and Drug Administration approved a monoclonal antibody (anti-α_4 integrin) that inhibits the trafficking of leukocytes across the CNS endothelium by blocking binding of $\alpha_4\beta_1$ integrin to a vascular cell adhesion molecule [5], but natalizumab (Tysabri) was voluntarily suspended from the market based on safety concerns as progressive multifocal leucoencephalopathy (PML) was discovered with an occurrence greater than expected as it occurred in a few trial patients on combination therapy. The effectiveness of immunomodulatory or other therapies is more difficult to demonstrate in secondary progressive MS, in part because these treatments probably do not target already injured tissue. Betaseron and mitoxantrone are approved for treatment of secondary progressive MS. There are no proved therapies for primary progressive MS [1]. MR imaging–based outcome measures have been instrumental in the approval process for the MS therapies. The cumulative number of gadolinium-enhancing lesions on monthly MR imaging is the primary outcome measure for many phase II trials [6]. Enhancing lesions, number of new and enlarging T2 lesions, and T2 lesion volume change are important secondary outcome measures in phase III (definitive) trials [6,7].

The focal and diffuse multiple sclerosis pathology by MR imaging

The MS pathology detected by direct neuropathologic examination or MR imaging is both focal and diffuse. Focal, classic MS lesions represent a range of pathology from nondestructive edema to injury from demyelination and most severe injury related to axonal loss [8]. The diffuse pathology may be evident by MR imaging only indirectly as indicated by atrophy [9–11], or detected in the normal-appearing white or gray matter by the advanced quantitative MR imaging methodologies [12,13]. As discussed later, there is mounting evidence that the clinical and cognitive consequences of the MS pathology require an understanding of the focal pathology, yet the diffuse pathology may be equally if not more important.

Enhancing lesions, the blood-brain barrier, and inflammation

The acute enhancing MS lesion, which is almost always associated with hyperintensity on T2-weighted imaging, is visualized as a result of abnormal leakage and accumulation of contrast material across disrupted tight junctions of the vascular endothelium that are a crucial component of the blood-brain barrier [14]. The factors associated with the initial barrier disruption are complex, but central to this process is entrance of activated T cells through the junctions of the capillary endothelium. These activated lymphocytes recognize CNS antigen and trigger a cytokine-chemokine cascade that further mediates disruption of the blood-brain barrier [15,16] with additional cellular infiltration that is characteristic of this inflammatory process. Contrast enhancement in MS serves as a convenient marker for the events associated with macroscopic inflammation in MS [17–19], appearing at the time inflammation can be easily observed under the microscope, and lasting for the same time course, about 4 to 8 weeks in most cases (range <1–16 weeks) [Fig. 1] [20,21]. There is strong evidence, however, that weeks to months before lesions become evident on contrast-enhanced MR imaging, changes occur in the corresponding NAWM that can be detected by the quantitative MR imaging methodologies [22–26] including measures of perfusion [26]. Unfortunately, these measures to detect the earliest stages of MS lesions are not practical for evaluation of individual patients at this time and they remain research tools.

The enhancement pattern (size, shape, solid versus ring) may be strikingly variable within and more so between patients, which is highly suggestive of a heterogeneous pathology, possibly related to the host response and severity [Fig. 2] [27–29]. Ring enhancement, for example, may suggest a more severe pathology [29]. Enhancement seen only after high (triple dose) MR imaging contrast infusion tends to be smaller and may indicate less destruction than that detected by single (standard) dose MR imaging contrast [30,31]. The correlation between pattern of enhancement, the underlying pathology, and clinical course in individual patients may not be straightforward, however, and is not well understood at this time.

Enhancement, which is associated with early lesions and inflammation in MS, is now also known to be associated with axonal injury. Biopsy and autopsy series show that acute, inflammatory MS lesions are accompanied by an impressive degree of axonal injury that includes axonal transection, in addition to the classic findings of demyelination [32]. Axonal injury, which is mostly irreversible, is an important factor even in early MS and is thought to contribute to progression to secondary progressive stages or further disability. The MR spectroscopy literature supports early axonal degeneration in the NAWM and in focal, enhancing-inflammatory lesions based on the finding of reduced *N*-acetyl aspartate (NAA), a neuronal marker [33–35].

The number and volume of enhancing lesions within individual MS patients varies over time, as most dramatically documented in high-frequency (weekly and monthly) MR imaging series [Fig. 3] [6,20,21]. General activity patterns, however, can often be recognized in individuals. Some individuals on most monthly enhanced MR imaging studies show little or no enhancing lesion activity, whereas others are more likely than not to have one or more lesions on most observations. These trends are used to great advantage in MS clinical trials where pooled results for many, often hundreds of patients are analyzed. Analysis based on individual patients can be informative but must be understood in the context of expected intraindividual variation over time.

Cellular imaging

Contrast enhancement suggests inflammation, but is more accurately a measure of leakage of

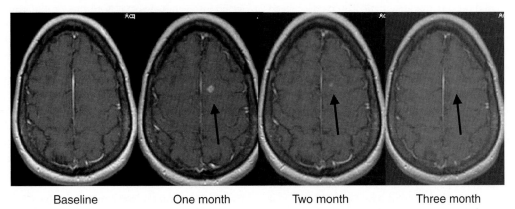

Baseline — One month — Two month — Three month

Fig. 1. Time course for enhancing lesion. Serial monthly MR imaging shows development of a new enhancing lesion (*arrows*) at 1 month, and the typical decrease in size over the subsequent 2 months. The duration of enhancement can range from less than 1 week to about 16 weeks. The time course for enhancement in MS parallels that for inflammation, but more accurately enhancement measures the integrity of the blood-brain barrier.

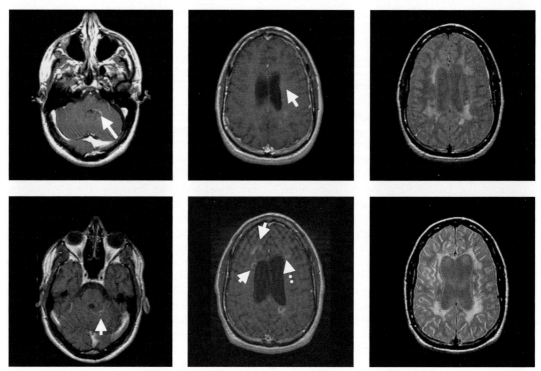

Fig. 2. Aggressive MS over 2 years. Patient with relatively early disease onset at age 15 and death 7 years later related to MS. Disease was initially relapsing-remitting but converted relatively quickly to secondary progressive MS (progression without relapses). Top row: contrast-enhancement left pons (*left*) and left frontal-parietal white matter (*middle*) both showing a relatively rare edge enhancement pattern (*arrows*). Typical confluent T2 hyperintensities and mild-moderate volume loss based on lateral ventricle size (*right*). Bottom row: two years later MR imaging shows different edge enhancing lesions (*arrows*) in posterior fossa (*left*) and both edge enhancement (*arrows*) and ring enhancement (*dotted arrow*) in deep white matter along the lateral ventricles (*middle*). Progressive volume loss based on moderately large lateral ventricles and more extensive confluent T2 hyperintensity (*right*). This enhancement pattern is relatively rare (*arrows*), and in this case apparently related to an aggressive disease course. Ring enhancement has also been associated with more severe pathology, but not all patients with ring enhancement show an aggressive course by MR imaging.

moderate-size molecules across the damaged tight-junctions of the CNS endothelium. Cellular imaging based on superparamagnetic iron oxide–tagged cells is a more specific probe of the migration occurring at the level of the blood-brain barrier basic to the inflammatory process. In one approach, the superparamagnetic iron oxide particles after intravenous injection concentrate within macrophages and can then be followed in vivo in research studies in humans as they pass into the CNS. The intracellular particles exert a strong influence on the local magnetic field, which is detected as signal loss on T2 and T2*-weighted pulse sequences [36,37]. The location of lesions and their time-course based on superparamagnetic iron oxide imaging does not correlate strongly with that based on conventional contrast-enhanced MR imaging, suggesting that it provides different quantitative and qualitative information. In another approach, cell-type–specific tagging has been found to be feasible in animal studies. Superparamagnetic iron oxide particles

are introduced outside the body into isolated cells through transfection, and the tagged cells then injected intravenously [38]. Both these cellular imaging approaches may in the near future become practical methods to monitor individual patients, and could provide far more specific detail relevant to the inflammatory process in MS. Dissecting the inflammatory process in MS is important, because it is becoming clear that inflammation includes destructive components (bad inflammation), which clinicians want to treat, and potentially beneficial components (good inflammation), which should be enhanced or not disturbed by treatment [39,40].

The T2 hyperintense lesion

The T2 hyperintense focal areas observed on MR imaging in MS lesions are known by neuropathology studies to be caused by a wide range of pathology, and are described as nonspecific with regard to pathology. T2 hyperintensity (T2 lesions) can be the result of water space changes that include edema

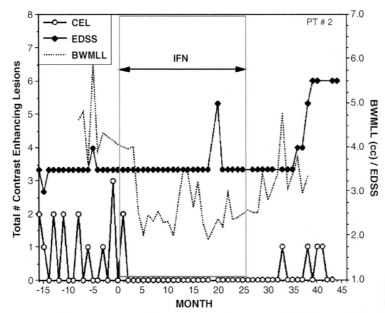

Fig. 3. High-frequency monthly MR imaging. The response to therapy may be followed by MR imaging because the MR imaging, even at yearly intervals, may suggest activity trends. In this idealized monthly MR imaging follow-up, responsiveness to initiation of therapy with interferon-□ is apparent, as is return toward baseline activity with cessation of therapy. Because monthly MR imaging is not practical in the clinic, counting new T2 lesions over a 1-year interval (not shown) provides a good estimate of intercurrent MR imaging activity, because most new lesions leave a permanent T2 residue, the footprint of prior activity. Enhancing lesions at any point in time provide a measure of inflammation around the time of MR imaging. BWMLL, brain white matter lesion load; CEL, contrast-enhancing lesion number; EDSS, expanded disability status scale; IFN, interferon. (*From* Richert ND, Zierak MC, Bash CN, et al. MRI and clinical activity in MS patients after terminating treatment with interferon beta-1b. Mult Scler 2000;6:86–90; with permission.)

(acute lesions), and other water compartment changes in chronic lesions; in acute and chronic lesions mild or severe demyelination, variable degrees of astrogliosis and matrix disruption; and axonal injury or loss [Fig. 4] [8,17]. Complicating the interpretation of T2-weighted imaging and T2 hyperintensity, the T2 lesion areas may include zones of active remyelination [41], although remyelination is often limited and the capacity for remyelination decreases in MS with time and severity of injury.

There is increasing evidence that the underlying MS pathology is variable across patients, yet may be more homogeneous within patients (see later) [27]. Consequently pathology in an individual expressed as T2 hyperintensity may also have variable significance. This heterogeneous pathology characteristic of T2 hyperintense lesions is thought to account in part for the poor correlation between total T2 lesion volume in an individual patient's brain or spinal cord and their degree of disability [42].

After reaching a maximal lesion size over a period of about 4 to 8 weeks, the T2 hyperintensity almost always shrinks over a period of weeks to months [43], leaving a smaller residual area or T2 footprint

related to the prior acute event. Although many T2 lesions do not change over years, some lesions may expand through activity along their periphery or less commonly through central activation. Reactivation of focal lesions is thought to be an important mechanism accounting for more severe cumulative pathology, and in theory through loss of capacity for remyelination [41,44].

Over time the T2 lesion number and volume (the T2 burden of disease) increases on average in the brain or spinal cord in the absence of treatment, and most often less so when treatment is effective [Fig. 5]. In some individuals, the T2 burden of disease transiently decreases as lesions shrink to their footprint size and edema resolves, a finding that is not uncommon during effective treatment. With disease progression, however, lesions often become confluent because of expansion and crowding. A more minor contribution to an increasing T2 burden of disease is the result of the T2 hyperintensity that develops with secondary (fiber) degeneration that sometimes can be visualized outside focal lesions [see Fig. 5] [45,46]. The T2 burden of disease is an important MS trial metric, as a measure of change in total (albeit nonspecific) abnormal tissue. New or enlarging individual T2 lesions are

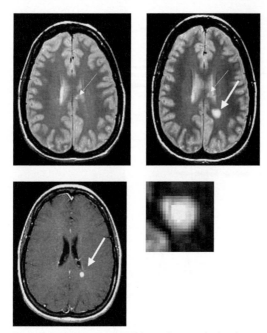

Fig. 4. Development of a T2 hyperintense lesion by serial MR imaging. Upper left: case of relapsing MS with low T2 hyperintense lesion burden including chronic lesions in the corpus callosum (*arrow*). Upper right: 1 month later, a new T2 hyperintense lesion develops in the left parietal-occipital white matter (*solid arrow*), whereas the corpus callosum lesions remain stable (*dotted arrow*). Lower left: corresponding enhancement in acute lesion (*arrow*), from blood-brain barrier breakdown and concurrent inflammation. Lower right: exploded view of the new lesion shows the complex structure, centrally hyperintense most likely from mixed pathology including demyelination, matrix including glial change, and importantly axonal degeneration. The intermediate black ring may be a zone of macrophage infiltration, and the outer ring is likely from edema.

also often measured, as an indication of new MS events within an interval between imaging studies.

Chronic T1 hypointense lesions (T1 black holes)

T1-weighted imaging separates chronic MS lesions into two groups [Fig. 6]. One group of lesions, evident on T2-weighted imaging, is isointense to normal white matter on T1-weighted imaging. A smaller fraction of T2 lesions (5%–20%) are hypointense to normal white matter on T1-weighted imaging [47,48]. The chronic T1 hypointense lesion fraction (the classic T1 black hole) is important because it represents white matter that has suffered relatively more severe injury. These T1 black holes are characterized by greater reduction in axonal density and matrix disruption as compared with

T2 lesions that are not chronically T1 hypointense. These T1 black holes have relatively reduced magnetization transfer ratios (MTR), elevated diffusion coefficient, and reduced NAA, also indicative of more severe focal injury [47].

In evaluating an image, it is important to distinguish acute T1 hypointense areas, which are T1 hypointense on the basis of edema, and may show considerable or complete recovery, from chronic T1 hypointense lesions, which are the classic T1 black holes. Because serial studies are not always available to assess the chronicity of a T1 hypointense lesion, chronicity is assumed based on T1 hypointensity after contrast enhancement. High-dose corticosteroids can confound this interpretation by rapidly suppressing enhancement. In reality, acute T1 hypointense (edematous) lesions often evolve slowly over many months to their final T1 isointense or hypointense state, the latter occurring about one third of the time. Transition of an acute MS lesion to normal signal intensity on T1-weighted imaging reflects recovery from the edematous stage, and potentially partial remyelination [41]. Unfortunately, there is no specific remyelination MR imaging measure [41,44], although MTR recovery may have some potential in this regard [49].

In populations, the correlation between chronic T1 hypointense lesions and disability is thought to be stronger than the correlation between T2 lesions and disability, but the correlation is more often than not still poor. As an indication of severe injury, however, many clinicians value this parameter as a means to assess the pathologic significance of lesions (which are most often subclinical) in individuals. Chronic T1 hypointense lesion volume (T1 burden of disease) is an important MS trial measure because it is more specific than T2 burden of disease. T1 black holes are also sometimes followed in MS trials to determine if treatment has the effect of decreasing the rate of evolution of acute focal lesions to regions of severe damage [50,51].

Multiple sclerosis lesion heterogeneity by neuropathology

Recent neuropathology studies from biopsy material suggest that MS and its variants may be characterized as a heterogeneous pathology (between individuals) although relatively homogeneous within individuals [27]. The hypothesis from these studies is that the underlying pathology of MS remains a chronic T-lymphocyte–mediated inflammation, accompanied by activated macrophages and microglia and their toxic products (pattern I), but additional amplification factors generate patterns known as II, III, and IV [52]. Pattern II is based on deposition of immunoglobulins and activated

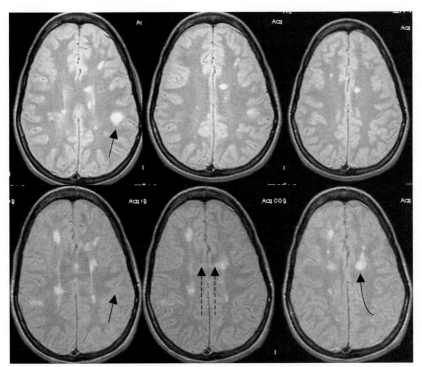

Fig. 5. Five-year follow-up after a clinically isolated syndrome shows the natural history of MS from the early stages. Proton density weighted images at three levels show accumulation of multiple new T2 hyperintense lesions and increase in T2 burden of disease. One large left frontal lesion (*arrow*) observed at baseline has shrunk leaving only a tiny T2 footprint. Note the transcallosal band (*dashed arrows*), an indication of secondary, possibly wallerian degeneration extending through the corpus callosum originating in the left frontal periventricular T2 lesion (*curved arrow*).

complement, resembling an antibody-mediated process, and has been associated with Devic's neuromyelitis optica [53]. Pattern III is characterized by a process known as "distal dying back oligodendrogliopathy with oligodendrocyte apoptosis," and has been associated with hypoxia and perfusion abnormalities [52]. Perfusion abnormality has been recently described in MS lesions and MS NAWM [54]. There has been speculation that pattern III may also underlie Balœ's concentric sclerosis. Pattern IV, thought to be rare, is based on degeneration and oligodendrocyte death in the periplaque white matter [52]. It should be noted that this classification scheme (patterns I–IV pathology) is not free from healthy controversy [55], and is best described as a working and stimulating model for understanding MS.

Distribution of focal lesions in the brain and spinal cord

Characteristics and distribution of lesions in the brain

The characteristic distributions of focal MS lesions in the brain are well known to radiologists, and have been reviewed [8,56]. In recent years, there has been some precision added to the lesion nomenclature relevant to the new MS diagnostic criteria discussed later [57,58]. The T2 hyperintense lesions that occur throughout the CNS show a typical distribution in the periventricular (touching ventricle surface) more so than the peripheral white matter, but they occur commonly in both regions [56]. Within the white matter T2 lesions may be discrete (separate from ventricle surface), and when peripheral, many touch the gray matter (juxtacortical). Lesions may straddle both gray and white matter (juxtacortical-cortical), or only rarely by MR imaging may lie entirely within the cortical gray matter (cortical). Many periventricular lesions extend at a right angle from the lateral ventricle surfaces, and have an ovoid shape reminiscent of the pathology described as Dawson's fingers, which are cellular infiltrates oriented along the periventricular veins. Infratentorial lesions are frequent in MS compared with their occurrence from small vessel disease. Deep cerebellar hemisphere, cerebellar peduncle, and brainstem surface lesions are common, the latter more typical of demyelination than infarction.

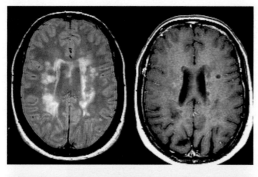

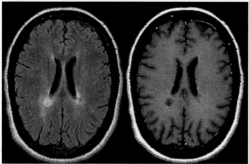

Fig. 6. Nonspecific T2 hyperintense lesions, based on comparison with postcontrast T1-weighted images that show T1 black holes. Top left shows a patient with extensive T2 hyperintense lesions, a small fraction of which (10%–20%) are T1 hypointense and nonenhancing (*right*), and considered to be classic T1 black holes. T1 black holes under the microscope characteristically are focal areas of more severe injury with loss of axons, demyelination, and matrix disruption, and show low NAA content. Bottom left shows in another patient a fast-FLAIR image with a higher ratio of T1 black hole to T2 lesion area (about 60%). The correlation between T1 black hole volume and disability tends to be slightly stronger as shown by population studies than the correlation between T2 lesion volume and disability, but in individuals T1 black hole volume is still only weakly correlated with disability. The importance of T1 black holes is that they reflect focal areas of more severe injury, and some patients may be more prone to this type of injury for reasons that are not understood.

Corpus callosum lesions are frequent, and often lie within the inner or deep surfaces. Although not always seen in the earliest stages of disease, corpus callosum lesions are often early characteristic findings on MR imaging, well seen on thin section sagittal fast FLAIR sequences. These may be primary focal lesions or secondary neuronal tract lesions [46].

Optic nerve lesions are not difficult to visualize in the acute stages of optic neuritis by thin-section high-resolution fat-suppression techniques, and show strong correlations with visual function and electrophysiologic impairment [59]. In later stages,

the imaging consequences of optic neuritis may only be detected by MR imaging based on atrophy or in population studies by techniques, such as magnetization transfer imaging [59]. In typical clinical optic neuritis, imaging of the optic nerve is usually not indicated, whereas a positive brain MR imaging at the time of optic neuritis may provide diagnostic criteria for possible MS [57,60] or risk for MS [61,62] or if negative suggest a low (but not zero) risk for MS [58,60]. Strong clinical MR imaging correlations are also seen for brainstem lesions causing internuclear ophthalmoplegia [63].

Brain atrophy, often apparent on inspection in midrelapsing stages of MS, is not a rare or a late event in MS, and may progress at a surprisingly rapid pace in some individuals. In population studies, atrophy can be measured over 1-year intervals [9–11]. CNS atrophy detected by MR imaging in MS can be focal or regional affecting the central white matter and resulting in ventricular expansion or corpus callosum atrophy [Fig. 7], may affect the cerebellum or result in sulcal widening, and can cause global brain volume loss [64]. Atrophy is considered an important measure in MS because it likely reflects in most cases irreversible injury, much of which is from axonal loss, but additionally with contributions from myelin loss and other structural changes (those from astrogliosis) also contributory. Under relatively extreme conditions (dehydration, corticosteroid usage, malnutrition), visible atrophy may reflect reversible factors.

Characteristics and distribution of lesions in the spinal cord

Most patients with early MS have lesions within the spinal cord [65,66]. In one study of 115 patients who had optic neuritis, only 12% had an abnormal spinal cord MR imaging when the brain MR imaging was normal. However, an abnormal spinal cord was found in 45% of patients with nine or more brain lesions, the latter group known to be at higher risk for a second attack and a diagnosis of clinical MS [67].

Because spinal cord T2 hyperintense lesions are relatively rare incidental findings, and not typically observed with normal aging, in contrast to the frequent nonspecific brain T2 hyperintensities, their observation and typical features can be helpful in increasing confidence in a diagnosis of MS [Fig. 8] [66]. On sagittal imaging, most T2 hyperintense MS lesions in the spinal cord are vertically oriented and less than 10 to 15 mm in height or less than two vertebral segments [66]. On axial T2-weighted images, lesion distribution across the spinal cord is typically (but not always) asymmetric, corresponding to the frequent asymmetric clinical presentation of partial transverse myelitis. Acute

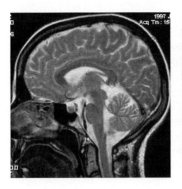
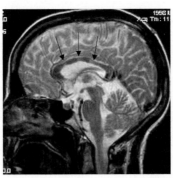

Fig. 7. Extensive corpus callosum atrophy over a 1-year interval. Note that volume loss is most extensive in the region of each T2 hyperintensity (*arrows*), but also is generalized. Atrophy in MS in the brain is likely multifactorial but based on autopsy series and MR spectroscopy thought to be principally from axonal loss. Loss of myelin and changes in the glia and water spaces likely also affect tissue volume.

spinal cord lesions might be expected to enhance; however, enhancement is frequently not seen probably related to technical issues and structural considerations. Chronic T1 black holes are rare in the spinal cord in MS. A diffusely swollen, T1 hypointense spinal cord is more characteristic of Devic's neuromyelitis optica [53,68] or viral or idiopathic myelitis rather than MS [Fig. 9]. Acute disseminated encephalomyelitis may also show an impressively swollen spinal cord. A focally swollen spinal cord, for example over one segment, although rare, occurs with sufficient frequency in MS at clinical onset that this finding should not discourage consideration of MS in the differential. Brain MR imaging is often diagnostic in that setting. Later secondary changes in the spinal cord from MS include focal and diffuse volume loss [9,11,65,69,70], the atrophy related to demyelination and more so axonal loss in focal lesions, and secondary to wallerian degeneration from distant lesions [71–73].

The normal-appearing white and gray matter

From the pathology literature and now from the MR imaging literature much of the injury in MS seems to reside in the NAWM [12,49,74] and the NAGM, collectively referred to as the normal-appearing brain tissue. In the NAWM microglial inflammatory pathology may exceed that of lymphocytic inflammatory pathology, the latter so characteristic of focal lesions [12]. Axonal loss and loss or disruption of myelin may also occur in the normal-appearing brain tissue [71–73,75–77]. The abnormalities of normal-appearing brain tissue, which are difficult to detect in the earliest stages of disease, seem to increase in magnitude as disease advances, and may vary in the different MS phenotypes [12,78].

The advanced quantitative MR imaging techniques are required to detect abnormalities of the normal-appearing brain tissue in vivo. Magnetization transfer imaging is sensitive to disruption of the macromolecular environment of membrane, cells, and tissue, and has been especially valuable

in characterizing the pathology in the NAWM and NAGM in MS [78]. Loss of structure, such as when myelin fragments or is destroyed, influences the structure and concentration of macromolecules and results in a reduction in the transfer of magnetization from these to the free water fractions. These changes are readily measured by MR imaging as a decrease in the MTR. MTR changes are thought principally to reflect changes in myelin, but in the complex environment of CNS tissue, the MTR change must also reflect other factors, such as those from axonal injury and inflammation and less so edema. Typically in MS studies the average MTRs from NAWM or NAGM from groups of MS patients are evaluated using histogram analyses, based on mean MTR or other parameters, such as histogram peak height or peak location [79].

Several water diffusion-based measures also are sensitive to abnormality in the NAWM in MS [80,81]. Increased diffusivity is a relatively nonspecific finding, and is seen in focal MS lesions and normal-appearing brain tissue, in contrast to the reduced diffusivity (restricted diffusion) characteristic of cerebral infarction. Although cellular infiltrates characteristic of acute inflammation may counter increases in the apparent diffusion coefficient in MS lesions [80], the diffusion changes are not sufficiently specific to substitute for contrast-enhanced MR imaging. By measuring the directional components of water diffusion, the fractional anisotropy (the relative anisotropic compared with isotropic contribution) or alternatively the parallel (to fiber) versus perpendicular (to fiber) components of diffusion can be determined. Loss or decrease in anisotropy is a more specific finding than diffusivity changes in MS. Decreased anisotropy is characteristic of focal white matter MS lesions and diffuse abnormality of the NAWM. Although initially myelin was thought to be the basis for the strong diffusion anisotropy characteristic of white matter, it now seems that organized cellular orientation rather than myelin alone may account for much of the anisotropy measured in vivo [82]. Diffusion anisotropy is the basis for diffusion tractography, which

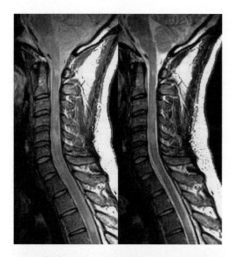

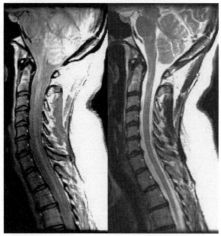

Fig. 8. MS in the spinal cord. Two patients with primary progressive MS. Top left (proton density) and top right (heavily T2-weighted) images show intrinsic multifocal T2 hyperintensities, which are vertically oriented and less than 2 vertebral segments in length. Axial sections in MS most often show an asymmetric distribution across the cord. These findings are typical for both relapsing and progressive forms of MS. Bottom left (proton density) and right (heavily T2-weighted) images show that the proton density series is frequently more sensitive to spinal cord pathology, showing both multifocal lesions and a diffuse cord hyperintensity (higher signal than cerebrospinal fluid). These findings are typical for relapsing and progressive forms of MS, but diffuse hyperintensity has been described as more common in primary progressive MS.

can be used as a research measure to identify the relationship between focal MS lesions and the neuronal tracts they intersect [Fig. 10].

The fundamental T1 (longitudinal) and T2 (transverse) relaxation rate measures are also sensitive to the underlying pathology in the NAWM. With specialized multiecho pulse sequences, it can be seen that T2 relaxation is multiexponential. The short T2 relaxation time fraction provides a measure that most likely is related to myelin content (myelin water fraction); a mid T2 relaxation time fraction is associated with other (interstitial) water; free water produces a long T2 relaxation time fraction [Fig. 11] [83,84]. A current practical limitation of this method is the long scan time for full brain coverage.

By MR spectroscopy, abnormally low NAA levels can be detected in the NAWM in both relapsing and progressive MS, generally more so in the latter [12,34,35,85,86]. A recent study suggests that in the early stages of disease increased *myo*-inositol may be found in the NAWM, more so than decreased NAA [87]. As in relapsing MS, *myo*-inositol and creatine are potentially relevant to the pathology from abnormal glial cells, the latter possibly accounting for their increased concentration in the NAWM [12,87,88].

Perfusion abnormalities in the NAWM may be relevant to MS clinical or pathologic subtypes [27,52]. Decreased perfusion reflecting microvascular change or injury has been detected in the NAWM in MS [54]. Increased perfusion precedes the development of enhancing lesions in the NAWM [26]. Other quantitative MR imaging measures (MTR, relaxation measures) are also sensitive to this pre-enhancing lesion pathology in the NAWM [22–26].

The quantitative MR imaging technologies are not commonly used and are not generally helpful in evaluating individual MS patients. Rarely, MR spectroscopy may be helpful in establishing tumefactive MS versus neoplasm, but metabolite ratios or magnitude often overlap. There are reports of normal NAWM in acute disseminated encephalomyelitis and early Devic's neuromyelitis [89,90], in contrast to abnormal NAWM in MS, but these observations are based on significant differences in pooled results from multiple patients and may not be applicable to individual patients.

MR imaging is insensitive to the focal gray matter pathology of MS that is well known from the pathology literature [91], although with effort focal lesions can be seen [Fig. 12]. Poor tissue contrast is thought to be the basis for this MR imaging insensitivity. Focal cortical lesions often involve the subcortical white matter with only about 15% to 25% exclusively cortical [92,93], including lesions extending from the pial surface into the cortex that are never seen by conventional MR imaging [94,95]. The pathology of gray matter MS lesions is different from that seen in white matter, with gray matter MS lesions being less inflammatory with fewer lymphocytes, with fewer activated microglia, and perivascular cuffs [94,95]. These gray matter lesions, however, may contain significant

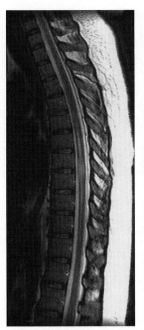

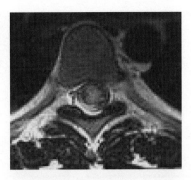
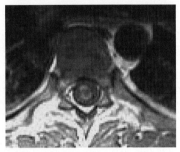

Fig. 9. Devic's neuromyelitis optica (DNO). This patient presented with bilateral visual symptoms related to demyelinating lesion of optic chiasm, and only later development of spinal symptoms. Brain white matter was otherwise normal. Sagittal images of the spinal cord show extensive thoracic cord T2 hyperintense lesion more than 2 segments in height with a cavitary enhancing pattern. The axial images show involvement of much of the cross-section of the cord. The length, ring enhancement, T1 hypointense core, and full-thickness involvement on axial images are all uncharacteristic for MS. Recent studies suggest that most but not all DNO patients are positive for a serum neuromyelitis optica (NMO)-IgG marker, whereas most MS patients are negative. The serum autoantibody data and MR imaging findings, such as normal initial brain MR imaging, support the concept that NMO is not simply an unusual manifestation of MS, and these findings expedite early aggressive therapy for DNO, which has a relatively poor prognosis.

destructive pathology with transected neurites (axons and dendrites) and loss of neurons from apoptosis [93]. Diffuse gray matter abnormality may also be present, because the quantitative MR imaging techniques find abnormal (but normal appearing) cortical gray matter in all MS phenotypes and stages of disease [12].

Deep gray matter involvement may also occur in MS, but disproportionate focal or diffuse T2 hyperintense or enhancing lesions in the deep gray matter suggests alternative diagnoses. Diffuse deep gray matter involvement in MS may be apparent based on volume loss [96], or by low signal on T2- or T2*-weighted imaging, which reflects increased hemosiderin or ferritin iron [97]. MS population studies suggest modest clinical correlations with this so-called "black T2" in the deep gray matter, which has potential as a neurodegeneration marker [98].

Axonal injury and neuronal tract degeneration

MS is the classic example of a primary demyelinating disorder, but demyelination alone does not account

for the persistent functional disturbances that characterize the disease as it progresses. Experimental studies have shown that after myelin is damaged, nerve conduction properties, initially abnormal, can recover in part related to redistribution of sodium channels [99]. A missing link in the understanding of irreversible injury could be filled by axonal injury. Axonal injury in MS, known from the work of Charcot in the mid nineteenth century but subsequently associated only with late disease, was recently rediscovered as an important early pathology of considerable importance in MS through studies that showed convincingly that axons were in fact injured in early inflammatory MS lesions. Axonal injury was documented based on two observations: inflammatory MS lesions were associated with increases in amyloid precursor protein as a result of reduction in axonal transport from the axonal injury [100], and direct three-dimensional visualization of axonal injury in inflammatory lesions by confocal microscopy of immunostained material, which showed loss of normal neurofilament and transected axons [75]. This and subsequent work indicated that axonal injury occurred in early lesions and potentially in early MS, and it was understood

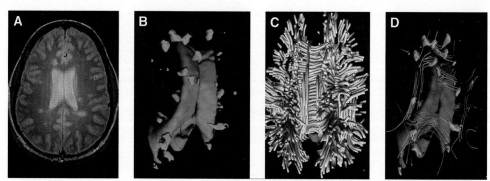

Fig. 10. Diffusion tensor imaging at 3T as basis for diffusion tractography in early relapsing MS. (*A*) The T2-weighted image reveals small lesion volume. (*B*) Computerized segmentation into lesion (*green*), ventricle (*blue*). (*C*) Stream tube tractography. The tubular structures are representations of neuronal fiber tracts with common properties that have reached a predetermined diffusion anisotropy threshold. (*D*) Final image shows only those fibers that intersect MS lesions. Note that this method allows determination as to how each lesion affects different fiber pathways, many coursing through the corpus callosum, others intersecting fibers running anteroposterior. Work based on collaboration between University of Colorado Brain Imaging Research Laboratory (J. Simon, D. Miller, M. Brown); Department of Neurology (J. Bennett and J. Corboy); and the Computer Science Department, Brown University (Song Zhang and David Laidlaw).

immediately that axonal injury was potentially an important factor in irreversible injury, disability, and the progressive stages of disease [101].

Researchers also quickly understood the potential for such injuries to contribute to the diffuse pathology in MS through retrograde and antegrade neuronal degeneration, originating in the focal lesions but extending outside the lesion. In vivo, acute enhancing (inflammatory) MS lesions can be the source of signal and anatomic changes suggestive of secondary wallerian (fiber) degeneration [45,46]. One informative case report linked an inflammatory MS lesion in the brainstem to distant spinal cord axonal degeneration [73]. Further support for neuronal tract degeneration in MS comes from in vivo studies showing reduced NAA [102]

and increased diffusivity potentially related to connected lesions [103], studies showing reduced fractional anisotropy remote from focal lesions [80], and reduced NAA in visual pathways [104].

Axonal loss can be profound in later stages of disease. In one study, there was a 53% reduction in axonal number in the NAWM of corpus callosum, which was proportionate to the reduction in cross-sectional area [105,106]. Reductions in nerve fiber density are also seen in spinal cord, including in otherwise normal-appearing tissue [72], and likely related to permanent disability [107]. Studies of fiber degeneration and connections between lesions and fiber pathways are becoming feasible in the clinical imaging environment through diffusion tensor MR imaging [see Fig. 10].

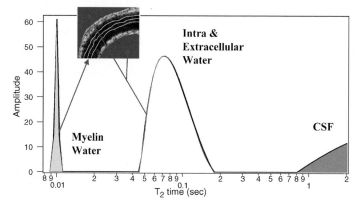

Fig. 11. Myelin water fraction. Myelin water fraction can be determined using a specialized multiecho fast spin echo pulse sequence. Analysis of the MR imaging data shows three water fractions in brain: (1) the short T2 time fraction representing myelin water, (2) the intermediate fraction intracellular and extracellular water, and (3) the long T2 time fraction cerebrospinal fluid water. The myelin water fraction is decreased in the NAWM in MS and in focal lesions (not shown). (Courtesy of C. Laule, PhD, University of British Columbia, Vancouver, Canada.)

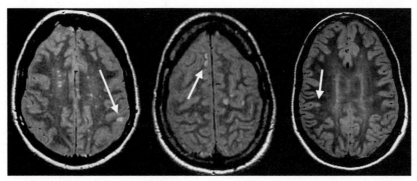

Fig. 12. Gray matter (cortical) MS. Pure cortical gray matter lesions are relatively rare by conventional MR imaging, but not uncommon by histopathology. Left panel (*arrow*) shows a focal T2 lesion centered on gray matter. Middle panel (*arrow*) shows a lesion that straddles gray and white matter (juxtacortical-cortical). Right panel (*arrow*) shows a juxtacortical (touching cortex) white matter lesion, a common finding in MS.

Functional MR imaging, plasticity, and adaptive mechanisms

Functional MR imaging methodologies are increasingly used to detect and explain sensorimotor and cognitive disturbances in MS. The most consistent finding by functional MR imaging studies in populations of patients with MS is impairment in sensorimotor activation indicated by abnormally increased contralateral blood oxygenation level dependent activation over larger than normal cortical regions, and increased ipsilateral supplementary motor activation [108]. Several studies suggest that sensorimotor functional MR imaging is sensitive even in the early stages of disease [109]. In secondary progressive MS [110] strong correlations have been noted between cortical activation and diffuse injury in the NAWM and NAGM. Disturbances in cognitive function including information processing can also be evaluated by functional MR imaging [111–113]. Functional disturbances detected through functional MR imaging have been the basis for hypotheses suggesting that compensatory mechanisms develop in early MS, which initially may mask injury and delay the appearance of dysfunction. Functional disturbance may only become apparent after exhaustion of these adaptive mechanisms [114–116]. Although abnormal functional MR imaging patterns may be observed in individual MS patients, their interpretation may not be straightforward, and this technique is not generally used in the clinic.

Disease course by MR imaging

At the time of the first clinical event, the CIS, many patients have multiple, previously unsuspected and widely distributed lesions in the brain or spinal cord, primarily in clinically silent areas of the white matter. These individuals are at high risk for a subsequent clinical attack or show new MR imaging evidence for ongoing demyelination, which has been recently recognized as indicative of a diagnosis of MS (see later). Alternatively, at the time of a CIS, a negative brain (and spinal cord) MR imaging suggests a low, but not zero probability of second clinical attack or MR imaging disease activity. Most of these individuals with negative MR imaging remain categorized as CIS even after prolonged clinical follow-up [117]. Although there can be striking inter-individual variability, most individuals with a CIS and a positive MR imaging have a small number (2 or 3–20) and volume (a few milliliters) of focal MS lesions [118] compared with the later relapsing (typically 5–15 mL) and secondary progressive stages of disease (typically 5–25 mL) [56].

In the earliest stages of disease, focal lesions are readily counted, confluent lesions are small or relatively rare, T1 black hole volume is low, and most cases show no signs of atrophy by visual criteria. Enhancing lesions in the brain are observed in about 30% to 60% of these patients [6]. The literature is not consistent regarding the degree of abnormality of the NAWM in early MS defined at the time of a CIS, some studies suggesting abnormality, others not, which may reflect patient selection factors, but also suggests that much of the NAWM may be normal or only minimally abnormal early on.

With clinical disease progression or greater disease duration, as patients progress through relapsing and secondary progressive stages of disease, the focal T1 and T2 lesion volume increases, lesions show an increasing tendency to become confluent, and atrophy may become apparent as thinning of the corpus callosum and enlarged third and lateral ventricles [11]. Some but not all studies suggest an increase in the relative T1 black hole lesion volume with an increase in the T1/T2 lesion volume ratio.

The likelihood of finding enhancing lesions on one examination in relapsing MS is similar to earlier stages of disease, ranging from about 50% to 65% in the larger studies [6]. Enhancing lesion number and volume decrease in secondary progressive MS, in parallel to the well-known decrease in clinical relapses, with enhancing lesions occurring in about 36% to 48% of patients [6].

Primary progressive multiple sclerosis

Primary progressive MS has several distinct clinical, neuropathologic, and immunologic features compared with relapsing and secondary progressive MS [119–122], but by MR imaging there is overlap with relapsing and secondary progressive MS such that by imaging alone these MS phenotypes are indistinguishable [123]. Patients classified as primary progressive on average have a decreased number and volume of enhancing lesions, which is believed to be related to the less intense inflammation observed by histopathology [120,123,124]. Spinal cord pathology has been hypothesized to be an important factor in disease progression in primary progressive MS, yet whereas patients may have severe and progressive disability localized to the spinal cord, the number or volume of T2 hyperintense spinal cord lesions does not always account for this difference in all cases [see Fig. 8]. Although not a distinguishing feature, there have been observations of increase in total T2 lesion volume based on expansion of pre-existing lesions more so than by additional lesions in primary progressive MS, and more diffuse rather than focal abnormality of the spinal cord in some patients [see Fig. 8] [65]. Although total T2 burden of disease may be lower on average in primary progressive MS, T2 lesion measures remain the principle clinical trial measures in primary progressive MS, with atrophy measures taking on new importance [125,126].

The clinical significance of the MR imaging pathology

Acute relapse in MS is essentially an inflammatory event [127]. MS relapse early in the disease may often show good or full clinical recovery, but many relapses leave some residual deficit [128]. Inflammatory, enhancing MS lesions, when they occur in functionally eloquent regions of the CNS, result in imaging findings, symptoms, and electrophysiologic disturbances with a similar time course [129]. Most often, however, the correlation between new enhancing lesions and new clinical activity is poor, with about 5 to 10 MR imaging events on average occurring for every clinical event [130], and cases with 50 to 100 MR imaging events have

been observed in the absence of any new clinical signs or symptoms [131].

Over short intervals (years), most studies find no or minimal relationships between enhancing lesions and disability. The relationship between enhancing lesions and significant injury, evidenced by atrophy, has been noted in some but not other series, but this too remains only weak at best [6,9]. One factor potentially accounting for this poor clinical (and pathology) relationship despite pathophysiologic connections is the location of lesions; for example, lesions occurring in relatively silent white matter may have only late effects when critical levels of injury (eg, fiber loss) occur, which may take years. Another factor is that much of the enhancing lesion burden may be missed with conventional imaging sensitive to only the macroscopic lesions. Also, injury associated with enhancement is likely heterogeneous and of variable severity, and measures do not account for this. Nevertheless, enhancing lesions do provide a measure of disease, with pathologic consequences, that is missed based on clinical evaluation alone.

The correlation between T2 lesion burden of disease and physical disability in population studies is significant, but very poor, and in individuals typically the relationship between lesion burden and disability can be strikingly poor. The MR imaging disability discrepancy is most likely multifactorial, related to the lack of pathologic specificity of the T2 lesion, imperfections of the disability scoring systems, and limited long-term observations. The latter is supported because the 14-year follow-up study of patients presenting initially with a CIS found a modest correlation between increasing T2 lesion load and disability [117]. The relationship between T2 burden of disease and neuropsychologic impairment is also modest at best, and in many studies poor [132].

Several studies suggest a stronger correlation between injury, indicated through the advanced quantitative MR imaging measures, and disability and cognitive dysfunction, compared with the T2 burden of disease measures. But these advanced measures in larger studies still provide only a modest at best correlation [12]. The strongest correlations between MR imaging measures and disability may be those provided by atrophy measures [132–134]. Although the limited MR imaging functional correlations are discouraging, the poor correlations may only realistically reflect the complex relationships between the pathology; its location and heterogeneity (severity); the long-term consequences that are not evaluated; and the limited measures of dysfunction (typically physical rather than cognitive or functional) that are usually used.

MR imaging in the diagnosis of multiple sclerosis

The classic diagnosis of relapsing MS until recently was based on demyelinating events occurring with dissemination in space (multiple anatomic regions) and dissemination in time based on clinical signs or symptoms. In 2001, however, new so-called "International Panel Criteria," also known as the "McDonald Criteria," were published for the diagnosis of MS [57]. The International Panel Criteria are applicable in individual patients; are well known to the neurologic community; are well (although not universally) accepted; and most important have several advantages in the early diagnosis of MS, including increased specificity and earlier diagnosis.

The International Panel Criteria are summarized in Box 1. After a clinically isolated syndrome, they are based on characteristic lesions and lesion distribution, and allow new MR imaging lesions in lieu of waiting for a second clinical attack. The latter is a key advance because substitution of an MR imaging–documented pathologic event has the potential to expedite diagnosis by months, years, or a lifetime, in contrast to requiring a second clinical event [Fig. 13]. Several studies have addressed the validation of these criteria [60]. They establish that earlier diagnosis is a frequent benefit of use of the International Panel Criteria, which allows earlier treatment in many instances, and improved counseling and support. In addition, the relatively specific dissemination in space criteria based on MR imaging can be useful in minimizing false-positive diagnoses related to incidental nonspecific T2 hyperintensities.

The basis for the new criteria were studies that showed that at the time of a CIS, a negative MR imaging study suggests a low (up to 20%), but not zero probability of a future second attack and a formal diagnosis of MS, whereas a positive MR imaging was associated with high probability of a second attack and a formal diagnosis of MS, ranging from about 50% to 90% of cases [57]. Operational refinements in the criteria evolved with observations suggesting that the number and volume of T2 lesions at the time of a CIS, the presence of enhancing lesions, and the characteristics of the lesions (location) also increased the specificity of the various criteria [57,58,60], increased accuracy, and limited false-positive diagnoses, however, at the expense of sensitivity. Because a positive cerebrospinal fluid also predicts second clinical attack after a CIS, in cerebrospinal fluid–positive patients the dissemination in space criteria can be relaxed to only two MR imaging lesions according to the International Panel Criteria. Lesions in the spinal cord may substitute for lesions in the brain.

> **Box 1: Summary of International Panel Criteria for diagnosis of multiple sclerosis after a clinically-isolated syndrome**
>
> *MR imaging criteria for dissemination in space (3 of 4 of the following)[a]*
>
> 1. 1 gadolinium-enhancing lesion or 9 T2-hypertense lesions if there is no gadolinium-enhancing lesion
> 2. ≥1 infratentorial lesion
> 3. ≥1 juxtacortical lesion
> 4. ≥3 periventricular lesions
>
> *MR imaging criteria for dissemination in time (DIT)*
>
> 1. If a first scan occurs ≥3 months after the onset of the clinical event, the presence of a gadolinium-enhancing lesion is sufficient to demonstrate DIT, provided that it is not at the site implicated in the original clinical event. If there is no enhancing lesion at this time, a follow-up scan is required. The timing of this follow-up scan is not crucial, but 3 months is recommended. A new T2- or gadolinium-enhancing lesion at this time then fulfills the criterion for DIT.
> 2. If the first scan is performed <3 months after the onset of the clinical event, a second scan ≥3 months after the clinical event showing a new gadolinium-enhancing lesion provides sufficient evidence for DIT; however, if no enchancing lesion is seen at this second scan, a further scan not <3 months after the first scan that shows a new T2 or enhancing lesion suffices.
>
> [a] One spinal cord lesion can be substituted for one brain lesion.
>
> *Data from* McDonald WI, Compston A, Edan G, et al. Recommended diagnostic criteria for multiple sclerosis: guidelines from International Panel on the diagnosis of multiple sclerosis. Ann Neurol 2001;50(1):121–7.

An alternative approach used by many MS neurologists in North America is to initiate therapy (in patients at risk for MS) based on positive MR imaging after a CIS, with the MR imaging positive based on at least two MR imaging lesions (periventricular or ovoid and at least 3 mm diameter), or three or more lesions [61]. The likelihood of ongoing demyelination in carefully selected individuals with a classic CIS and only a few MR imaging lesions is supported by results from the placebo arm of the CHAMPS Trial [62], which found that more than 50% of the patients not meeting the formal dissemination in space criteria of the International Panel still developed a second attack or had

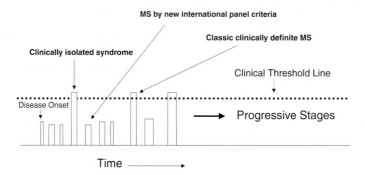

Fig. 13. Overview of relapsing-remitting MS. Vertical open bars represent MR imaging or pathologic events. Dotted line is a theoretical threshold above which lesions are clinically evident to the patient or physician. Before the first clinical event (the time of the clinically isolated syndrome), there are nearly always multiple subclinical pathologic events. Prior criteria required a second clinical event to establish a diagnosis of clinically definite MS (CDMS). By the new international panel criteria, an appropriate MR imaging event may substitute for a second clinical event in establishing dissemination in time, often expediting diagnosis. Most patients have less than one relapse per year. MR imaging events occur on average 5 to 10 times as frequently. After 5 to 10 years, most patients enter a secondary progressive stage of disease, characterized by increasing disability yet fewer relapses and focal MR imaging events.

evidence for ongoing demyelination based on new MR imaging lesions. Although relaxed criteria (fewer lesions, less formal anatomic characteristics) increase sensitivity and function well in formal trial settings, their use must be balanced against the possibility in clinical practice of increasing false-positive diagnoses in patients with nonspecific findings, including those associated with aging and small vessel disease [60,135]. Irrespective of the criteria that are used, a careful plan for MR imaging and clinical follow-up may be informative for any patient after a first attack with a positive MR imaging study, and may reduce the likelihood of delayed diagnosis or treatment in individuals with early subclinical disease, most importantly in those with aggressive disease.

Monitoring patients by MR imaging

Practice patterns for MR imaging after the diagnosis is made are varied, ranging from never acquiring an MR imaging study unless there is a clinical concern to annual MR imaging surveillance for subclinical activity, irrespective of the clinical course. In the clinic, where monthly MR imaging [see Fig. 3] is not feasible, MR imaging activity can be monitored based on counting new T2 hyperintense lesions as a measure of interval change (eg, on annual MR imaging examinations) and counting enhancing lesions at each study as a measure of inflammation around the time of the MR imaging evaluation. Because most enhancing lesions leave a T2 footprint, counting new T2 lesions provides a reasonable

estimate of new lesions that could have been more accurately determined by monthly MR imaging.

Several initiatives are underway to define criteria for successful or acceptable treatment versus treatment failure, based on both clinical and MR imaging activity [136]. Standardized MR imaging (see later) improves the accuracy of these interval assessments, and can be useful in assessing if the International Panel Criteria are met for diagnosis. Complicating the MR imaging interpretation, in addition to intraindividual variation in activity over time independent of treatment, the current therapies are only partially effective. Consequently, it may be impossible to differentiate partial but good responses (decreased lesions) versus poor responses to treatment. MR imaging monitoring, however, may increase confidence in a clinical impression of stable disease or help discount borderline symptoms or signs, supporting maintenance of the current therapy. Severe MR imaging activity may support a clinical impression or uncover a need to initiate aggressive and more risky therapy with immunosuppressive agents.

It is known that interferon-β may decrease enhancing lesions within weeks of initiation of therapy. There are only limited data regarding washout of effect after cessation of therapy, but one study found washout (return to active MR imaging disease) by 6 to 10 months after treatment with interferon beta-1b once halted [137]. Glatiramer acetate also suppresses enhancing lesions, the effect increasing to maximum benefit after an interval of about 4 to 6 months [138]. In phase II trials Tysirabi reduced enhancing and new T2 lesions in weeks [139,140]. High-dose corticosteroids may decrease enhancement within hours of administration, the effect lasting for weeks to months [141].

Clinical imaging technique

CT imaging is now used only in patients who are not appropriate subjects for MR imaging, or for indications unrelated to MS. There are multiple reasonable approaches to MR imaging for MS, and as a result there is a great deal of variability within and between institutions as to how the examination is acquired. Unfortunately, this creates a situation in which comparison of current with prior MR imaging studies can be compromised. With the more specific International Panel and other criteria, standardization can be helpful and ensure stability in decision-making over time. As a result, standardized MR imaging criteria for MS have been promoted for diagnosis and follow-up [142]. Elements of the standardized MR imaging include use of internal landmarks for setting slice location and angle; pulse sequences that are sensitive to MS pathology and comparable from scan-to-scan; and uniform standards for contrast administration including dose and sufficient interval from injection to scan. Triple-dose MR imaging contrast, delayed imaging after contrast administration, and magnetization transfer pulse sequences all increase the yield of enhancing lesions [143], but these are not required for good-quality clinical evaluation, and are not incorporated in the new MS diagnostic criteria.

The advanced quantitative imaging techniques, although invaluable in population studies, are not usually informative in individual patients. There are efforts, however, to develop reproducible acquisition and postprocessing methodologies that enable characterization of disease in individuals, such as measures of global atrophy or MTR and its change over time. Atrophy measures are increasingly used in MS clinical trials as a measure of irreversible injury [9,12], and this measure shows good long-term correlation with disability [134]. The advanced quantitative methodologies for evaluating the NAWM and NAGM are also being tested in formal clinical trial settings. These require stringent technical control to be useful in assessing individuals or populations over time [144].

References

[1] Goldman MD, Cohen JA. Multiple sclerosis. In: Rakel RE, Bope ET, editors. Conn's current therapy. Philadelphia: Elsevier Saunders; 2005. p. 1057–66.

[2] Noseworthy JH, Lucchinetti C, Rodriguez M, et al. Multiple sclerosis. N Engl J Med 2000; 343:938–52.

[3] Lublin FD, Reingold SC. Defining the clinical course of multiple sclerosis: results of an international survey. National Multiple Sclerosis Society (USA) Advisory Committee on Clinical Trials of New Agents in Multiple Sclerosis. Neurology 1996;46:907–11.

[4] Pittock SJ, McClelland RL, Mayr WT, et al. Clinical implications of benign multiple sclerosis: a 20-year population-based follow-up study. Ann Neurol 2004;56:303–6.

[5] Miller DH, Khan OA, Sheremata WA, et al. A controlled trial of natalizumab for relapsing-remitting multiple sclerosis. N Engl J Med 2003; 348:15–23.

[6] Simon JH. Measures of gadolinium enhancement in multiple sclerosis. In: Cohen JA, Rudick RA, editors. Multiple sclerosis therapeutics. 2nd edition. London: Martin Dunitz; 2003. p. 97–124.

[7] Miller DH, Albert PS, Barkhof F, et al. Guidelines for the use of magnetic resonance techniques in monitoring the treatment of multiple sclerosis. US National MS Society Task Force. Ann Neurol 1996;39:6–16.

[8] Simon JH. Pathology of multiple sclerosis as revealed by in vivo magnetic-resonance-based approaches. In: Herndon RM, editor. Multiple sclerosis: immunology, pathology, and pathophysiology. Ch 15. New York: Demos Medical Publishers; 2003. p. 199–213.

[9] Simon JH. Brain and spinal cord atrophy in multiple sclerosis: role as a surrogate measure of disease progression. CNS Drugs 2001;15:427–36.

[10] Miller DH, Barkhof F, Frank J, et al. Measurement of atrophy in multiple sclerosis: pathological basis, methodological aspects and clinical relevance. Brain 2002;125:1676–95.

[11] Simon JH. Brain and spinal cord atrophy in multiple sclerosis. Neuroimaging Clin N Am 2000;10:753–70.

[12] Miller DH, Thompson AJ, Filippi M. Magnetic resonance studies of abnormalities in the normal appearing white matter and grey matter in multiple sclerosis. J Neurol 2003;250:1407–19.

[13] Filippi M, Dousset V, McFarland HF, et al. Role of magnetic resonance imaging in the diagnosis and monitoring of multiple sclerosis: consensus report of the White Matter Study Group. J Magn Reson Imaging 2002;15:499–504.

[14] Sage MR, Wilson AJ, Scroop R. Contrast media and the brain: the basis of CT and MR imaging enhancement. Neuroimaging Clin N Am 1998; 8:695–707.

[15] Markovic-Plese S, McFarland HF. Immunopathogenesis of the multiple sclerosis lesion. Curr Neurol Neurosci Rep 2001;1:257–62.

[16] Oksenberg JR, Baranzini SE, Hauser SL. Emerging concepts of pathogenesis: relationship to therapies for multiple sclerosis. In: Cohen JA,

Rudick RA, editors. Multiple sclerosis therapeutics. 2nd edition. London: Martin Dunitz; 2003. p. 289–322.

[17] Bruck W, Bitsch A, Kolenda H, et al. Inflammatory central nervous system demyelination: correlation of magnetic resonance imaging findings with lesion pathology. Ann Neurol 1997;42:783–93.

[18] Katz D, Taubenberger JK, Cannella B, et al. Correlation between magnetic resonance imaging findings and lesion development in chronic, active multiple sclerosis. Ann Neurol 1993;34:661–9.

[19] Nesbit GM, Forbes GS, Scheithauer BW, et al. Multiple sclerosis: histopathologic and/or CT correlation in 37 cases at biopsy and three cases at autopsy. Radiology 1991;180:467–74.

[20] Lai M, Hodgson T, Gawne-Cain M, et al. A preliminary study into the sensitivity of disease activity detection by serial weekly magnetic resonance imaging in multiple sclerosis. J Neurol Neurosurg Psychiatry 1996;60:339–41.

[21] Cotton F, Weiner HL, Jolesz FA, et al. MRI contrast uptake in new lesions in relapsing-remitting MS followed at weekly intervals. Neurology 2003;60:640–6.

[22] Goodkin DE, Rooney WD, Sloan R, et al. A serial study of new MS lesions and the white matter from which they arise. Neurology 1998;51:1689–97.

[23] Filippi M, Rocca MA, Martino G, et al. Magnetization transfer changes in the normal appearing white matter precede the appearance of enhancing lesions in patients with multiple sclerosis. Ann Neurol 1998;43:809–14.

[24] Pike GB, De Stefano N, Narayanan S, et al. Multiple sclerosis: magnetization transfer MR imaging of white matter before lesion appearance on T2-weighted images. Radiology 2000;215:824–30.

[25] Narayana PA, Doyle TJ, Lai D, et al. Serial proton magnetic resonance spectroscopic imaging, contrast-enhanced magnetic resonance imaging, and quantitative lesion volumetry in multiple sclerosis. Ann Neurol 1998;43:56–71.

[26] Wuerfel J, Bellmann-Strobl J, Brunecker P, et al. Changes in cerebral perfusion precede plaque formation in multiple sclerosis: a longitudinal perfusion MRI study. Brain 2004;127(Pt 1):111–9.

[27] Lucchinetti C, Bruck W, Parisi J, et al. Heterogeneity of multiple sclerosis lesions: implications for the pathogenesis of demyelination. Ann Neurol 2000;47:707–17.

[28] Wingerchuk DM, Lucchinetti CF, Noseworthy JH. Multiple sclerosis: current pathophysiological concepts. Lab Invest 2001;81:263–81.

[29] Morgen K, Jeffries NO, Stone R, et al. Ring-enhancement in multiple sclerosis: marker of disease severity. Mult Scler 2001;7:167–71.

[30] Filippi M, Rocca MA, Rizzo G, et al. Magnetization transfer ratios in multiple sclerosis lesions enhancing after different doses of gadolinium. Neurology 1998;50:1289–93.

[31] Tortorella C, Codella M, Rocca MA, et al. Disease activity in multiple sclerosis studied by weekly triple-dose magnetic resonance imaging. J Neurol 1999;246:689–92.

[32] Bjartmar C, Trapp BD. Axonal and neuronal degeneration in multiple sclerosis: mechanisms and functional consequences. Curr Opin Neurol 2001;14:271–8.

[33] Bjartmar C, Battistuta J, Terada N, et al. *N*-acetylaspartate is an axon-specific marker of mature white matter in vivo: a biochemical and immunohistochemical study on the rat optic nerve. Ann Neurol 2002;51:51–8.

[34] Arnold DL, De Stefano N, Narayanan S, et al. Proton MR spectroscopy in multiple sclerosis. Neuroimaging Clin N Am 2000;10:789–98.

[35] Wolinsky JS, Narayana PA. Magnetic resonance spectroscopy in multiple sclerosis: window into the diseased brain. Curr Opin Neurol 2002;15:247–51.

[36] Dousset V, Ballarino L, Delalande C, et al. Comparison of ultrasmall particles of iron oxide (USPIO)-enhanced T2-weighted, conventional T2-weighted, and gadolinium-enhanced T1-weighted MR images in rats with experimental autoimmune encephalomyelitis. AJNR Am J Neuroradiol 1999;20:223–7.

[37] Rausch M, Hiestand P, Baumann D, et al. MRI-based monitoring of inflammation and tissue damage in acute and chronic relapsing EAE. Magn Reson Med 2003;50:309–14.

[38] Anderson SA, Shukaliak-Quandt J, Jordan EK, et al. Magnetic resonance imaging of labeled T-cells in a mouse model of multiple sclerosis. Ann Neurol 2004;55:654–9.

[39] Filippi M, Falini A, Arnold DL, et al. White Matter Study Group. Magnetic resonance techniques for the in vivo assessment of multiple sclerosis pathology: consensus report of the white matter study group. J Magn Reson Imaging 2005;21(6):669–75.

[40] Martino G, Adorini L, Rieckmann P, et al. Inflammation in multiple sclerosis: the good, the bad, and the complex. Lancet Neurol 2002;1:499–509.

[41] Barkhof F, Bruck W, De Groot CJ, et al. Remyelinated lesions in multiple sclerosis: magnetic resonance image appearance. Arch Neurol 2003;60:1073–81.

[42] Filippi M, Paty DW, Kappos L, et al. Correlations between changes in disability and T2-weighted brain MRI activity in multiple sclerosis: a follow-up study. Neurology 1995;45:255–60.

[43] Guttmann CR, Ahn SS, Hsu L, et al. The evolution of multiple sclerosis lesions on serial MR. AJNR Am J Neuroradiol 1995;16:1481–91.

[44] Bruck W, Kuhlmann T, Stadelmann C. Remyelination in multiple sclerosis. J Neurol Sci 2003;206:181–5.

[45] Simon JH, Kinkel RP, Jacobs L, et al. A wallerian degeneration pattern in patients at risk for MS. Neurology 2000;54:1155–60.

[46] Simon JH, Jacobs L, Kinkel RP. Transcallosal bands: a sign of neuronal tract degeneration in early MS? Neurology 2001;57:1888–90.

[47] van Walderveen MA, Barkhof F, Pouwels PJ, et al. Neuronal damage in T1-hypointense multiple sclerosis lesions demonstrated in vivo using proton magnetic resonance spectroscopy. Ann Neurol 1999;46:79–87.

[48] Van Walderveen MA, Kamphorst W, Scheltens P, et al. Histopathologic correlate of hypointense lesions on T1-weighted spin-echo MRI in multiple sclerosis. Neurology 1998;50:1282–8.

[49] Filippi M, Rocca MA. Magnetization transfer magnetic resonance imaging in the assessment of neurological diseases. J Neuroimaging 2004;14:303–13.

[50] Filippi M, Rovaris M, Rocca MA, et al. Glatiramer acetate reduces the proportion of new MS lesions evolving into "black holes". Neurology 2001;57:731–3.

[51] Dalton CM, Miszkiel KA, Barker GJ, et al. Effect of natalizumab on conversion of gadolinium enhancing lesions to T1 hypointense lesions in relapsing multiple sclerosis. J Neurol 2004; 251:407–13.

[52] Lassmann H. Hypoxia-like tissue injury as a component of multiple sclerosis lesions. J Neurol Sci 2003;206:187–91.

[53] Lennon VA, Wingerchuk DM, Kryzer TJ, et al. A serum autoantibody marker of neuromyelitis optica: distinction from multiple sclerosis. Lancet 2004;364:2106–12.

[54] Law M, Saindane AM, Ge Y, et al. Microvascular abnormality in relapsing-remitting multiple sclerosis: perfusion MR imaging findings in normal-appearing white matter. Radiology 2004;231:645–52.

[55] Barnett MH, Prineas JW. Relapsing and remitting multiple sclerosis: pathology of the newly forming lesion. Ann Neurol 2004;55:458–68.

[56] Simon JH. Magnetic resonance imaging in the diagnosis of multiple sclerosis, elucidation of disease, course, and determining prognosis. In: Burks JS, Johnson KP, editors. Multiple sclerosis: diagnosis, medical management, and rehabilitation. New York: Demos Medical Publishing; 2000. p. 99–126.

[57] McDonald WI, Compston A, Edan G, et al. Recommended diagnostic criteria for multiple sclerosis: guidelines from the International Panel on the diagnosis of multiple sclerosis. Ann Neurol 2001;50:121–7.

[58] Barkhof F, Filippi M, Miller DH, et al. Comparison of MRI criteria at first presentation to predict conversion to clinically definite multiple sclerosis. Brain 1997;120(Pt 11):2059–69.

[59] Hickman SJ, Toosy AT, Jones SJ, et al. Serial magnetization transfer imaging in acute optic neuritis. Brain 2004;127(Pt 3):692–700.

[60] Miller DH, Filippi M, Fazekas F, et al. Role of magnetic resonance imaging within diagnostic criteria for multiple sclerosis. Ann Neurol 2004;56:273–8.

[61] Frohman EM, Goodin DS, Calabresi PA, et al. The utility of MRI in suspected MS: report of the Therapeutics and Technology Assessment Subcommittee of the American Academy of Neurology. Neurology 2003;61:602–11.

[62] CHAMPS Study Group. MRI predictors of early conversion to clinically definite MS in the CHAMPS placebo group. Neurology 2002;59: 998–1005.

[63] Frohman EM, Zhang H, Kramer PD, et al. MRI characteristics of the MLF in MS patients with chronic internuclear ophthalmoparesis. Neurology 2001;57(5):762–8.

[64] Pelletier D, Garrison K, Henry R. Measurement of whole-brain atrophy in multiple sclerosis. J Neuroimaging 2004;14(3 Suppl):11S–9S.

[65] Bot JC, Barkhof F, Polman CH, et al. Spinal cord abnormalities in recently diagnosed MS patients: added value of spinal MRI examination. Neurology 2004;62:226–33.

[66] Lycklama G, Thompson A, Filippi M, et al. Spinal-cord MRI in multiple sclerosis. Lancet Neurol 2003;2:555–62.

[67] Dalton CM, Brex PA, Miszkiel KA, et al. Spinal cord MRI in clinically isolated optic neuritis. J Neurol Neurosurg Psychiatry 2003;74:1577–80.

[68] Filippi M, Rocca MA, Moiola L, et al. MRI and magnetization transfer imaging changes in the brain and cervical cord of patients with Devic's neuromyelitis optica. Neurology 1999;53: 1705–10.

[69] Lin X, Tench CR, Evangelou N, et al. Measurement of spinal cord atrophy in multiple sclerosis. J Neuroimaging 2004;14(3 Suppl):20S–6S.

[70] Stevenson VL, Ingle GT, Miller DH, et al. Magnetic resonance imaging predictors of disability in primary progressive multiple sclerosis: a 5-year study. Mult Scler 2004;10:398–401.

[71] Bergers E, Bot JC, De Groot CJ, et al. Axonal damage in the spinal cord of MS patients occurs largely independent of T2 MRI lesions. Neurology 2002;59:1766–71.

[72] Ganter P, Prince C, Esiri MM. Spinal cord axonal loss in multiple sclerosis: a post-mortem study. Neuropathol Appl Neurobiol 1999;25: 459–67.

[73] Bjartmar C, Kinkel RP, Kidd G, et al. Axonal loss in normal-appearing white matter in a patient with acute MS. Neurology 2001;57:1248–52.

[74] Allen IV, McQuaid S, Mirakhur M, et al. Pathological abnormalities in the normal-appearing white matter in multiple sclerosis. Neurol Sci 2001;22:141–4.

[75] Trapp BD, Peterson J, Ransohoff RM, et al. Axonal transection in the lesions of multiple sclerosis. N Engl J Med 1998;338:278–85.

[76] Evangelou N, Konz D, Esiri MM, et al. Regional axonal loss in the corpus callosum correlates

with cerebral white matter lesion volume and distribution in multiple sclerosis. Brain 2000; 123(Pt 9):1845–9.

[77] Coombs BD, Best A, Brown MS, et al. Multiple sclerosis pathology in the normal and abnormal appearing white matter of the corpus callosum by diffusion tensor imaging. Mult Scler 2004;10:392–7.

[78] Filppi M, Rocca MA, Comi G. The use of quantitative magnetic-resonance-based techniques to monitor the evolution of multiple sclerosis. Lancet Neurol 2003;2:337–46.

[79] Zhou LQ, Zhu YM, Grimaud J, et al. A new method for analyzing histograms of brain magnetization transfer ratios: comparison with existing techniques. AJNR Am J Neuroradiol 2004;25:1234–41.

[80] Bammer R, Augustin M, Strasser-Fuchs S, et al. Magnetic resonance diffusion tensor imaging for characterizing diffuse and focal white matter abnormalities in multiple sclerosis. Magn Reson Med 2000;44:583–91.

[81] Werring DJ, Clark CA, Barker GJ, et al. Diffusion tensor imaging of lesions and normal-appearing white matter in multiple sclerosis. Neurology 1999;52:1626–32.

[82] Beaulieu C. The basis of anisotropic water diffusion in the nervous system: a technical review. NMR Biomed 2002;15:435–55.

[83] Laule C, Vavasour IM, Moore GR, et al. Water content and myelin water fraction in multiple sclerosis: a T2 relaxation study. J Neurol 2004; 251:284–93.

[84] Whittall KP, MacKay AL, Li DK, et al. Normal-appearing white matter in multiple sclerosis has heterogeneous, diffusely prolonged T(2). Magn Reson Med 2002;47:403–8.

[85] Fu L, Matthews PM, De Stefano N, et al. Imaging axonal damage of normal appearing white matter in multiple sclerosis. Brain 1998;121:103–13.

[86] Arnold D, Matthews PM. Measures to quantify axonal damage in vivo based on magnetic resonance spectroscopy in multiple sclerosis. In: Cohen JA, Rudick RA, editors. Multiple sclerosis therapeutics. 2nd edition. London: Martin Dunitz; 2003. p. 193–205.

[87] Fernando KT, McLean MA, Chard DT, et al. Elevated white matter myo-inositol in clinically isolated syndromes suggestive of multiple sclerosis. Brain 2004;127(Pt 6):1361–9.

[88] Rooney WD, Goodkin DE, Schuff N, et al. 1H MRSI of normal appearing white matter in multiple sclerosis. Mult Scler 1997;3:231–7.

[89] Ghezzi A, Bergamaschi R, Martinelli V, et al. Clinical characteristics, course and prognosis of relapsing Devic's neuromyelitis optica. J Neurol 2004;251:47–52.

[90] Filppi M, Rocca MA, Moiola L, et al. MRI and magnetization transfer imaging changes in the brain and cervical cord of patients with Devic's neuromyelitis optica. Neurology 1999;53: 1705–10.

[91] Catalaa I, Fulton JC, Zhang X, et al. MR imaging quantitation of gray matter involvement in multiple sclerosis and its correlation with disability measures and neurocognitive testing. AJNR Am J Neuroradiol 1999;20:1613–8.

[92] Kidd D, Barkhof F, McConnell R, et al. Cortical lesions in multiple sclerosis. Brain 1999;122 (Pt 1):17–26.

[93] Peterson JW, Bo L, Mork S, et al. Transected neurites, apoptotic neurons, and reduced inflammation in cortical multiple sclerosis lesions. Ann Neurol 2001;50:389–400.

[94] Bo L, Vedeler CA, Nyland HI, et al. Subpial demyelination in the cerebral cortex of multiple sclerosis patients. J Neuropathol Exp Neurol 2003;62:723–32.

[95] Bo L, Vedeler CA, Nyland H, et al. Intracortical multiple sclerosis lesions are not associated with increased lymphocyte infiltration. Mult Scler 2003;9:323–31.

[96] Bermel RA, Innus MD, Tjoa CW, et al. Selective caudate atrophy in multiple sclerosis: a 3D MRI parcellation study. Neuroreport 2003;14:335–9.

[97] Schenck JF, Zimmerman EA. High-field magnetic resonance imaging of brain iron: birth of a biomarker? NMR Biomed 2004;17:433–45.

[98] Bakshi R, Benedict RH, Bermel RA, et al. T2 hypointensity in the deep gray matter of patients with multiple sclerosis: a quantitative magnetic resonance imaging study. Arch Neurol 2002;59: 62–8.

[99] Waxman SG. Demyelinating diseases: new pathological insights, new therapeutic targets. N Engl J Med 1998;338:323–5.

[100] Ferguson B, Matyszak MK, Esiri MM, et al. Axonal damage in acute multiple sclerosis lesions. Brain 1997;120:393–9.

[101] Bjartmar C, Wujek JR, Trapp BD. Axonal loss in the pathology of MS: consequences for understanding the progressive phase of the disease. J Neurol Sci 2003;206:165–71.

[102] De Stefano N, Narayanan S, Matthews PM, et al. In vivo evidence for axonal dysfunction remote from focal cerebral demyelination of the type seen in multiple sclerosis. Brain 1999;122(Pt 10): 1933–9.

[103] Werring DJ, Clark CA, Droogan AG, et al. Water diffusion is elevated in widespread regions of normal-appearing white matter in multiple sclerosis and correlates with diffusion in focal lesions. Mult Scler 2001;7:83–9.

[104] Heide AC, Kraft GH, Slimp JC, et al. Cerebral N-acetylaspartate is low in patients with multiple sclerosis and abnormal visual evoked potentials. AJNR Am J Neuroradiol 1998;19: 1047–54.

[105] Evangelou N, Esiri MM, Smith S, et al. Quantitative pathological evidence for axonal loss in normal appearing white matter in multiple sclerosis. Ann Neurol 2000;47:391–5.

[106] Evangelou N, Konz D, Esiri MM, et al. Regional axonal loss in the corpus callosum correlates

with cerebral white matter lesion volume and distribution in multiple sclerosis. Brain 2000; 123(Pt 9):1845–9.

[107] Wujek JR, Bjartmar C, Richer E, et al. Axon loss in the spinal cord determines permanent neurological disability in an animal model of multiple sclerosis. J Neuropathol Exp Neurol 2002; 61:23–32.

[108] Filippi M, Rocca MA, Mezzapesa DM, et al. A functional MRI study of cortical activations associated with object manipulation in patients with MS. Neuroimage 2004;21:1147–54.

[109] Filippi M, Rocca MA, Mezzapesa DM, et al. Simple and complex movement-associated functional MRI changes in patients at presentation with clinically isolated syndromes suggestive of multiple sclerosis. Hum Brain Mapp 2004; 21:108–17.

[110] Rocca MA, Gavazzi C, Mezzapesa DM, et al. A functional magnetic resonance imaging study of patients with secondary progressive multiple sclerosis. Neuroimage 2003;19:1770–7.

[111] Mainero C, Caramia F, Pozzilli C, et al. fMRI evidence of brain reorganization during attention and memory tasks in multiple sclerosis. Neuroimage 2004;21:858–67.

[112] Audoin B, Ibarrola D, Ranjeva JP, et al. Compensatory cortical activation observed by fMRI during a cognitive task at the earliest stage of MS. Hum Brain Mapp 2003;20:51–8.

[113] Staffen W, Mair A, Zauner H, et al. Cognitive function and fMRI in patients with multiple sclerosis: evidence for compensatory cortical activation during an attention task. Brain 2002; 125(Pt 6):1275–82.

[114] Cifelli A, Matthews PM. Cerebral plasticity in multiple sclerosis: insights from fMRI. Mult Scler 2002;8:193–9.

[115] Filippi M, Rocca MA. Cortical reorganisation in patients with MS. J Neurol Neurosurg Psychiatry 2004;75:1087–9.

[116] Filippi M. MRI-clinical correlations in the primary progressive course of MS: new insights into the disease pathophysiology from the application of magnetization transfer, diffusion tensor, and functional MRI. J Neurol Sci 2003; 206:157–64.

[117] Brex PA, Ciccarelli O, O'Riordan JI, et al. A longitudinal study of abnormalities on MRI and disability from multiple sclerosis. N Engl J Med 2002;346:158–64.

[118] CHAMPS Study Group. Baseline MRI characteristics of patients at high risk for multiple sclerosis: results from the CHAMPS trial. Mult Scler 2002;8:332–8.

[119] Pender MP. The pathogenesis of primary progressive multiple sclerosis: antibody-mediated attack and no repair? J Clin Neurosci 2004;11: 689–92.

[120] Thompson AJ, Polman CH, Miller DH, et al. Primary progressive multiple sclerosis. Brain 1997;120:1085–96.

[121] Wolinsky JS. The diagnosis of primary progressive multiple sclerosis. J Neurol Sci 2003;206: 145–52.

[122] Bruck W, Lucchinetti C, Lassmann H. The pathology of primary progressive multiple sclerosis. Mult Scler 2002;8:93–7.

[123] Kremenchutzky M, Lee D, Rice GP, et al. Diagnostic brain MRI findings in primary progressive multiple sclerosis. Mult Scler 2000;6: 81–5.

[124] Filippi M, Rovaris M, Rocca MA. Imaging primary progressive multiple sclerosis: the contribution of structural, metabolic, and functional MRI techniques. Mult Scler 2004; 10(Suppl 1):S36–44 [discussion: S44–5].

[125] Stevenson VL, Miller DH, Leary SM, et al. One year follow up study of primary and transitional progressive multiple sclerosis. J Neurol Neurosurg Psychiatry 2000;68:713–8.

[126] Leary SM, Miller DH, Stevenson VL, et al. Interferon beta-1a in primary progressive MS: an exploratory, randomized, controlled trial. Neurology 2003;60:44–51.

[127] McDonald WI. Relapse, remission, and progression in multiple sclerosis. N Engl J Med 2000; 343:1486–7.

[128] Lublin FD, Baier M, Cutter G. Effect of relapses on development of residual deficit in multiple sclerosis. Neurology 2003;61:1528–32.

[129] Youl BD, Turano G, Miller DH, et al. The pathophysiology of acute optic neuritis: an association of gadolinium leakage with clinical and electrophysiological deficits. Brain 1991;114(Pt 6): 2437–50.

[130] Barkhof F, Scheltens P, Frequin ST, et al. Relapsing-remitting multiple sclerosis: sequential enhanced MR imaging vs clinical findings in determining disease activity. AJR Am J Roentgenol 1992;159:1041–7.

[131] Jacobs LD, Beck RW, Simon JH, et al. Intramuscular interferon beta-1a therapy initiated during a first demyelinating event in multiple sclerosis. CHAMPS Study Group. N Engl J Med 2000;343: 898–904.

[132] Benedict RH, Weinstock-Guttman B, Fishman I, et al. Prediction of neuropsychological impairment in multiple sclerosis: comparison of conventional magnetic resonance imaging measures of atrophy and lesion burden. Arch Neurol 2004;61:226–30.

[133] Amato MP, Bartolozzi ML, Zipoli V, et al. Neocortical volume decrease in relapsing-remitting MS patients with mild cognitive impairment. Neurology 2004;63:89–93.

[134] Fisher E, Rudick RA, Simon JH, et al. Eight-year follow-up study of brain atrophy in patients with MS. Neurology 2002;59:1412–20.

[135] Simon JH, Thompson AJ. Is multiple sclerosis still a clinical diagnosis? Neurology 2003;61: 596–7.

[136] Rudick RA, Lee JC, Simon J, et al. Defining interferon beta response status in multiple

sclerosis patients. Ann Neurol 2004;56: 548–55.

[137] Richert ND, Zierak MC, Bash CN, et al. MRI and clinical activity in MS patients after terminating treatment with interferon beta-1b. Mult Scler 2000;6:86–90.

[138] Comi G, Filippi M, Wolinsky JS. European/ Canadian multicenter, double-blind, randomized, placebo-controlled study of the effects of glatiramer acetate on magnetic resonance imaging: measured disease activity and burden in patients with relapsing multiple sclerosis. European/Canadian Glatiramer Acetate Study Group. Ann Neurol 2001;49:290–7.

[139] Miller DH, Khan OA, Sheremata WA, et al. International Natalizumab Multiple Sclerosis Trial Group. A controlled trial of natalizumab for relapsing multiple sclerosis. N Engl J Med 2003;348:15–23.

[140] O'Connor PW, Goodman A, Willmer-Hulme AJ, et al. Randomized multicenter trial of natalizumab in acute MS relapses: clinical and MRI effects. Neurology 2004;62:2038–43.

[141] Miller DH, Thompson AJ, Morrissey SP, et al. High dose steroids in acute relapses of multiple sclerosis: MRI evidence for a possible mechanism of therapeutic effect. J Neurol Neurosurg Psychiatry 1992;55:450–3.

[142] Simon JH, Li D, Traboulsee A, et al. Standardized MRI protocol for multiple sclerosis: Consortium of MS Centers (CMSC) consensus guidelines. AJNR 2005;. in press.

[143] Silver NC, Good CD, Sormani MP, et al. A modified protocol to improve the detection of enhancing brain and spinal cord lesions in multiple sclerosis. J Neurol 2001;248: 215–24.

[144] Horsfield MA, Barker GJ, Barkhof F, et al. Guidelines for using quantitative magnetization transfer magnetic resonance imaging for monitoring treatment of multiple sclerosis. J Magn Reson Imaging 2003;17:389–97.

MAGNETIC
RESONANCE
IMAGING CLINICS

Magn Reson Imaging Clin N Am 14 (2006) 225–247

ELSEVIER
SAUNDERS

MR Imaging of Epilepsy: Strategies for Successful Interpretation

Venkatramana R. Vattipally, MD, Richard A. Bronen, MD*

- Overview of epilepsy
- Role of MR imaging
- MR imaging of epileptogenic substrates
  Hippocampal sclerosis
  Malformations of cortical development
  Neoplasms
  Vascular malformations
  Gliosis and miscellaneous abnormalities
  Prenatal, perinatal, and postnatal insults
  Posttraumatic epilepsy
- Imaging issues: strategies for successful interpretation
  Normal variations
  Differential diagnosis: avoiding the pitfalls
  Postoperative imaging
  Interpretation of MR images: a systematic approach
  Recommendations for imaging protocols
- Summary
- References

The first half of this article is devoted to providing an introduction and overview for MR imaging of epilepsy. Several MR imaging epilepsy topics will be discussed in great detail in separate articles, such as hippocampal sclerosis, developmental disorders, and functional MR imaging. The remainder of this review will discuss strategies for successful interpretation of MR images from the seizure patient and how to avoid potential pitfalls.

Overview of epilepsy

Epilepsy is a chronic, neurologic disorder characterized by spontaneous, recurrent seizures. Seizures are caused by excessive and abnormal electrical discharges from the cortical neurons.

The epilepsies and epilepsy syndromes are broadly classified into generalized and focal [1]. Partial (focal) seizures originate from a localized area of the brain, whereas generalized seizures originate simultaneously from both cerebral hemispheres. Partial seizures are further subdivided into simple partial, without loss of any consciousness, and complex partial, with loss of consciousness. Partial seizures can spread from one area to another and become secondarily generalized seizures. Though most patients with epilepsy caused by generalized seizures respond to antiepileptic drugs, 30% of those with partial seizures are resistant to antiepileptic drugs [2,3]. In these patients, surgical resection of the brain region provoking seizures is often the only effective treatment. Medically refractory epilepsy is a social, economic, and medical burden not only to the affected individual but also the community in general. Thus, the classification of seizures has prognostic and therapeutic values that help in the improved management and care of patients with epilepsy.

Epilepsy is a common disorder, with a prevalence of 0.4% to 1% of the population [4–6]. MR imaging is an excellent tool for detecting anatomic substrates that underlie regional brain epileptogenesis, but this potential is dependent on the particular population that is being examined. In a study of

This article was originally published in *Neuroimaging Clinics of North America* 14:349–72, 2004.
Yale University School of Medicine, New Haven, CT, USA
* Corresponding author. Yale University School of Medicine, 333 Cedar Street, New Haven, CT 06510.
E-mail address: richard.bronen@yale.edu (R.A. Bronen).

doi:10.1016/j.mric.2006.06.006

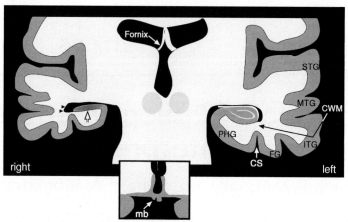

Fig. 1. Coronal T1-weighted diagram of hippocampal sclerosis. Hippocampal atrophy (*open arrow*), the primary finding of hippocampal sclerosis, is demonstrated on the right (the other primary finding of abnormal increased T2 signal intensity is not depicted). The right hippocampus shows loss of the normal alternating gray and white matter internal architecture (compare with the normal left hippocampus). Secondary MR findings of mesial temporal sclerosis include ipsilateral atrophy of the temporal lobe, parahippocampal white matter (PHG), fornix, and mammilary body (mb). The *insert* represents the mammilary body on a more anterior image. Ipsilateral temporal horn dilatation (*arrowheads*) and atrophy of the white matter (CWM) between the hippocampus and gray matter overlying the collateral sulcus (CS) is also depicted. (*From* Bronen RA. MR of mesial temporal sclerosis: how much is enough? AJNR Am J Neuroradiol 1998;19(1):15–8; with permission.)

300 consecutive patients presenting with first seizure, an epileptogenic lesion was identified by MR imaging in 14% (38/263) [7]. In another study, MR imaging detected etiologically relevant structural abnormalities in 12.7% (62/388) of children with newly diagnosed epilepsy [8]. In intractable epilepsy, the overall sensitivity of MR imaging in identifying substrates is in the range of 82% to 86% [9,10]. In a study of 117 patients with intractable epilepsy who underwent surgery, the sensitivities of CT and MR imaging in detecting structural abnormalities were 32% (35/109) and 95% (104/109) respectively [9]. However, MR imaging is of little benefit in those with idiopathic generalized epilepsy. One study found no structural abnormalities

in subjects with idiopathic generalized epilepsy or benign rolandic epilepsy [7]. Based on these and other studies, published guidelines indicate that MR imaging must always be performed in the nonemergent setting in patients with epilepsy, with the exception of primary idiopathic generalized epilepsy. CT still has a role in the initial evaluation of seizures when associated with focal neurologic changes, fever, trauma, or in an emergency setting [11–14].

Role of MR imaging

The main purpose of neuroimaging in epilepsy patients is to identify underlying structural abnormalities that require specific treatment (ie, surgery in

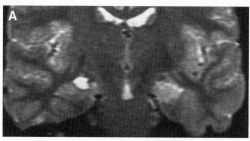

Fig. 2. Hippocampal sclerosis and choroidal fissure cyst. Coronal T2-weighted image (*A*) shows a hyperintense lesion adjacent to the right hippocampus, which did not match a left temporal lobe clinical seizure source. If one focused solely on this obvious lesion, one would neglect the small hyperintense left hippocampus (*arrow*), which was surgically proven to represent hippocampal sclerosis (*B*). The right-sided lesion was a choroidal fissure cyst. It was isointense to CSF on all pulse sequences and located in choroidal fissure above the hippocampus. (*From* Bronen RA, Cheung G, Charles JT, et al. Imaging findings in hippocampal sclerosis: correlation with pathology. AJNR Am J Neuroradiol 1991;12(5):933–40; with permission.)

most instances) and also to aid in formulating a syndromic or etiologic diagnosis. With recent advances in techniques, previously undetectable subtle structural abnormalities are now routinely demonstrated by MR imaging. As compared with CT, MR imaging—with its higher sensitivity, better spatial resolution, excellent soft tissue contrast, multiplanar imaging capability, and lack of ionizing radiation—emerged as primary modality of choice in the evaluation of patients with epilepsy.

In epilepsy surgery, MR plays a crucial role not only in identifying the anatomic location of a substrate but also in depicting the relationship of the substrate to the eloquent regions of the brain (eg, cortices involved with motor, speech, or memory function). Correlation and concordance of MR imaging identified substrate with clinical and electrophysiologic data is essential to avoid false positive localization of the epileptogenic substrate [15]. Concordance of noninvasive electrophysiologic data with MR may obviate the need for invasive electroencephalographic monitoring.

Postoperative MR imaging may identify the complications of surgery as well as causes for the surgical treatment failure, such as residual/recurrent lesion. MR imaging can also prognosticate the postoperative seizure control of epileptogenic substrates. Postoperative seizure control depends on

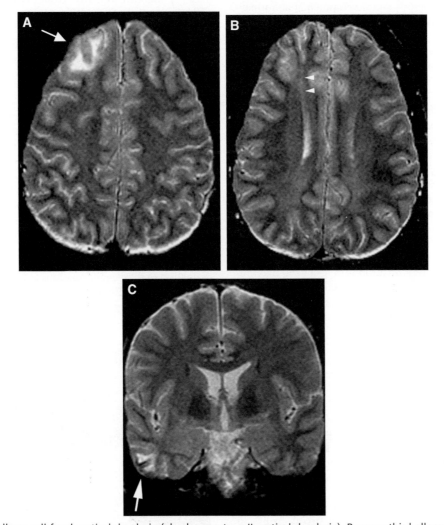

Fig. 3. Balloon cell focal cortical dysplasia (also known type II cortical dysplasia). Because this balloon cell focal cortical dysplastic lesion (*A, B*) has hyperintense signal changes in the subcortical white matter (*A*) on long TR images, it may be confused with a neoplasm (*C*). However, unlike tumors, balloon cell focal cortical dysplasia is associated with cortical thickening (compare the thickened cortex in (*A*) to the normal cortex in (*C*) (*arrows*). A radial band (*arrowheads* in *B*) in this case of dysplasia also helps to distinguish this from neoplasm. (*From* Bronen RA, Vives KP, Kim JH, et al. Focal cortical dysplasia of Taylor balloon cell subtype: MR differentiation from low-grade tumors. AJNR Am J Neuroradiol 1997;18(6):1141–51; with permission.)

the identification of the substrate by MR imaging and the characteristics of the MR abnormality [16].

MR imaging of epileptogenic substrates

Focal epilepsy can be categorized into the following five groups or substrates: (1) hippocampal sclerosis, (2) malformations of cortical development, (3) neoplasms, (4) vascular abnormalities, and (5) gliosis and miscellaneous abnormalities [17]. Each substrate can be defined by a set of characteristic parameters, which unite all abnormalities within each particular substrate category. These parameters include etiology, mechanism of action, treatment options, and postoperative outcome. Because hippocampal sclerosis and developmental abnormalities are discussed separately, here the authors concentrate on the vascular, neoplastic, gliosis, and miscellaneous substrates, with brief references to hippocampal sclerosis and developmental disorders.

Hippocampal sclerosis

Hippocampal sclerosis is the most common epileptogenic substrate seen throughout various surgical epilepsy series. Anterior temporal lobectomy cures the epilepsy in 67% of patients with hippocampal sclerosis [18]. Hippocampal sclerosis is characterized by neuronal loss and gliosis [19,20]. The most important MR findings in hippocampal sclerosis are atrophy and abnormal T2 signal [Figs. 1 and 2] [20–22]. Other minor findings include loss of internal architecture, loss of hippocampal head interdigitations [23], atrophy of ipsilateral mammillary body and fornix [24], dilatation of the ipsilateral temporal horn, volume loss of the temporal lobe, and atrophy of the collateral white matter between the hippocampus and collateral sulcus [25]. The sensitivity of MR in detecting hippocampal sclerosis by qualitative assessment is in the range of 80% to 90%, and by quantitative methods, the sensitivity climbs to 90% to 95% in surgical intractable epilepsy patients [26–28]. Bilateral hippocampal atrophy without obvious signal changes on long TR images, which occurs in 10% to 20% of cases, can be diagnosed by hippocampal volumetry and T2 relaxometry. Hippocampal volumetry and T2 relaxometry can also be useful in lateralizing the epileptogenic lesion [29,30]. Dual pathology is the coexistence of hippocampal sclerosis with another epileptogenic substrate. It occurs in 8% to 22% of surgical epilepsy patients [31]. The most common substrate visualized along with hippocampal sclerosis is cortical dysgenesis. Lesionectomy and hippocampectomy may improve the surgical success in controlling seizures in patients with dual pathology [32,33].

Malformations of cortical development

Developmental malformations are increasingly recognized by MR imaging as causes of epilepsy in children and young adults. At the present time, developmental malformations constitute 10% to 50% of pediatric epilepsy cases being evaluated for surgery and 4% to 25% of adult cases [34–36]. The most widely used classification of malformations of cortical development (MCD) divides these entities into four categories: (1) malformations due to abnormal neuronal and glial proliferation or apoptosis, (2) malformations due to abnormal neuronal migration [Figs. 3 and 4], (3) malformations due to abnormal cortical organization [Fig. 5], and (4) malformations of cortical development, not otherwise classified [37].

MR imaging findings in MCD include cortical thickening, morphologic abnormalities in sulci and gyri, blurring of gray/white matter junction, areas of T2 prolongation in the cortex or subjacent white matter with/without extension toward the ventricles, heterotopic gray matter [21,38], and cerebral spinal fluid (CSF) clefts and cortical dimple [Box 1] [39]. Many developmental malformations are intrinsically epileptogenic. It is important to be aware that the extent of the epileptogenic zone may be more extensive than the structural abnormalities visible on MR images and that epileptogenic zone may not correlate directly to the malformation but may be at a distance from the malformation [34,40,41]. Thus, invasive electrophysiologic studies (ie, subdural and depth electrodes) are usually considered in the presurgical evaluation of these malformations [35,42]. Because many of these malformations may be subtle, high-resolution imaging with good gray-white matter

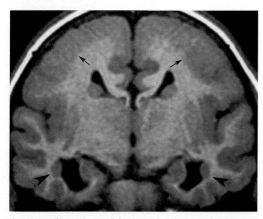

Fig. 4. Pachygyria and heteropia. T1-weighted coronal image demonstrates pachygyria with macrogyria, cortical thickening, and loss of gray-white distinction (*arrows*) as well as heterotopia (*arrowheads*) and agenesis of corpus callosum.

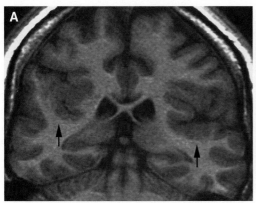
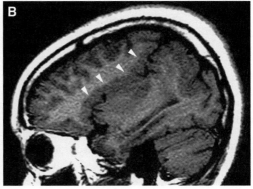

Fig. 5. Polymicrogyria. (*A*) Coronal T1-weighted imaging shows an abnormal sylvian fissure morphology associated with marked cortical thickening (*arrows*). The sagittal image (*B*) demonstrates an abnormal sylvian fissure (*arrowheads*), which has become contiguous with the central sulcus.

differentiating sequences and a systemic approach in interpretation of images are essential for identification and characterization of these substrates [43].

Neoplasms

Brain tumors constitute 2% to 4% of epileptogenic substrates in the general epilepsy population. MR imaging has a sensitivity of nearly 100% in detecting neoplastic lesions, 68% of which are located in temporal lobes in epilepsy patients [9]. Epileptogenic neoplasms associated with chronic epilepsy are located near the cortex in 90% of patients, in the temporal lobe in 68%, and not usually associated with mass effect or vasogenic edema [44]. These focal lesions are often associated with calvarial remodeling corresponding with their indolent nature and chronic presence. The epileptogenic focus is usually localized in the surrounding brain parenchyma, but in some cases, such as hypothalamic hamartomas, the neoplasm has intrinsic epileptogenicity. Complete resection of the neoplasm and overlying cortex results in successful control of seizures in most cases; partial resection of tumor can

Box 1: Imaging features of cortical dysgenesis
Cortical thickening
Blurring of gray-white junction
Irregularity of gray-white junction
Macrogyria
Mini-gyria (polymicrogyria)
Paucity of gyri
Sulcal cleft and cortical dimple
Sulcal morphologic changes
Radial bands of hyperintensity
Transmantle gray matter
Gray matter heterotopia
Band heterotopia

result in improvement in quality of life by decrease in the frequency of seizures [44,45].

Various neoplasms are found in patients with seizures, including low-grade astrocytic tumors, ganglioglioma, dysembryoplastic neuroepithelial tumor (DNET), oligodendroglioma, pleomorphic xanthoastrocytoma, and cerebral metastasis. Most neoplasms are hypointense on T1-weighted images and hyperintense on T2-weighted images. It is often difficult to predict tumor histology in an individual from the MR imaging findings, although certain characteristics tend to be associated with some types of tumors.

Astrocytomas

Astrocytomas have nonspecific imaging features. As a group, the fibrillary subtype (WHO grade 2) is often a low-grade, ill-defined infiltrative tumor that usually does not enhance with contrast, whereas pilocytic astrocytomas are well-defined lesions that usually enhance with contrast [45,46].

Oligodendroglioma

Oligodendroglioma is a slow-growing, peripherally located lesion commonly seen in the frontal or frontotemporal cortex. On MR imaging, these tumors may appear as cortical-based lesions in the frontal lobe with calcifications and adjacent calvarial changes. Contrast enhancement is variable.

Ganglioglioma

Ganglioglioma is commonly seen in temporal lobe, usually occurring in patients less than 30 years old (peak age is 10 to 20 years). These are benign, mixed solid and cystic lesions, cortically based with minimal or no mass effect or edema. Calcification is often present. Contrast enhancement is variable [47,48]. The combination of calcification and cysts in a cortically based lesion in a patient with seizures should make the practitioner consider this diagnosis.

Dysembryoplastic neuroepithelial tumors

DNETs are benign, low-grade, multicystic, and multinodular cortical-based tumors predominantly seen in children and young adults. These lesions may be associated with calvarial remodeling or cortical dysplasia. The MR imaging appearance and contrast enhancement is variable and nonspecific, unless the imaging features present as a multicystic cortically based tumor [Fig. 6] [46,47].

Pleomorphic xanthoastrocytomas

Pleomorphic xanthoastrocytomas are peripherally located (adjacent to the leptomeninges) cystic lesions with enhancing mural nodule. Involvement of the leptomeninges is the characteristic feature of this tumor. Prognosis is good after surgical resection; however, local recurrence and malignant transformation can occur in these tumors [46,47].

Vascular malformations

Vascular malformations constitute 5% of epileptogenic substrates in the generality of epilepsy patients. Arteriovenous malformations (AVMs) and cavernous malformations (also known as cavernomas or cavernous hemangiomas) are the most common vascular malformations causing seizures in epilepsy patients. The sensitivity of MR imaging is close to 100% in detecting these malformations [44].

Arteriovenous malformations

AVMs are congenital, developmental anomalies of blood vessels. AVMs consist of a tangle of blood vessels lacking intervening capillary network and leading to direct arteriovenous shunting of blood. Thrombosis, calcification, hemorrhage, and fibrosis are common secondary changes in these lesions. The possible mechanisms for seizure generation include (1) focal cerebral ischemia from steal phenomena due to arteriovenous shunting, and (2) gliosis and hemosiderin deposition from subclinical hemorrhage in the brain parenchyma [45]. T1- and T2-weighted images demonstrate serpigenous flow voids with areas of T2 prolongation in the adjoining brain parenchyma. Surgical resection of the AVM is effective in controlling seizures in patients with epilepsy [49].

Cavernous malformations

Cavernous malformations are composed of well-circumscribed vascular spaces containing blood in various stages of evolution. The absence of any intervening neural tissue within the lesion is the hallmark of this lesion. From 15% to 54% of these lesions are multiple, and 50% to 80% of multiple lesions occur on a familial basis [50]. The typical MR appearance of a cavernous malformation is popcorn-like with a heterogeneous hyperintense signal centrally on all pulse sequences, surrounded by a rim of low signal intensity from hemosiderin [Fig. 7]. Because hemosiderin results in magnetic susceptibility artifacts (which are visualized as signal voids on MR images), sequences that are more affected by magnetic susceptibility artifacts will tend to have the greatest sensitivity for detecting small cavernomas. Thus, gradient echo images have a much higher sensitivity when compared with conventional or fast spin echo sequences. Though MR imaging has high sensitivity in detecting these lesions, it cannot reliably differentiate between

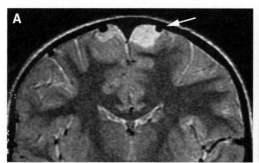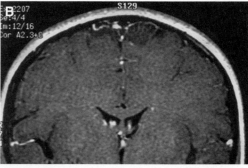

Fig. 6. Dysembyroplastic neuroepithelial tumor. Coronal proton density-weighted image (*A*) and postcontrast (*B*) images demonstrate a peripherally based lesion (*arrow*) with trabeculated enhancement. Based solely on these images, it appears that the lesion is extra-axial because gray matter can be seen surrounding the lesion, especially in (*A*). However, it is not uncommon for an intra-axial neoplasm causing chronic epilepsy to appear extra-axial because it is situated within or replaces the cortex and has the appearance of being outside the cortex in some cross-sectional planes. Thin section imaging allowed visualization of the multicystic nature of this lesion on the enhanced image (*B*).

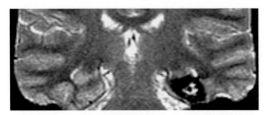

Fig. 7. Cavernous malformation. Coronal T2-weighted image with a temporal lobe lesion. The central hyperintense signal intensity (due to chronic blood products, methemoglobin) surrounded by a rim of signal void (due to hemosiderin) is typical of an occult vascular malformation, which is usually the result of a cavernous malformation, as in this case.

a cavernous hemangioma, a partially thrombosed AVM, or a hemorrhagic metastatic lesion [44]. However, in a patient with epilepsy and typical MR imaging popcorn lesion with a hemosiderin ring, the most likely diagnosis is cavernous malformation.

Developmental venous malformations are discussed in the normal variant section that follows.

Gliosis and miscellaneous abnormalities

A number of disparate entities that are associated with intractable epilepsy have certain histologic findings, with gliosis (and neuronal loss) in common. Gliosis is the end result of various focal and diffuse central nervous system injuries. Examples include trauma, infection, and infarctions, which may be focal or diffuse. Stroke is a common cause of epilepsy in the elderly population [51]. Rasmussen's encephalitis, perinatal insults, and Sturge-Weber syndrome are examples of diffuse entities, which may involve an entire cerebral hemisphere and lead to atrophy of that hemisphere. MR imaging findings of gliosis are nonspecific, consisting of hyperintense changes on long TR sequences and hypointense signal intensity on T1-weighted images, which may be associated with volume loss, encephalomalacia, sulcal widening, and ventricular enlargement. Some of the more important epileptogenic entities in this gliosis and miscellaneous category will be discussed in detail.

Prenatal, perinatal, and postnatal insults

Diffuse and focal destructive lesions of the brain constitute a major group of pathologic processes in children presenting with seizures [52]. The appearance of these lesions depends on the timing of the insults to the brain.

Early injury to the brain of the developing fetus (less than 6 months) leads to the formation of smooth-walled porencephalic cavities with minimal or no glial reaction in the surrounding brain parenchyma [53]. These porencephalic cavities are commonly located in perisylvian regions and are filled with CSF and may communicate with the ventricles, subarachnoid space, or both. Porencephaly is associated with increased incidence of hippocampal sclerosis ipsilateral to the porencephalic cavity, or bilateral [52].

Brain injury occurring in the perinatal or postnatal period leads to a pattern of encephalomalacia or ulegyria. Encephalomalacia (diffuse or focal) results from late gestational, perinatal, and postnatal injuries to the brain. Encephalomalacia results in multiple, irregular cystic cavities with prominent astrocytic proliferation [Fig. 8] [53]. Ulegyria, also a result of perinatal insult to the brain, is commonly seen in the parieto-occipital region. It is characterized by destruction of the gray matter in the depths of the sulci, sparing the crowns of gyral convolutions [54]. MR imaging is useful not only in identifying these lesions and defining their extent in surgically fit patients but also in diagnosing periventricular leucomalacia and multicystic encephalomalacia.

Posttraumatic epilepsy

Posttraumatic epilepsy may be considered a specialized form of postnatal injury epilepsy. The overall risk of seizures is in the range of 1.8% to 5% for civilian injuries, but can be as high as 53% for war injuries [55]. In closed head injuries, the most common sites of injury are along the inferior anterior regions of the brain because of irregularities of the skull base at these locations—the orbital surfaces of the frontal lobe, the undersurface of the temporal lobe, the frontal pole, and the temporal

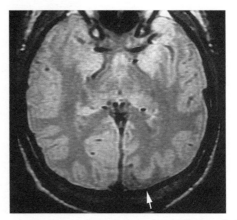

Fig. 8. Gliotic scar. This region of encephalomalacia and gliosis (arrow) appears as a widened CSF space on this proton density-weighed image. Surgical removal cured the seizures. (From Bronen RA, Fulbright RK, Kim JH, et al. A systematic approach for interpreting MR images of the seizure patient. AJR Am J Roentgenol 1997;169(1):241–7; with permission.)

pole. These traumatic shearing injuries of the brain, or contusions, are often associated with hemorrhage, which eventually results in hemosiderin deposition and reparative gliotic changes [56]. Hemosiderin and gliosis are known to be involved in seizure generation/propagation [57].

Risk factors for late posttraumatic epilepsy include (1) early posttraumatic seizures, (2) severe initial brain injury (loss of consciousness or amnesia for more than 24 hours), (3) complex depressed skull fracture, (4) subdural hematoma, (5) penetrating injury, (6) intracranial hemorrhage, (7) brain contusion, and (8) age over 65 years [55,58]. Depressed skull fractures, intracerebral hematoma and subdural hematoma carry a risk of 25% for

developing post traumatic seizures [58]. MR imaging is an effective modality for demonstrating diffuse axonal injury, intracerebral hematoma, subdural hematoma, contusions, and gliosis. Because hemosiderin is not completely removed from the brain, MR imaging can detect evidence of old hemorrhagic lesions. Thus, MR imaging plays a role in the management of patients with trauma and may be a useful tool in predicting the prognosis for the patient in the long run.

Infections

Seizures can be an early clinical sign in bacterial, viral, fungal, mycobacterial, and parasitic infections. In the acute phase, the seizures may be related to

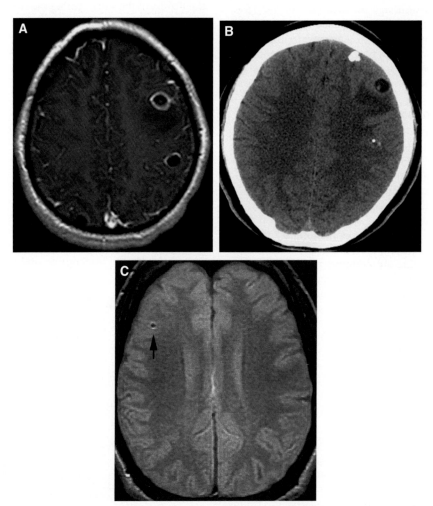

Fig. 9. Cysticercosis. (*A*) Multiple ring enhancing lesions with surrounding edema represent the inflammatory reactive stage of cysticercosis on this contrast enhanced T1-weighted axial image. Corresponding CT scan (*B*) shows calcification of these lesions. In a different patient, the only MR abnormality was the punctate signal void (*arrow*) in the right frontal lobe on this proton density-weighted image (*C*). This was surgically proven to represent a calcified granuloma due to cysticercosis that caused chronic epilepsy. (*Fig. 9C from* Bronen RA, Fulbright RK, Kim JH, et al. A systematic approach for interpreting MR images of the seizure patient. AJR Am J Roentgenol 1997;169(1):241–7; with permission.)

the host's inflammatory response, and may be due to gliotic changes in the chronic phase. With the recent advances in imaging and increase in the immigrant population, tuberculosis and neurocysticercosis are increasingly documented as the most common infections, with seizure presentation in developed and developing countries.

Neurocysticercosis results from infestation with larval form of pig tapeworm *Taenia solium*. Neurocysticercosis can be seen in parenchyma, ventricles, subarachnoid spaces, or a combination of these. Seizures are the result of the inflammatory response to the dying and degenerating parasite.

In the active parenchymal form, cysticercosis is visualized on MR images as thin-walled nonenhancing cystic lesions isointense to CSF on all pulse sequences. Within the cyst, an eccentrically located scolex may be seen, which usually enhances. In the inactive parenchymal or dying form, with increasing inflammatory changes from the host response, the cyst wall thickens and enhances after contrast administration. Vasogenic edema is usually seen in the adjoining brain parenchyma, and the fluid in the cyst also increases in signal on T1-weighted images. With further progression of inflammatory changes, the cystic lesion is replaced by granuloma, seen on MR imaging as an enhancing nodule. After the death of the larvae, the cysts and scolices are replaced by dense calcification, which are visualized as signal voids on gradient echo images as a result of susceptibility artifacts [59]. Most of the calcified lesions are located at the gray/white matter junction [Fig. 9].

Tuberculosis is a chronic granulomatous infection caused by *Mycobacterium*. It is characterized by caseous central necrosis and the presence of multinucleated giant cells in the granuloma. Risk factors include elderly age, poverty, human immunodeficiency virus (HIV), immunosuppression, and lymphoma. Incidence of central nervous system tuberculosis in the HIV-negative pulmonary tuberculosis population is 2%, and 19% in the HIV-positive pulmonary tuberculosis patients [60]. Central nervous system tuberculosis can involve the meninges and brain parenchyma, and the leptomeningeal version can cause hydrocephalus, neuropathies, arthritis, and deep gray matter infarction.

Parenchymal tuberculomas can be single or multiple. The MR imaging findings are nonspecific and depend on the host hypersensitivity reaction to the bacillus. The amount of host hypersensitivity reaction predicts the amount of inflammatory cells, gliosis, and free radical deposition in the granuloma. The noncaseating tuberculoma can be seen as an iso- to hypointense lesion on T1-weighted images and as a variable signal intensity lesion on T2-weighted images, with surrounding edema.

The granuloma enhances homogenously after contrast administration. Caseating granulomas are hypo- to isointense on T1-weighted images and hypointense to brain parenchyma on T2-weighted images, enhancing in a ring-like manner. Small lesions detected by MR imaging are more amenable to medical treatment, and thus MR imaging can have a prognostic value by identifying and determining their size [60].

Rasmussen's encephalitis

Rasmussen's encephalitis is chronic encephalitis characterized by partial motor seizures and progressive neurologic and cognitive deterioration [54,61,62]. It usually affects one cerebral hemisphere, which later becomes atrophic. Most cases are seen in children, though some are also reported in adolescents and adults.

The disease progresses through three phases. In the initial prodromal phase, the patient presents with few partial motor seizures. The second phase, the acute stage, is characterized by an increase in frequency of partial motor seizures. In the last or residual phase, there are permanent and stable neurologic deficits [61]. MR imaging findings in the acute phase include areas of T2 prolongation in the cortex and subcortical white matter, usually starting in the frontoinsular region and extending to other parts of the brain. These signal changes in the cortex and subcortical white matter can be fleeting—changing in size and location over time. Cortical atrophy with ventricular enlargement and caudate nucleus atrophy can be seen as the disease progresses [61]. In late stages of this disorder, atrophy of the entire cerebral hemisphere with

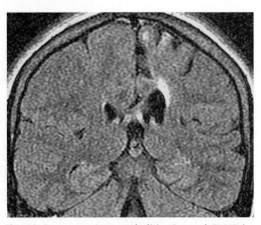

Fig. 10. Rasmussen's encephalitis. Coronal FLAIR image demonstrates encephalomalacia in the left frontoparietal region with abnormal signal in the left paracentral lobule and exvacuo dilatation of the left lateral ventricle in a patient with pathologically proven Rasmussen's encephalitis.

hemi-atrophy of the ipsilateral brain stem may be seen, and when associated with contralateral cerebellar diaschis is due to degeneration of corticopontocerebellar fibers [Fig. 10].

Sturge-Weber syndrome

Sturge-Weber syndrome is a sporadic, congenital neurocutaneous syndrome characterized by the association of ipsilateral facial angioma in the distribution of the trigeminal nerve with angiomatosis of the leptomeninges. Clinically, patients present with facial angioma, intractable seizures, hemiparesis, hemianopsia, and mental retardation. A dysgenetic venous system is responsible for most of the imaging and clinical findings in these patients.

Intractable epilepsy is the earliest and most common clinical presentation in these patients. MR can demonstrate the structural abnormalities in the brain, which include (1) pial angiomata in the parietal occipital region on post–contrast-enhanced images, (2) cortical calcifications subjacent to the cortex and white matter in the parieto-occipital region, which are depicted as signal voids or hypointense curvilinear structures, (3) enlarged choroid plexus, especially on postcontrast enhanced images, (4) atrophy of the ipsilateral cerebral hemisphere (angioma side), and (5) enlarged and elongated globe of the eye [Fig. 11] [63]. The pial angioma is believed to be due to the persistence of embryonic vasculature. It is generally accepted that the

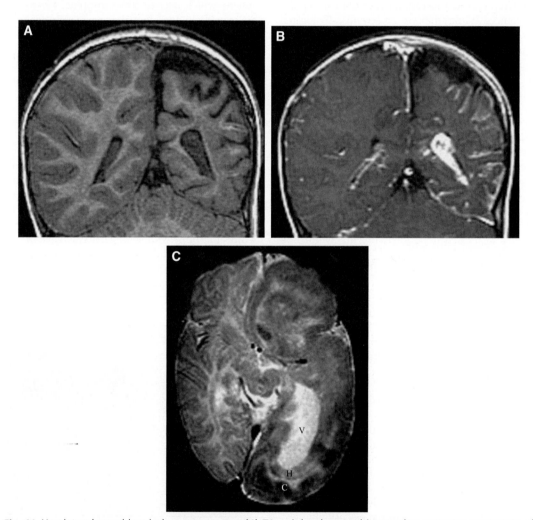

Fig. 11. Hemiatrophy and hemisphere asymmetry. (*A*) T1-weighted coronal image demonstrates asymmetry of the hemispheres. Because the CSF spaces and ventricle are larger ipsilateral to the smaller hemisphere, this represents hemiatrophy. Based solely on this image, it is difficult to distinguish the cause of the hemiatrophy. However, in this case of Sturge-Weber syndrome, a contrast-enhanced scan (*B*) is helpful, depicting marked enhancement along the pial surface and ipsilateral choroidal plexus. (*C*) Hemimegalencephaly is also associated with hemisphere and ventricular asymmetry, but the larger ventricle (V) is ipsilateral to the larger hemisphere. This entity is also associated with heterotopias (H) and cortical thickening (C).

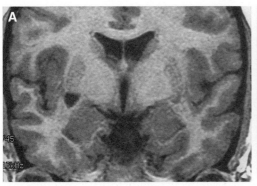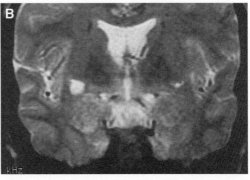

Fig. 12. Subcapsular Virchow Robbin spaces. This subcapsular lesion is isointense to CSF on coronal T1-weighted (*A*) and T2-weighted (*B*) images. This unilateral lesion may give one pause, but Virchow Robbin spaces in this location inferior to the basal ganglia are common, although they are usually bilateral and smaller in size.

calcifications in the cortex and the subjacent white matter are caused by chronic ischemia, and enlarged choroids plexus is the result of shunted venous drainage from the cerebral hemisphere to the choroids plexus. Other associated features include prominent and enlarged subependymal and medullary veins (due to dysgenetic superficial venous system) and secondary signs of cerebral atrophy, which include dilated paranasal sinuses, mastoid air cells, and thickened calvarium.

Imaging issues: strategies for successful interpretation

Successful MR imaging of the seizure patient can be more demanding than brain imaging of other patients because the abnormalities may be subtle and not easily visualized with routine brain imaging sequences. This necessitates dedicated imaging sequences, a high index of suspicion, and careful review of imaging studies. Some abnormalities present as minor asymmetries of brain structure, so practitioners must be able to differentiate normal variations from pathologic conditions. This section discusses some practical issues with respect to MR imaging of epilepsy: normal anatomic and imaging variations, an approach to image interpretation, differential diagnosis, and imaging protocol.

Normal variations

CSF or cystlike structures are frequently present in healthy individuals. The following CSF structures have no relationship to epilepsy in general and must be differentiated from pathologic conditions. One correlative MR-histologic study found cysts and punctate foci of T2 signal changes in 17% (n = 17) of patients with surgical intractable epilepsy [9]. Arachnoid cysts and choroidal fissure cysts are isointense to CSF on all pulse sequences [see

Fig. 2] [64]. Perivascular Virchow-Robbin spaces are commonly visualized in patients with seizures because the dedicated imaging sequences allow for better detail than routine sequences. Asymmetric large Virchow-Robbin spaces in the region of the anterior perforated substance and subcapsular region may give pause to the uninitiated, but are common occurrences [Fig. 12]. Virchow-Robbin spaces in the subinsular zone (ie, between the extreme and external capsules) may appear lesion-like on T2-weighted fast spin echo sequences [Fig. 13] [65]. However, because Virchow-Robbin spaces represent CSF in perivascular space, these "anomalies" are always isointense to CSF. Feather-like configurations may be detected on T2-weighted

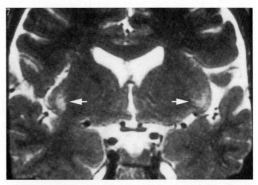

Fig. 13. Subinsular Virchow Robbin spaces. The hyperintense signals (*arrows*) in the extreme and external capsules on this T2-weighted coronal image are caused by Virchow Robbin spaces. Their true nature can be recognized by noting the feathered configuration, typical location, and isointensity to CSF on all sequences. (*From* Song CJ, Kim JH, Kier EL, Bronen RA. MR and histology of subinsular T2-weighted bright spots: Virchow-Robbin spaces of the extreme capsule and insula cortex. Radiology 2000;214:671–7; with permission.)

images. Partial volume effects with the brain may lead to mild hypointense signal intensity compared with brain on T1-weighted images rather than the more marked hypointensity of CSF that is found in the ventricles. Punctate or linear enhancement within the center of these represents the vasculature and confirms the diagnosis (but there should be no other enhancement associated with these). Similar findings may be found along the subcortical zone of the anterior temporal lobe cortex, which also represents Virchow-Robbin spaces (Zhang W, et al, unpublished data) and these again need to be distinguished from pathologic conditions. A normal variant seen in 10% to 15% of the normal population is the cyst of hippocampal sulcal. The hippocampal sulcus, located between the cornu ammonis and dentate gyrus, normally involutes in utero. In some cases, a cystic fluid collection forms if the lateral potion of the sulcus fails to involute. This cyst is located in the hippocampus itself, between dentate gyrus and cornua ammonis and is isointense to CSF in all pulse sequences [Fig. 14]. It does not demonstrate any contrast enhancement [66,67]. The uncal recess or anterior-most portion of the temporal horn is asymmetric in 60% of epilepsy patients as well as healthy individuals and has no relationship to epileptogenic zone (Messinger JM, Bronen RA, Kier EL, unpublished data), and is easily misinterpreted by those unfamiliar with this finding [Fig. 15].

Isolated developmental venous malformations, also known as venous angiomas or developmental venous anomalies, have not been implicated in epileptogenesis [68,69]. However, venous anomalies are not infrequently found in conjunction with other abnormalities that have been linked to epilepsy, such as cavernous malformations and malformations of cortical development (such as the perisylvian polymicrogyria and other polymicrogyrial syndromes).

Detection of cortical abnormalities underlying malformations of cortical development can be difficult, and practitioners need to be cognizant about the normal variants of gyral and sulcal configurations. The cortex adjoining the superior temporal sulcus on the right side is usually slightly thicker than that of the left side (Zhang W, Schultz R, Bronen RA, unpublished data) and can be misinterpreted as a region of dysplasia. Similarly, the gyri surrounding the calcarine sulcus usually indents the occipital horn (in an area known as the calcar avis), giving rise to the appearance of thickened gyri, which can be misinterpreted as cortical dysplasia if it is asymmetric [70]. Because of the normal undulations of the cortex, there are frequently brain regions with the appearance of cortical thickening on cross-sectional images, if the gyrus is parallel to cross-sectional plane. Dysplasia can be distinguished from this normal finding by observing cortical thickening on multiple images (usually at least three contiguous this section images) or confirming that cortical thickening is present in another plane [Fig. 16]. The signal intensity of gray and white matter in the immature myelinated infant can be confusing and lead to misinterpretations. For instance, the myelinated optic radiation surrounded by unmyelinated white matter could be mistaken for gray matter and labeled as band heterotopia (ie, the double-cortex syndrome) [Fig. 17].

Another potential area for confusing normal findings for cortical dysplasia is in the perirolandic fissure region. On coronal images, there is often poorer visualization of the gray matter thickness in the perirolandic fissure region compared with the rest of the frontal lobes as well as poor distinction between gray and white matter (Bronen RA, unpublished data). This variation appears to be

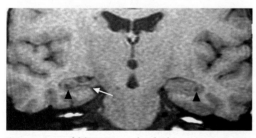

Fig. 14. Cyst of hippocampal sulcal remnant. A common variation occurs when the lateral portion of the hippocampal sulcus (*arrow*) does not normally involute and instead forms a hippocampal sulcal remnant cyst (*arrowheads*). (*From* Bronen RA, Cheung G. MRI of the normal hippocampus. Magn Reson Imaging 1991;9(4):497–500; with permission.)

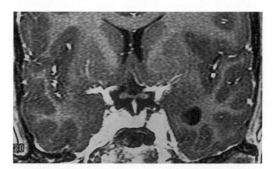

Fig. 15. Uncal recess. The hypointense finding in the left temporal lobe on this contrast-enhanced T1-weighted coronal image could easily be misinterpreted as a cystic lesion. However, it represents CSF in the uncal recess or anterior recess of the temporal horn and is contiguous with the temporal horn (although the bridging CSF may be small). The uncal recess is normally asymmetric in 60% of individuals.

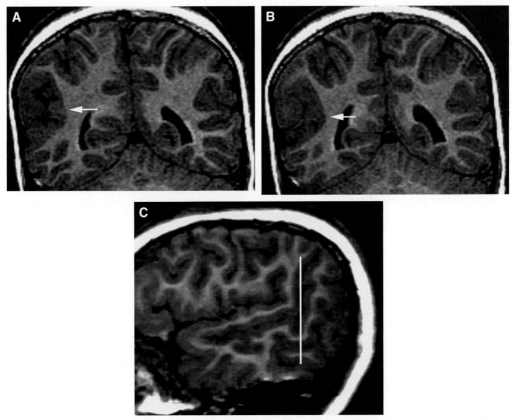

Fig. 16. Polymicrogyria differential diagnosis. Coronal T1-weighted images demonstrate a conglomeration of gray matter (*arrows*) in (*A*) and (*B*), which could represent polymicrogyria. Sagittal reformatted images (*C*) show that this is caused by gray matter along a prominent vertical portion of the posterior extent of the superior temporal sulcus (*line*). The cortical thickness is normal on sagittal images.

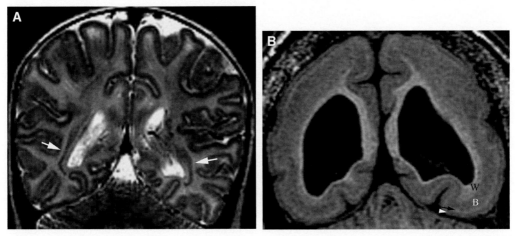

Fig. 17. Band heterotopia differential diagnosis. (*A*) Coronal T2-weighted image shows a bilateral structure (*arrows*) that is isointense to gray matter. This represents myelinated optic radiations against a backdrop of unmyelinated white matter in this infant and should not be confused with band heterotopia. (*B*) Compare with true band heterotopia in (*B*). B, band hetertopia; W, periventricular white matter; black arrow, subcortical white matter; white arrowhead, cortex.

caused by a combination of factors, one of which is that the gray matter surrounding the rolandic fissure is normally thinner than cortices in the rest of the brain. Another factor is that the frontal sulci and gyri anterior to the rolandic fissure (ie, superior, middle, and inferior frontal gyri) are perpendicular to the coronal plane, allowing for good definition of their cross-sectional surfaces; whereas the rolandic fissure and adjacent gyri are parallel to the coronal plane, allowing for partial volume effects with white matter. Because of the difficulty interpreting this region on coronal images, reference to axial (or axial reformatted) images should be performed, especially as frontal lobe epilepsy is secondary only to temporal lobe epilepsy in terms of the most common regions of partial seizures.

Other potential sources for errors with interpretation include evaluation of the hippocampus. As previously discussed, the key features of hippocampal sclerosis are hippocampal asymmetry and signal hyperintensity on FLAIR imaging. Artificial hippocampal size asymmetry can be created by head rotation because the cross-sectional size of the hippocampus is greatest anteriorly (at its head) and progressively tapers on more posterior sections. Correct interpretation depends on (1) accurate alignment of the patients head in the scanner and (2) taking head rotation into account for determining hippocampal symmetry in those subjects who fail to be properly aligned [Fig. 18]. Caution is also advised when interpreting FLAIR sequence images. The signal intensity of the hippocampi on FLAIR sequences is slightly greater than the cortex in healthy individuals and this has the potential of leading to a false diagnosis of bilateral hippocampal sclerosis in seizure patients. The

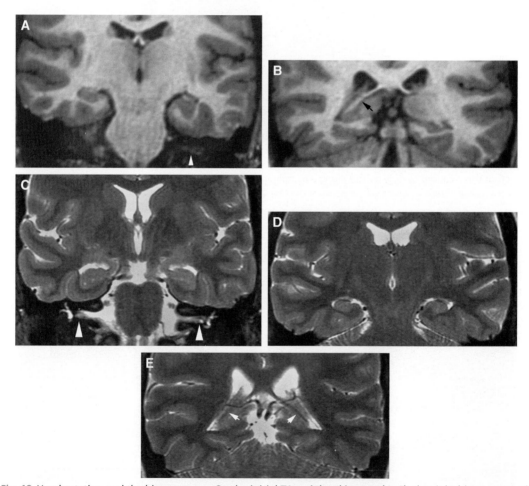

Fig. 18. Head rotation and the hippocampus. On the initial T1-weighted images (*A, B*), the right hippocampus is markedly smaller than the left, suggesting hippocampal sclerosis (*A*). However, this is the result of marked head rotation as confirmed by the marked asymmetry of the internal auditory canal (*arrowhead*) and fornix (*arrow*). After patient repositioning (*C–E*), head rotation is corrected as noted by the symmetry of the IACs (*arrowheads*) and fornices (*arrows*) on the T2-weighted coronal images. With head rotation corrected, there is no longer apparent hippocampal asymmetry.

configuration of the hippocampus can be variable, and this may also lead to difficulties with interpretation. The hippocampal body usually has an oval or round shape in the coronal plane. Infrequently, it may have a more vertical configuration, which may lead to an erroneous diagnosis of cortical dysgenesis. In cases of corpus callosum agenesis or holoprosencephaly, there may be associated incomplete infolding of the cornu ammonis and dentate gyrus, which manifests as a vertically shaped hippocampus with a (shallow) medial cleft on coronal images [Fig. 19].

Differential diagnosis: avoiding the pitfalls

Potential misinterpretations of imaging findings in seizure patients may be due to a number of situations in addition to the normal variations listed above. Perhaps the most troubling are transient lesions, because of the potential for performing lesional resective surgery in a setting where epileptogenesis is either widespread (eg, Rasmussen's encephalitis) or outside the lesional area. Focal transient signal abnormalities in seizure patients may be the result of infections or of prolonged or frequent seizures [20]. Postictal changes can present as focal or multifocal hyperintense abnormalities of the cortex or hippocampus on long TR images and as restricted diffusion (ie, hyperintensity) on diffusion-weighted images [Fig. 20]. Though these latter findings may indicate ischemic changes, perfusion studies show increased blood flow rather than decreased blood flow associated

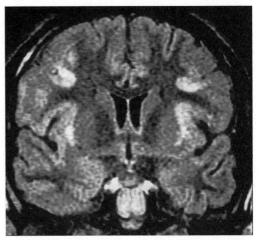

Fig. 20. Postictal changes. Multifocal regions of hyperintensity of the cortex are present on this coronal FLAIR image from a patient that was in status epilepticus. This is more problematic when postictal changes occur in the hippocampus unilaterally.

with infarction. In Rasmussen's syndrome, signal changes may not only be transient, but also move from location to location. Therefore, caution should be exercised in interpreting findings and recommending invasive studies for actively seizing patients [21,71]. Morphologic and signal abnormalities are also reported in recurrent focal or febrile seizures in the hippocampus [72,73]. Transient lesions may also affect the splenium of the corpus callosum [74]. This rare isolated focal lesion, occurring in 0.5% epilepsy patients, is characterized by hyperintensity on long TR images, restricted diffusion, and

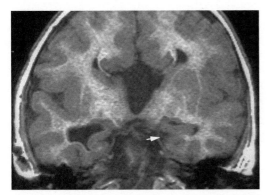

Fig. 19. Unfolded hippocampus. In this patient with agenesis of the corpus callosum, the hippocampi have characteristic features of an unfolded hippocampus—a medial CSF cleft (*arrow*) with a vertically oriented hippocampus, typical of a hippocampus that failed to completely infold the dentate gyrus and cornu ammonis together during development. (*From* Kier EL, Kim JH, Fulbright RK, Bronen RA. Embryology of the human fetal hippocampus: MR imaging, anatomy, and histology. AJNR Am J Neuroradiol 1997;18:525–32; with permission).

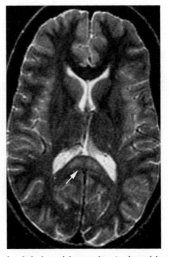

Fig. 21. Splenial signal intensity. Isolated hyperintensity of the splenium of the corpus callosum (*arrow*) on this axial T2-weighted image in this patient with epilepsy.

lack of enhancement [Fig. 21]. This particular lesion is thought to result from either frequent seizures or abrupt changes in antiepileptic drug concentrations that may elevate arginine vasopressin and possibly cause cytotoxic edema in the splenium.

Differentiating neoplasms from either focal cortical dysplasia or hippocampal sclerosis may be problematic at times. Hyperintense signal changes on T2-weighted images in the subcortical white matter may be present in neoplasms as well as focal cortical dysplasia (particularly balloon cell focal cortical dysplasia). Surgical strategies may differ for these entities, especially if an epileptogenic lesion is located in an eloquent area of the cortex (ie, primary motor or speech). Imaging findings suggestive of dysplasia rather than neoplasm include cortical thickening, the presence of a radial band extending from lesion to the ventricle, and homogenous appearance of subcortical white matter hyperintensity [see Fig. 3]. High-resolution imaging, perhaps with a high field-strength magnet or phased array surface coils may be helpful for demonstrating cortical thickening. A frontal lobe location is more commonly seen in dysplasias, whereas a temporal lobe location is more commonly seen in tumors. The presence of subependymal or multiple subcortical lesions should raise concerns for tuberous sclerosis.

In individuals with a hyperintense hippocampus on long TR images, practitioners must distinguish tumor from hippocampal sclerosis. This is not particularly difficult if the hippocampus is ipsilaterally small, which represents the cardinal finding of hippocampal sclerosis. However, the hippocampus is not small in all cases of hippocampal sclerosis. Findings suggestive of neoplasm include heterogeneous signal changes and extension of signal changes beyond the hippocampus into the parahippocampal white matter [Fig. 22].

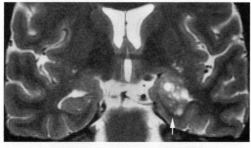

Fig. 22. Hippocampal hyperintensity differential diagnosis. Heterogeneous signal intensity, extension beyond the confines of the hippocampus, and lack of hippocampal atrophy are signs of neoplastic involvement as opposed to hippocampal sclerosis. This heterogeneous hippocampal lesion (*arrow*) was a neoplasm.

Malformations of cortical development can sometimes be difficult to distinguish from one another and from normal structures. Differentiating polymicrogyria from the pachygyria/agyria (lissencephaly) spectrum appears to be a particular problem [compare Figs. 4 and 5]. Both entities present with cortical thickening on imaging, which may be bilateral and appear as smooth cortices (because of the "micro" gyri in polymicrogyria entity). One differentiating feature is the tendency for polymicrogyria to affect the sylvian fissure and to be associated with a CSF cleft. Sagittal images may be particularly helpful—perisylvian polymicrogyria often results in a sylvian fissure that is continuous with the central sulcus, which is easily depicted on the sagittal images. Though polymicrogyria may be bilateral, it is not as diffuse and pervasive as pachygyria (even though pachygyria may affect the brain regionally, such as the frontal lobes). With high-resolution imaging, multiple gyri in polymicrogyria may be visualized.

The differential diagnosis for periventricular findings that are isointense to gray matter on T1-weighted images include periventricular heterotopia, normal caudate nucleus, and subependymal tuberous sclerosis hamartomas. True gray matter follows the signal intensity of the cortex on all pulse sequences, not only T1-weighted sequences. Regarding the caudate nucleus, the head is easily identified, allowing the identification of body and tail on subsequent slices and differentiation from heterotopia.

The asymmetric hemisphere may also be problematic—hemimegalencephaly may sometimes be mistaken for the hemiatrophic syndromes [see Fig. 11]. In both entities, there is ventricular enlargement (and one hemisphere is larger than the other), and there may be diffuse white matter hyperintensity. However, the ventricular enlargement in hemiatrophy is in the smaller hemisphere; ventricular enlargement occurs in the larger hemisphere in hemimegalencephaly. Unlike hemiatrophy, hemimegalencephaly is associated with cortical thickening, sulcal abnormalities, heterotopias, and radial bands.

An important pitfall to avoid relates to dual pathology. As discussed previously, dual pathology refers to the presence of an extrahippocampal lesion and hippocampal sclerosis [Fig. 23]. It is easy to focus on an obvious lesion and neglect assessment of the hippocampus, especially if there are correlative electroclinical features. However, coincidental hippocampal sclerosis is not infrequent, especially with developmental anomalies.

The temporal lobe encephalocele is an extremely rare cause of epilepsy that can lead to errors in interpretation (occurring in 1 of 600 patients who have undergone epilepsy surgery in the last 18 years at

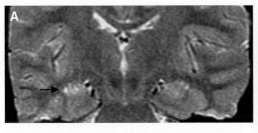
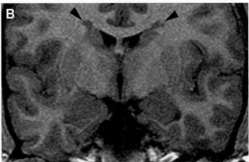

Fig. 23. Dual pathology (A) Coronal T2-weighted image shows findings of hippocampal sclerosis—hippocampal atrophy and hyperintensity (*arrow*). (B) Coronal T1-weighted image in this same patient demonstrates an additional finding of bilateral heterotopia (*arrowheads*).

the authors' institution). Because it occupies an extra-axial location, it is easily overlooked unless the basal temporal lobe is specifically scrutinized for this disorder. The need to distinguish this pathologic condition from the normal protrusions of brain tissue occurring along the basal temporal lobes is important [Fig. 24].

Postoperative imaging

MR imaging plays a crucial role not only in the presurgical evaluation of patients with medically refractory epilepsy but also in the postoperative imaging of these patients. MR imaging can determine the extent of surgical resection for epileptogenic substrates and surgical divisions for functional hemispherectomies. In patients who have not had success with surgery, MR imaging can identify (1) residual substrate at the operative site, (2) any other previously unrecognized epileptogenic substrates at other locations in the brain,

and (3) persistent connections in functional hemispherectomies [11].

Knowledge of the normal patterns of enhancement is essential to avoid misinterpretation of the benign findings in the postoperative MR imaging scans. During the first postoperative week, a thin linear enhancement can be seen at the pial margins of the resection site [75]. In those with temporal lobe surgery, enlargement and enhancement of the choroid plexus occurs on the ipsilateral side [76]. Pneumocephalus is commonly present during the first 4 to 5 days after surgery. In patients with persistence of this finding after 5 days, a fistula or infectious process may need to be excluded.

One week to 1 month after surgery, the resection margin enhances with a thick linear or nodular pattern and may mimic residual neoplastic or inflammatory processes [Fig. 25]. Sometime between 1 month and 3 to 5 months after surgery, the

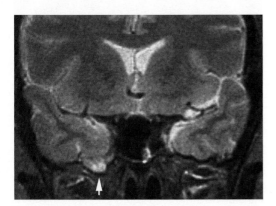

Fig. 24. Temporal lobe encephalocele. This rare cause of temporal lobe epilepsy was visualized retrospectively on MR (*arrow*) after it was discovered at surgery. This is easily overlooked when concentrating on the hippocampus and cortex, if it is not scrutinized for prospectively.

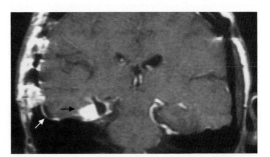

Fig. 25. Postoperative enhancement. Coronal enhanced image 3 weeks after temporal lobectomy for hippocampal sclerosis shows nodular enhancement (*black arrow*) that could be mistaken for tumor, if this resection had been performed for a neoplasm. Dural enhancement (*white arrow*) is usually seen postoperatively as well. (*From* Sato N, Bronen RA, Sze G, Kawamura Y, Coughlin W, Putman CM, et al. Postoperative changes in the brain: MR imaging findings in patients without neoplasms. Radiology 1997; 204(3):839–46; with permission.)

resection margin stops enhancing. The course for dural enhancement mimics that of pial enhancement, except that dural enhancement persists and can last for years [75].

MR imaging is more sensitive in detecting complications of hemispherectomy, such as extra- or intra-axial hemorrhage, hydrocephalus, or infections. MR imaging can also demonstrate sequela of placement of intraparenchymal depth electrodes. Punctate hyperintense signal abnormalities on long TR sequences can be seen in these cases, representing gliosis along the tracks of the electrode [77]. Rarely, punctate hemosiderin is visualized along a depth electrode tract, representing evidence of prior hemorrhage.

Interpretation of MR images: a systematic approach

Many epileptogenic lesions are subtle and can be easily missed unless a systematic approach is used during the interpretation of MR images from a seizure patient [43]. One approach can be followed using the mnemonic "HIPPO SAGE" [Box 2]. The hypothalamus is reviewed to detect a hypothalamic hamartomas, particularly in children. These can be subtle and overlooked, especially if the patient does not present with gelastic seizures [Fig. 26]. Hippocampal size, symmetry, and signal abnormalities are assessed in the coronal plane to evaluate for hippocampal sclerosis. Because head rotation may lead to a false diagnosis of hippocampal atrophy, head rotation is assessed based on symmetry of the internal auditory canals and symmetry of the atria of the left lateral ventricles [see Fig. 18]. If head rotation is present, assessment of hippocampal symmetry must be compensated for by comparing compatible coronal hippocampal sections (ie, the right hippocampal section adjacent to the right internal auditory canal should be compared with left hippocampal section adjacent to the left internal auditory canal). Periventricular regions should be scrutinized for

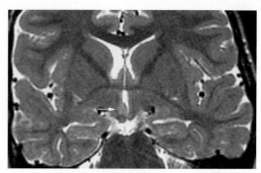

Fig. 26. Hypothalamic hamartoma. Coronal T2-weighted image shows a hypothalamic hamartoma (*white arrow*), causing mass effect on the third ventricle and ipsilateral mammillary body. This patient presented with right frontal seizures, and this lesion was not detected on the initial MR study because the hypothalamus was not scrutinized. It was detected on this subsequent MR study after the seizures took on a gelastic quality.

subependymal gray matter heterotopias, which occur most commonly adjacent to the atria of lateral ventricles. Gray matter inferior-lateral to the temporal horns is abnormal [see Fig. 4; Fig. 27].

Because focal epilepsy is a cortical-based process, the periphery of the brain should be carefully scrutinized for developmental anomalies, atrophic processes, and small neoplasms or vascular malformations. The authors closely inspect for the sulcal and gyral morphologic changes (which underlie developmental disorders) [Fig. 28], atrophic processes (which may underlie glottic substrates or represent developmental CSF clefts) [see Fig. 8], and gray matter thickening and indistinctness of

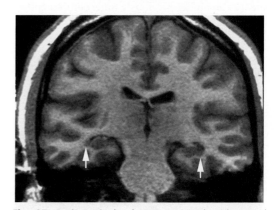

Fig. 27. Periventricular heterotopia. The abnormal gray matter (*arrows*) on this coronal T1-weighted image may be difficult to detect because it blends in with the normal gray matter of the hippocampus. The periventricular regions need to be scrutinized for heterotopia in all seizure patients. (*From* Bronen RA, Fulbright RK, Kim JH, et al. A systematic approach for interpreting MR images of the seizure patient. AJR Am J Roentgenol 1997;169(1):241–7; with permission).

Box 2: Systematic evaluation of MR scans of seizure patients (HIPPO SAGE)

- **H**ypothalamic hamartoma; hippocampal size and signal abnormality
- **I**nternal auditory canal and atrial assymmetry
- **P**eriventricular heterotopia
- **P**eripheral abnormalities

  - ○ **S**ulcal morphologic abnormalities
  - ○ **A**trophy
  - ○ **G**ray matter thickening
  - ○ **E**ncephalocele of anterior temporal lobe

- **O**bvious lesion

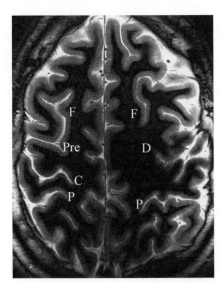

Fig. 28. Sulcal morphologic changes, cortical dysplasia. The perirolandic region is a common location for frontal lobe dysplasias causing epilepsy. Detection requires assessment of the normal cortical anatomy on axial images. This inversion recovery image shows the normal perirolandic fissure configurations on the right side, the superior frontal sulcus (F), precentral sulcus (Pre), central sulcus (C), and postcentral sulcus (P). On the left side, the normal anatomic configuration is distorted by the dysplastic cortex (D), which has caused loss of the typical superior frontal, precentral, and central sulci pattern.

gray-white matter junction (associated with developmental disorders) [see Figs. 3–5, 11C]. The inferior aspect of the anterior temporal lobe is assessed to exclude a temporal lobe encephalocele, an extremely uncommon cause of epilepsy but one that is easily overlooked if not specifically assessed for [see Fig. 24] [43].

Finally, the authors evaluate the obvious lesion in the brain and assess its characteristics. The obvious lesion could be an incidental finding, an epileptogenic substrate, or an additional lesion. By concentrating only on an obvious lesion, there is a chance that concurring hippocampal sclerosis will not be detected in those patients with dual pathology [see Figs. 2 and 23].

Recommendations for imaging protocols

Most standard or routine MR imaging protocols typically used to evaluate intracranial disease are suboptimal in the identification of epileptogenic substrates, such as cortical dysplasia, hippocampal sclerosis, and band heterotopia [78]. Optimal imaging parameters (image orientation, slice thickness, and pulse sequences) need to be employed to identify these substrates [Fig. 29].

With regard to hippocampal sclerosis, the most ideal plane for depicting the findings of hippocampal atrophy, signal changes and disruption of internal architecture is the oblique coronal (ie, the imaging plane perpendicular to the long axis of the hippocampus). FLAIR sequences appear to have the best sensitivity for demonstrating abnormal signal in the hippocampus [79], though the authors use a combination of coronal FLAIR and fast spin echo T2-weighted sequences to assess signal intensity because the hippocampus is normally slightly hyper-intense compared with gray matter on FLAIR sequences in certain individuals [80], making interpretation difficult if relying solely on the FLAIR images. Most epileptic centers employ T1-weighted gradient volume acquisitions (SPGR or MP-RAGE) to help assess the morphology of the hippocampus and to evaluate for developmental disorders. The raw data from these high-resolution images can be reconstructed in any plane and aid in qualitative, morphometric, and volumetric analysis of the hippocampus. Inversion recovery sequences with good gray/white matter differentiation also provide information regarding morphology and signal abnormalities. Some centers use T2 relaxometry or spectroscopy to further assess the

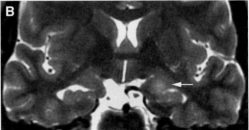

Fig. 29. Technique. Coronal T2-weighted images demonstrate the value of high-quality techniques for detecting epileptogenic abnormalities. (A) The left temporal lobe lesion cannot be visualized on this 5-mm thick slice with a gap of 2.5 mm (ie, effective slice thickness of 7.5 mm) and a 256 × 192 matrix. (B) On this higher resolution image, the lesion (arrow) is easily seen on this and adjacent sections. This scan was performed with 3-mm thick contiguous slices and a 256 × 256 matrix.

hippocampus and medial temporal lobes. T2 relaxometry is useful in cases where the findings on visual analysis are equivocal or in lateralization of seizure focus when bilateral abnormalities exist in the hippocampi.

Recommended sequences for developmental anomalies include FLAIR sequence to assess for hyperintense signal changes and radial bands and a sequence capable of depicting good contrast between gray matter and white matter, particularly with thin slices. Malformations of cortical development are subtle abnormalities and can be missed easily without employing high-resolution imaging and sequences with good gray/white matter differentiation [81,82]. Coronal T1-weighted gradient volume sequences (SPGR or MP-RAGE) with thin slice thickness (1 to 1.6 mm) can demonstrate subtle developmental malformations [83]. There are many additional measures that can be used to increase the yield for detecting MCD. Postprocessing of the raw data from a 3D volume set can yield high-resolution 3D reformations, which can demonstrate cortical dysplasia, abnormal sulcal morphology, gray/white matter indistinctiveness, and the relationship of developmental abnormalities to the eloquent cortical regions [84]. High-resolution imaging with phased array coils, image registration and averaging, and high-field scanners (greater than 3T) can provide adequate information in locating the cortical dysplasia [81,82]. FLAIR/T2-weighted images demonstrate abnormal signal in the subcortical/deep white matter associated with developmental malformations. Quantitative analysis of gray and white matter, when compared with normal controls, may show widespread developmental abnormalities. However, the location and extent of cortical dysplasia identified by MR imaging may not correlate with the seizure semiology or the electrophysiologic studies [34].

Routine use of intravenous contrast (gadolinium) is not indicated in the evaluation of chronic epilepsy patients but may play a role in the evaluation of patients with new onset of epilepsy to look for infectious, inflammatory and neoplastic processes, especially in those over 50 years old [85–87]. One clear exception to this is in the patient with hemiatrophy, where contrast may diagnosis Sturge-Weber syndrome [see Fig. 11]. However, after identification of a lesion on MR imaging, contrast is often helpful. Infusion of intravenous contrast increases the diagnostic confidence, delineates the extent of lesion, differentiates between an aggressive and a nonaggressive lesion, and may be useful for guidance for obtaining the biopsy specimen [86].

Some techniques appear to be useful, but are not easily implemented on a routine basis or early in the evaluation process. Apparent diffusion coefficient maps and diffusion tensor imaging can identify the abnormal diffusion at the epileptogenic foci in normal-appearing standard MR imaging studies [88–90]. Abnormal magnetization transfer ratios in epilepsy patients with negative conventional MR imaging may detect and delineate the extent of occult malformations of cortical development [91]. Various image analysis, segmentation, and quantitative techniques have shown benefits in the detection of epileptogenic abnormalities but are not routinely available with commercial clinical MR scanners or work stations. Functional MR imaging is useful in preoperative localization of the motor strip in relation to the epileptogenic foci in this region [92]. fMR imaging information of lateralization of memory and language is promising and may be useful in the prediction of postsurgical seizure relief and cognitive deficits after anterior temporal lobectomy [93]. fMR imaging has also been shown to detect the cortical activation in the brain before the clinical seizure activity, but this appears to be a rare finding [94].

Summary

MR imaging plays a pivotal role in the evaluation of patients with epilepsy. With its high spatial resolution, excellent inherent soft tissue contrast, multiplanar imaging capability, and lack of ionizing radiation, MR imaging has emerged as a versatile diagnostic tool in the evaluation of patients with epilepsy. MR imaging not only identifies specific epileptogenic substrates but also determines specific treatment and predicts prognosis. Employing appropriate imaging protocols and reviewing the images in a systematic manner helps in the identification of subtle epileptogenic structural abnormalities. With future improvements in software, hardware, and post-processing methods, MR imaging should be able to throw more light on epileptogenesis and help physicians to better understand its structural basis.

References

[1] Commission on Classification and Terminology of the International League against Epilepsy. Proposal for revised classification of epilepsies and epileptic syndromes. Epilepsia 1989;30:389–99.

[2] Kwan P, Brodie M. Early identification of refractory epilepsy. N Engl J Med 2000;342:314–9.

[3] Arroyo S. Evaluation of drug-resistant epilepsy. Rev Neurol 2000;30:881–9.

[4] Bell GS, Sander JW. The epidemiology of epilepsy: the size of the problem. Seizure 2001;16: 165–70.

[5] Sander JW. The epidemiology of epilepsy revisited. Curr Opin Neurol 2003;16:165–70.

[6] Bernal B, Altman N. Evidence-based medicine: neuroimaging of seizures. Neuroimaging Clin N Am 2003;13:211–24.

[7] King MA, Newton MR, Jackson GD, et al. Epileptology of the first-seizure presentation: a clinical, electroencephalographic, and magnetic resonance imaging study of 300 consecutive patients. [see comment]. Lancet 1998;352:1007–11.

[8] Berg A, Testa FM, Levy SR. Neuroimaging in children with newly diagnosed epilepsy: a community based study. Pediatrics 2000;106:527–32.

[9] Bronen RA, Fulbright RK, Spencer DD, et al. Refractory epilepsy: comparison of MR imaging, CT, and histopathologic findings in 117 patients. Radiology 1996;201:97–105.

[10] Scott CA, Fish DR, Smith SJ, et al. Presurgical evaluation of patients with epilepsy and normal MRI: role of scalp video-EEG telemetry. [see comment]. J Neurol Neurosurg Psychiatry 1999;66:69–71.

[11] Commission on Neuroimaging of the International League against Epilepsy. Guidelines for neuroimaging evaluation of patients with uncontrolled epilepsy considered for surgery. Epilepsia 1998;39:1375–6.

[12] Commission on Neuroimaging of the International League against Epilepsy. Recommendations for neuroimaging of patients with epilepsy. Epilepsia 1997;38:1255–6.

[13] Anonymous. Practice parameter: the neurodiagnostic evaluation of the child with a first simple febrile seizure. Pediatrics 1996;97:769–75.

[14] Anonymous. Practice parameter: neuroimaging in the emergency patient presenting with seizure. Summary statement. Neurology 1996;47:288–91.

[15] Holmes MD, Wilensky AJ, Ojemann GA, Ojemann LM. Hippocampal or neocortical lesions on magnetic resonance imaging do not necessarily indicate site of ictal onsets in partial epilepsy. Ann Neurol 1999;45:461–5.

[16] Berkovic SF, McIntosh AM, Kalnios RM, et al. Preoperative MRI predicts outcome of temporal lobectomy: an actuarial analysis. Neurology 1995;45:1358–63.

[17] Spencer D. Classifying the epilepsies by substrate. Clin Neurosci 1994;2:104–9.

[18] Spencer SS. When should temporal lobe epilepsy be treated surgically? Lancet Neurol 2002;1:375–82.

[19] Jackson G, VanPaesschen W. Hippocampal sclerosis in the MR era. Epilepsia 2002;43:4–10.

[20] Bronen RA. Epilepsy: the role of MR imaging. AJR Am J Roentgenol 1992;159:1165–74.

[21] Bronen RA, Gupta V. Epilepsy. In: Atlas S, editor. MRI of brain and spine. New York: Lippincott Williams & Wilkins; 2002. p. 415–55.

[22] Jack CJ, Sharbrough FW, Cascino GD, et al. Magnetic resonance image-based hippocampal volumetry: correlation with outcome after temporal lobectomy. Ann Neurol 1992;31:138–46.

[23] Oppenheim C, Dormont D, Biondi A, et al. Loss of digitations of the hippocampal head on high resolution fast spin echo MR: a sign of mesial temporal sclerosis. AJNR Am J Neuroradiol 1998;19:457–63.

[24] Baldwin GN, Tsuruda JS, Maravilla KR, et al. The fornix in patients with seizures caused by unilateral hippocampal sclerosis: detection of unilateral volume loss on MR images. AJR Am J Roentgenol 1994;162:1185–9.

[25] Meiners LC, Witkamp TD, de Kort GA, et al. Relevance of temporal lobe white matter changes in hippocampal sclerosis. Magnetic resonance imaging and histology. Invest Radiol 1999;34:38–45.

[26] Jack CJ, Sharbrough FW, Twomey CK, et al. Temporal lobe seizures: lateralization with MR volume measurements of the hippocampal formation. Radiology 1990;175:423–9.

[27] Bronen RA, Anderson AW, Spencer DD. Quantitative MR for epilepsy: a clinical and research tool? AJNR Am J Neuroradiol 1994;15:1157–60.

[28] Jack CR Jr. MRI-based hippocampal volume measurements in epilepsy. Epilepsia 1994;35:S21–9.

[29] Arruda F, Cendes F, Andermann F, et al. Mesial atrophy and outcome after amygdalohippocampectomy or temporal lobe removal. Ann Neurol 1996;40:446–50.

[30] Quigg M, Bertram EH, Jackson T, Laws E. Volumetric magnetic resonance imaging evidence of bilateral hippocampal atrophy in mesial temporal lobe epilepsy. Epilepsia 1997;38:588–94.

[31] Cendes F, Cook MJ, Watson C, et al. Frequency and characteristics of dual pathology in patients with lesional epilepsy. Neurology 1995;45:2058–64.

[32] Sisodiya SM, Moran N, Free SL, et al. Correlation of widespread pre-operative magnetic resonance imaging changes with unsuccessful surgery for hippocampal sclerosis. Ann Neurol 1997;41:490–6.

[33] Li LM, Cendes F, Andermann F, et al. Surgical outcome in patients with epilepsy and dual pathology. Brain 1999;122:799–805.

[34] Raymond AA, Fish DR, Sisodiya SM, et al. Abnormalities of gyration, heterotopias, tuberous sclerosis, focal cortical dysplasia, microdysgenesis, dysembryo-plastic neuroepithelial tumour and dysgenesis of the archicortex in epilepsy. Clinical, EEG and neuroimaging features in 100 adult patients. Brain 1995;118:629–60.

[35] Kuzniecky R. Magnetic resonance imaging in cerebral developmental malformations and epilepsy. In: Cascino GD, Jack CJ, editors. Neuroimaging in epilepsy: principles and practice. Newton (MA): Buttetworth-Heinemann; 1996. p. 51–63.

[36] Wyllie E, Comair YG, Kotagal P. Seizure outcome after epilepsy surgery in children and adolescents. Ann Neurol 1998;44:740–8.

[37] Barkovich AJ, Kuzniecky RI, Jackson GD, et al. Classification system for malformation of

cortical development: update 2001. Neurology 2001;57:2168–78.

[38] Barkovich AJ. Congenital malformations of the brain and skull. In: Barkovich A, editor. Pediatric imaging. New York: Lippincott Williams & Wilkins; 2000. p. 251–381.

[39] Bronen RA, Spencer DD, Fulbright RK. Cerebrospinal fluid cleft with cortical dimple: MR imaging marker for focal cortical dysgenesis. Radiology 2000;214:657–63.

[40] Palmini A, Gambardella A, Andermann F, et al. Operative strategies for patients with cortical dysplastic lesions and intractable epilepsy. Epilepsia 1994;35:S57–71.

[41] Sisodiya SM, Free SL, Stevens JM, et al. Widespread cerebral structural changes in patients with cortical dysgenesis and epilepsy. Brain 1995;118:1039–50.

[42] Cascino G. Selection of candidates for surgical treatment of epilepsy. In: Cascino G, Jack CJ, editors. Neuroimaging in epilepsy: principles and practice. Newton (MA): Butterworth-Heinemann; 1996. p. 219–34.

[43] Bronen RA, Fulbright RK, Kim JH, et al. A systematic approach for interpreting MR images of the seizure patient. AJR Am J Roentgenol 1997; 169:241–7.

[44] Bronen RA, Fulbright RK, Spencer DD, et al. MR characteristics of neoplasms and vascular malformations associated with epilepsy. Magn Reson Imaging 1995;13:1153–62.

[45] Friedland R, Bronen R. Magnetic resonance imaging of neoplastic, vascular, and indeterminate substrates. In: Cascino G, Jack CJ, editors. Neuroimaging in epilepsy: principles and practice. Newton (MA): Butterworth-Heinemann; 1996. p. 29–50.

[46] Atlas S, Lavi E, Fisher P. Intra-axial brain tumors. In: Atlas S, editor. MRI of the brain and spine. New York: Lippincott Williams & Wilkins; 2002. p. 565–693.

[47] Koeller KK, Henry JM. From the archives of the AFIP Superficial gliomas: radiologic-pathologic correlation. Radiographics 2001;21:1533–56.

[48] Provanzale J. Comparison of patient age with MR imaging features of gangliogliomas. AJR Am J Roentgenol 2000;174:859–62.

[49] Piepgras DG, Sundt TJ, Ragoowansi AT, Stevens L. Seizure outcome in patients with surgically treated cerebral arteriovenous malformations. J Neurosurg 1993;78:5–11.

[50] Rivera PP, Willinsky RA. Intracranial cavernous malformations. Neuroimaging Clin N Am 2003; 13:27–40.

[51] Bladin CF, Alexandrov AV, Bellavance A, et al, for the Seizures after Stroke Study Group Seizures after stroke. Arch Neurol 2000;57:1617–22.

[52] Ho SS, Kuzniecky RI. Congenital porencephaly: MR features and relationship to hippocampal sclerosis. AJNR Am J Neuroradiol 1998;19:135–41.

[53] Barkovich AJ. Brain and spine injuries in infancy and childhood. In: Barkovich A, editor. Pediatric neuroimaging. New York: Lippincott Williams & Wilkins; 2000. p. 157–249.

[54] Kuzniecky R, Jackson G. Disorders of cerebral hemispheres. In: Kuzniecky R, Jackson G, editors. Magnetic resonance in epilepsy. New York: Raven-Press; 1995. p. 213–33.

[55] Annegers J. A population based study of seizures after traumatic brain injuries. N Engl J Med 1998;338:20–4.

[56] Hardman JM, Manoukian A. Pathology of head trauma. Neuroimaging Clin N Am 2002;12: 175–87.

[57] Willmore LJ. Post-traumatic epilepsy: cellular mechanisms and implications for treatment. Epilepsia 1990;31:s67–73.

[58] Frey LC. Epidemiology of posttraumatic epilepsy: a critical review. Epilepsia 2003;44(Suppl 10): 11–7.

[59] White AC Jr. Neurocysticercosis: updates on epidemiolgy, pathogenesis, diagnosis, and management. Annu Rev Med 2000;51:187–206.

[60] Shah G. Central nervous system tuberculosis: imaging manifestations. Neuroimaging Clin N Am 2000;10:355–74.

[61] Bien CG, Widman G, Urbach H, et al. The natural history of Rasmussen's encephalitis. Brain 2002;125:1751–9.

[62] Chiapparini L, Granata T, Farina L, et al. Diagnostic imaging in 13 cases of Rasmussen's encephalitis: can early MRI suggest the diagnosis? Neuroradiology 2003;45:171–83.

[63] Barkovich AJ. The phakomatoses. In: Barkovich AJ, editor. Pediatric neuroimaging. New York: Lippincott Williams & Wilkins; 2000. p. 383–441.

[64] Arroyo S, Santamaria J. What is the relationship between arachnoid cysts and seizure foci? [see comment]. Epilepsia 1997;38:1098–102.

[65] Song CJ, Kim JH, Kier EL, Bronen RA. MR imaging and histologic features of subinsular bright spots on T2-weighted MR images: Virchow-Robin spaces of the extreme capsule and insular cortex. Radiology 2000;214:671–7.

[66] Kier EL, Kim JH, Fulbright RK, Bronen RA. Embryology of the human fetal hippocampus: MR imaging, anatomy, and histology. AJNR Am J Neuroradiol 1997;18:525–32.

[67] Sasaki M, Sone M, Ehara S, Tamakawa Y. Hippocampal sulcus remnant: potential cause of change in signal intensity in the hippocampus. Radiology 1993;188:743–6.

[68] Topper R, Jurgens E, Reul J, Thron A. Clinical significance of intracranial developmental venous anomalies. J Neurol Neurosurg Psychiatry 1999; 67:234–8.

[69] Naff NJ, Wemmer J, Hoenig-Rigamonti DR. A longitudinal study of patients with venous malformations: documentation of a negligible hemorrhage risk and benign natural history. Neurology 1998;50:1709–14.

[70] Savas R, Sener RN. Deep calcarine sulcus and prominent calcar avis. J Neuroradiol 1998;25: 144–6.

[71] Chan S, Chin SS, Kartha K, et al. Reversible signal abnormalities in the hippocampus and neocortex after prolonged seizures. AJNR Am J Neuroradiol 1996;17:1725–31.

[72] Tien RD, Felsberg GJ. The hippocampus in status epilepticus; demonstration of signal intensity and morphologic changes with sequential fast spin-echo MR imaging. Radiology 1995;194:249–56.

[73] VanLandingham KE, Heinz ER, Cavazos JE, et al. Magnetic resonance imaging evidence of hippocampal injury after prolonged focal febrile convulsions. Ann Neurol 1998;43:413–26.

[74] Mirsattari SM, Lee DH, Jones MW, et al. Transient lesion in the splenium of the corpus collosum in an epileptic patient. Neurology 2003;60:1838–41.

[75] Sato N, Bronen RA, Sze G, et al. Postoperative changes in the brain: MR imaging findings in patients without neoplasms. Radiology 1997;204:839–46.

[76] Saluja S, Sato N, Kawamura Y, et al. Choroid plexus changes after temporal lobectomy. AJNR Am J Neuroradiol 2000;21:1650–3.

[77] Merriam MA, Bronen RA, Spencer DD, McCarthy G. MR findings after depth electrode implantation for medically refractory epilepsy. AJNR Am J Neuroradiol 1993;14:1343–6.

[78] McBride MC, Bronstein KS, Bennett B, et al. Failure of standard magnetic resonance imaging in patients with refractory temporal lobe epilepsy. Arch Neurol 1998;55:346–8.

[79] Jack CR Jr, Rydberg CH, Krecke KN, et al. Mesial temporal sclerosis: diagnosis with fluid-attenuated in-version-recovery versus spin-echo MR imaging. Radiology 1996;199:367–73.

[80] Hirai T, Yoshizunmi K, Shigematsu Y, et al. Limbic lobe of the human brain: evaluation with turbo fluid inversion-recovery MR imaging. Radiology 2000;215:470–5.

[81] Bronen RA, Knowlton R, Garwood M, et al. High resolution imaging in epilepsy. Epilepsia 2002;43:11–8.

[82] Grant PE, Barkovich AJ, Wald LL, et al. High-resolution surface-coil MR of cortical lesions in medically refractory epilepsy: a prospective study. AJNR Am J Neuroradiol 1997;18:291–301.

[83] Barkovich AJ, Rowley HA, Andermann F. MR in partial epilepsy: value of high resolution volumetric techniques. AJNR Am J Neuroradiol 1995;16:339–44.

[84] Ruggieri PM, Najm I, Bronen R, Campos M, Cendes F, Duncan JS, et al. Neuroimaging of the cortical dysplasias. Neurology 2004;62(6 Suppl 3):S27–9.

[85] Bronen RA. Is there any role for gadopentetate dime-glumine administration when searching for mesial temporal sclerosis in patients with seizures? AJR Am J Roentgenol 1995;164:503.

[86] Bradley WG, Shey RB. MR imaging evaluation of seizures. Radiology 2000;214:651–6.

[87] Elster AD, Mirza W. MR imaging in chronic partial epilepsy: role of contrast enhancement. AJNR Am J Neuroradiol 1991;12:165–70.

[88] Rugg-Gunn FJ, Eriksson SH, Symms MR, et al. Diffusion tensor imaging in refractory epilepsy. Lancet 2002;359:1748–51.

[89] Yoo SY CK, Song IC, Han MH, et al. Apparent diffusion coefficient value of the hippocampus in patients with hippocampal sclerosis and in healthy volunteers. AJNR Am J Neuroradiol 2002;23:809–12.

[90] Wieshmann UC, Clark CA, Symms MR, et al. Water diffusion in the human hippocampus in epilepsy. Magn Reson Imaging 1999;17:29–36.

[91] Rugg-Gunn FJ, Eriksson SH, Symms MR, et al. Magnetization transfer imaging in focal epilepsy. Neurology 2003;60:1638–45.

[92] Hollaway V, Chong WK, Connelly A. Somatomotor fMRI in the presurgical evaluation of a case of focal epilepsy. Clin Radiol 1999;54:301–3.

[93] Killgore WD, Glosser G, Casasanto DJ, et al. Functional MRI and the Wada test provide complementary information for predicting postoperative seizure control. Seizure 1999;8:450–5.

[94] Jackson GD, Connelly A, Cross JH, et al. Functional magnetic resonance imaging of focal seizures. Neurology 1994;44:850–6.

MAGNETIC
RESONANCE
IMAGING CLINICS

Magn Reson Imaging Clin N Am 14 (2006) 249–270

Anatomy and Pathology of the Eye: Role of MR Imaging and CT

Mahmood F. Mafee, MD[a],*, Afshin Karimi, MD, PhD, JD[b], Jai D. Shah, MD, MBA, MPH[b], Mark Rapoport, BS[b], Sameer A. Ansari, MD, PhD[b]

Since the development of CT and MR imaging, significant progress has been made in ophthalmic imaging. As the technology advanced and MR imaging units improved their ability in terms of spatial resolution, the role of MR imaging in ophthalmic imaging has increased accordingly. This article considers the role of MR and CT imaging in the diagnosis of selected pathologies of the eye.

Ocular anatomy

The globe is formed from the neuroectoderm of the forebrain (prosencephalon), the surface ectoderm of the head, the mesoderm lying between these layers, and neural crest cells [1–4]. The neuroectoderm gives rise to the retina, the fibers of the optic nerve, and smooth muscles (the sphincter and dilator papillae) of the iris [3]. The surface ectoderm on the side of the head forms the corneal and conjunctival epithelium, the lens, and the lacrimal and tarsal glands [1–4]. The surrounding mesenchyme forms the corneal stroma, the sclera, the choroids, the iris, the ciliary musculature, part of the vitreous body, and the cells lining the anterior chamber [1,4]. The eyeball (eye, globe) is made up of three primary layers [Fig. 1]: (1) the sclera, or outer layer,

This article was originally published in *Neuroimaging Clinics of North America* 15:23–47, 2005.

[a] Department of Radiology, University of Illinois at Chicago Medical Center, Chicago, IL, USA
[b] Department of Radiology, University of Illinois Hospital at Chicago, University of Illinois College of Medicine, Chicago, IL, USA
* Corresponding author. Department of Radiology, University of Illinois at Chicago Medical Center, 1740 West Taylor Street, MC 931, Chicago, IL 60612.
E-mail address: mfmafee@uic.edu (M.F. Mafee).

which is composed of collagen-elastic tissue; (2) the uvea (uveal tract), or middle layer, which is richly vascular and contains pigmented tissue consisting of the choroid, ciliary body, and iris; and (3) the retina, or inner layer, which is the neural, sensory stratum of the eye. The eyeball is enveloped by a fascial sheath, known as the "fascia bulbi" or "Tenon's capsule." Tenon's capsule forms a socket for the eyeball and is separated from the sclera by Tenon's (episcleral) space [5]. Tenon's capsule is perforated near the equator by the vortex (vorticose) veins, the draining veins of the choroid and sclera [1,5]. Tenon's capsule is also perforated by the optic nerve and its sheath, the ciliary nerves and vessels. Tenon's capsule fuses with the sclera and the sheath of the optic nerve around the entrance of the optic nerve [5]. Tenon's capsule blends with the sclera just behind the corneoscleral junction and fuses

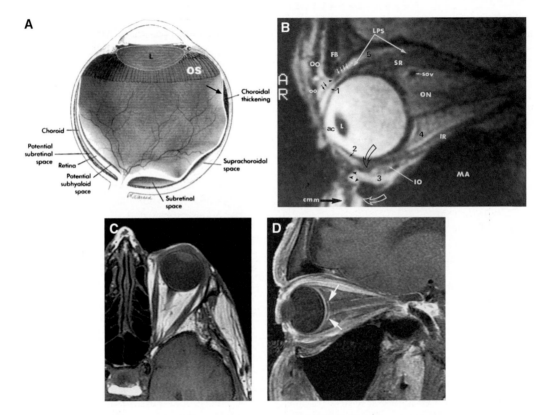

Fig. 1. (*A*) Ocular structures and various intraocular potential spaces. C, ciliary body; L, lens; OS, ora serrata. (*Modified from* Mafee MF, Inoue Y, Mafee RF. Ocular and orbital imaging. Neuroimaging Clin North Am 1996;6:292.) (*B*) Sagittal T2-weighted MR image (1.5 T) shows fibers of orbicilaris oculi (OO), frontal bone (FB), levator palpebrae superioris (LPS), extraconal fat (5), superior rectus muscle (SR), superior ophthalmic vein (SOV), optic nerve (ON), intraconal fatty reticulum (4), inferior rectus muscle (IR), maxillary antrum (MA), inferior oblique muscle (IO), extraconal fat (3), anterior wall of maxillary sinus (*white open arrow*), complex muscles of the mouth (cmm), orbital septum (*arrowheads*), presumed suspensory ligament of Lockwood (*black open arrow*), inferior (2) and superior fornices (1), anterior chamber (ac), lens (L), superior tarsal plate (*black arrows*), and the tendon of insertion of levator palpebrae superioris (*white arrows*). This tendon is an aponeurosis that descends posterior to the orbital septum (the orbital septum is depicted as an ill-defined image [*arrowhead*] in this section). The tendinous fibers then pierce the orbital septum and become attached to the anterior surface of the superior tarsal plate. Some of its fibers pass forward between the muscle bundles of the orbicularis oculi (OO) to attach to the skin. (*From* Mafee MF, Valvassori GE, Becker M, editors. Imaging of the head and neck. Stuttgart (Germany): Thieme; 2005; with permission.) (*C*) Axial T1-weighted image (566/12 ms, repetition time/echo time [TR/TE], 2.5-mm thick section, 352 × 192 matrix, 2 NEX, 160 × 160-mm field of view) obtained on a 3-T MR imaging unit, using eight-channel head coil, showing normal eye and orbit. (*D*) Sagittal fat-suppressed T1-weighted image (416/12 ms, TR/TE, 3-mm thick section, 320 × 192 matrix, 2 NEX, 140 × 140-mm field of view) obtained on a 3-T MR imaging unit using eight-channel head coil, showing normal eye and orbit. Note normal enhancement of uveoretinal coat and optic nerve meninges. Arrows point most likely to chemical shift artifact, rather than Tenon's capsule enhancement.

with the bulbar conjunctiva [1]. The tendons of the extrinsic ocular muscles pierce Tenon's capsule to reach the sclera. At the site of perforation, Tenon's capsule is reflected back along these muscle sheaths to form a tubular sleeve [6]. The connection between the muscle fibers, sheath, and the tubular sheath is especially strong at the point where the two fuse [5,6]. For this reason, the muscles retain their attachment to the capsule and do not retract extensively after enucleation (tenotomy) [5,6].

Sclera

The sclera is the outer supporting layer of the globe, extending from the limbus at the margin of the cornea to the optic nerve, where it becomes continuous with the dural sheath of the optic nerve [1]. The potential episcleral (Tenon's) space is between the outer aspect of the sclera and inner aspect of Tenon's capsule. The potential suprachoroidal space is between the inner aspect of the sclera and the outer aspect of the choroid [1,2]. In adults the sclera is 1 mm thick posteriorly, thinning at the equator to 0.6 mm. It is thinnest (0.3 mm) immediately posterior to the tendinous insertions of the rectus muscles [1,2]. The posterior scleral foramen is the site of scleral perforation by the optic nerve. At this site, the sclera is fused with the dural and arachnoid sheaths of the optic nerve. The lamina cribrosa is where the optic nerve fibers pierce the sclera.

Uvea (choroid, ciliary body, and iris)

The uveal tract (from the Latin *uva* or grape) is a pigmented vascular layer that lies between the sclera and the retina [see Fig. 1]. It consists of the choroid, the ciliary body, and the iris.

Choroid

The choroid is the section of the uveal tract that extends from the optic nerve to the ora serrata (where the sensory retina ends), beyond which it continues as the ciliary body [1,2]. The thickness of the choroid varies from 0.22 mm at the posterior pole to 0.10 mm near the ora serrata, at the optic nerve head, where it forms part of the optic nerve canal, and at the point of internal penetration of the vortex veins [1,2]. The uvea is supplied by the ophthalmic artery. The inner surface of the choroid is smooth and firmly attached to the retinal pigment epithelium (RPE). Its outer surface is roughened and is firmly attached to the sclera in the region of the optic nerve and where the posterior ciliary arteries and ciliary nerve enter the eye. It is also tethered to the sclera where the vortex veins leave the eyeball. This accounts for the characteristic shape of choroidal detachment (CD), which shows tethering at the site of the vortex veins and posterior ciliary arteries and ciliary nerves. Grossly,

the choroid can be divided into four layers, extending from internally to externally as (1) Bruch's membrane, (2) the choriocapillaris, (3) the stroma, and (4) the suprachoroid [1]. Bruch's membrane (2–4 μm thick) is a rough, acellular, amorphous, bilamellar structure, situated between the retina and the rest of the choroid. Microscopically, Bruch's membrane consists of five layers: (1) the basement membrane of the RPE, (2) the inner collagenous zone, (3) a meshwork of elastic fibers, (4) the outer collagenous zone, and (5) the basement membrane of the choriocapillaris [4,7,8]. When a choroidal malignant melanoma penetrates through Bruch's membrane, it results in a characteristic mushroom-shaped (collar button) growth configuration.

Ciliary body

The ciliary body is continuous posteriorly with the choroid and anteriorly with the iris [see Fig. 1]. The ciliary body can be considered as a complete ring that runs around the inside of the anterior sclera. The anterior surface of the ciliary body is ridged or plicated and is called the pars plicata. The pars plicata is 2 mm in length and is composed of about 70 ciliary processes arranged radially [9]. The posterior surface of the ciliary body is smooth and flat and is called the pars plana. The pars plana is 4 mm in length and is located between pars plicata and the ora serrata. The ciliary body is made up of (1) the ciliary epithelium, (2) the ciliary stroma, and (3) the ciliary muscle. The epithelium consists of two layers of cuboidal cells that cover the inner surface of the ciliary body [1,2,4,9]. The inner layer is comprised of pigmented epithelial cells, whereas the outer layer is comprised of nonpigmented epithelial cells [9]. The ciliary stroma consists of loose connective tissue, rich in blood vessels and melanocytes, containing the embedded ciliary muscle [1]. The aqueous humor is produced in the nonpigmented epithelial layer of the ciliary body [9]. The nonpigmented epithelial cells secrete mucopolysaccharide acid, one of the main components of the vitreous [9].

Iris

The iris forms the anterior portion of the uvea. It is a thin, contractile, pigmented diaphragm with a central aperture, the pupil [see Fig. 1]. It is suspended in the aqueous humor between the cornea and the lens and divides the anterior ocular compartment (segment) into anterior and posterior chambers. The aqueous humor, formed by the ciliary processes in the posterior chamber, circulates through the pupil into the anterior chamber and exits into the sinus venous (canal of Schlemm) at the iridocorneal angle [1,2,4]. The iris consists of a stroma and two epithelial layers. The stroma consists of vascular connective tissue containing melanocytes, nerve fibers, the smooth muscle of the sphincter papillae, and the myoepithelial cells of the dilator papillae [4]. The iris pigment epithelium is continuous with the pigmented and nonpigmented layers of the ciliary body.

Retina

The retina is the sensory inner layer of the globe. The internal surface of the retina is in contact with the vitreous body and its external surface is in contact with the choroid. Grossly, the retina can be considered as having two layers: the inner layer, which is the sensory retina (ie, photoreceptors) and the first- and second-order neurons (ganglion cells) and neuroglial elements of the retina (Müller's cells, or sustentacular gliocytes); and the outer layer, which is the RPE, consisting of a single layer of cells whose nuclei are adjacent to the basal lamina (Bruch's membrane) of the choroid [1,10,11]. The retina is very thin, measuring 0.056 mm near the disk and 0.1 mm anteriorly at the ora serrata. It is thinnest at the fovea of the macula [1]. The sensory retina extends forward from the optic disk to a point just posterior to the ciliary body. Here the nervous tissues of the retina end and its anterior edge forms a crenated wavy ring called ora serrata [1]. The RPE at the ora serrata becomes continuous with the pigmented and nonpigmented cell layers of the ciliary body and its processes [1,2]. The macula, the center of the retina, lies 3.5 mm temporal to the optic disk. The retina is attached very tightly at the margin of the optic disk and at its anterior termination at the ora serrata. It is also firmly attached to the vitreous, but loosely to the RPE and it is nourished by the choroid and the RPE [1,2]. The disk is pierced by the central retinal artery and vein. At the disk, there is complete absence of rods and cones. The disk is insensitive to light and is referred to as the "blind spot." The RPE cells are joined to each other by tight junctions. This arrangement forms a barrier, the so-called "retinal blood barrier." This limits the flow of ions and prevents diffusion of large toxic molecules from the choroid capillaries to the photoreceptors of the retina. The blood supply to the retina is from two sources: the outer lamina, including the rods and cones is supplied by the choroidal capillaries (the vessels do not enter the tissues, but tissue fluid exudes between these cells); the inner parts of the retina are supplied by the central retinal artery [1,2]. The retina depends on both of these circulations, neither of which alone is sufficient [1,2,4]. Small anastomoses occur between the branches of the posterior ciliary arteries and the central retinal artery (cilioretinal artery). The central retinal vein leaves the eyeball through the lamina cribrosa. The vein crosses the subarachnoid space and drains directly into the cavernous sinus or the superior ophthalmic vein. The retina has no lymphatic vessels.

Vitreous

The vitreous body occupies the space between the lens and retina and represents two thirds of the volume of the eye or approximately 4 mL [12]. All but 1% to 2% of the vitreous is water, bound to a fibrillar collagen meshwork of soluble proteins, some salts, and hyaluronic acid [1,2,10]. The clear, gel-like fluid that fills the vitreous chamber possesses a network of fine collagen fibrils that form scaffolding [1,2,4]. The vitreous body is the largest and simplest connective tissue present as a single structure in the human body [11]. Any insult to the vitreous body may result in a fibroproliferative reaction (eg, vitreoretinopathy of prematurity or diabetes), which can subsequently result in a tractional retinal detachment (RD) [10]. The vitreous body is bounded by the anterior and posterior hyaloid membranes. As one ages, the vitreous gel may undergo changes and start to shrink or thicken, forming strands or clumps inside the vitreous chamber, causing the so-called "floaters." Floaters are in fact tiny clumps of gel or cells inside the vitreous chamber. When the vitreous gel shrinks, it creates traction on the posterior hyaloid membrane, resulting in posterior vitreous detachment [Figs. 2 and 3]. The vitreous body is attached to the sensory retina, especially at the ora serrata and the margin of the optic disk [4]. It is also attached to the ciliary epithelium in the region of the pars plana [4]. The attachment of the vitreous to the lens is firm in young people and weakens with age [1,2]. During the first month of gestation, the space between the lens and the retina contains the primary vitreous. It consists of the embryonic intraocular hyaloid vascular system, embryonic connective tissue, and fibrillar meshwork. Shortly, collagen fibers and a ground substance or gel component consisting of hyaluronic acid are produced. They form the secondary vitreous and begin to replace the vascular elements of the primary vitreous [1]. By the fourteenth week of gestation, the secondary vitreous begins to fill the vitreous cavity. By the sixth month of fetal development, the cavity of the eye is filled with the secondary vitreous, which is identical to the adult vitreous. The primary vitreous is reduced to a small central space, Cloquet's canal (hyaloid canal), which runs in an S-shaped course between the optic disk and the posterior surface of the lens. During fetal life this channel contains the hyaloid artery. The artery disappears about 6 weeks before birth, and the canal becomes filled with liquid [4]. The vitreous body transmits lights, supports the posterior surface of the lens, and assists in holding the sensory retina against the RPE.

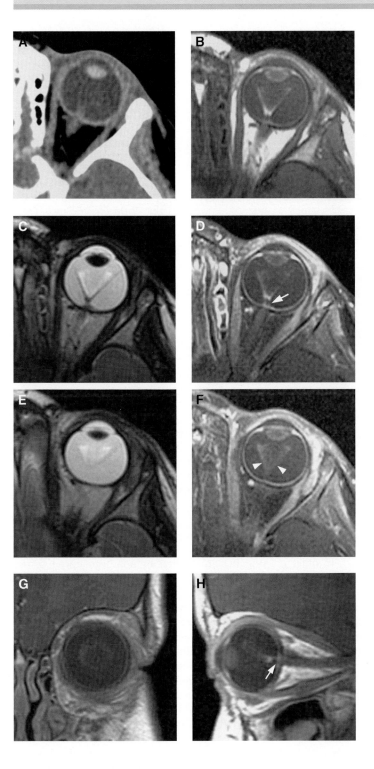

Fig. 2. Presumed posterior hyaloid detachment. An 18-month-old child who has leukocoria of the left eye. Retinoblastoma could not be excluded on clinical evaluation. (*A*) Axial CT scan shows a noncalcified lesion, presumed to be hematoma at the left optic disk. Note a faint V-shaped linear image, extending toward the optic disk. Axial unenhanced T1-weighted (*B*), axial T2-weighted (*C*), axial enhanced fat-suppressed T1-weighted (*D*), axial T2-weighted (*E*), axial enhanced fat-suppressed T1-weighted (*F*), coronal enhanced T1-weighted (*G*), and sagittal enhanced T1-weighted (*H*) MR images showing the detached posterior hyaloid membrane (*arrowheads* in *F*). Note that the apex of the V-shaped detachment, is connected to the optic disk by a faint ill-defined linear tissue (*arrows* in *D* and *H*), representing the attached part of the vitreous to the retina at the edge of the optic disk. (A–C *from* Mafee MF, Valvassori GE, Becker M, editors. Imaging of the head and neck. Stuttgart (Germany): Thieme; 2004; with permission.)

Ocular pathology

Intraocular potential spaces and ocular detachments

There are basically three potential spaces in the eye [see Fig. 1] that can accumulate fluid, causing detachment of various layers of the eyeball: (1) the posterior hyaloid space, the potential space between the base of the vitreous (posterior hyaloid membrane) and the sensory retina; (2) the subretinal space, the potential space between the sensory retina and the RPE; and (3) the suprachoroidal

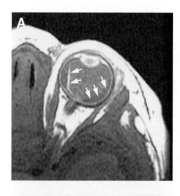
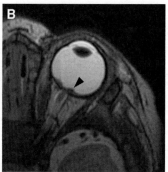
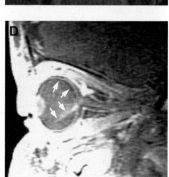

Fig. 3. Posterior hyaloid detachment. Axial unenhanced T1-weighted (*A*), axial T2-weighted (*B*), axial enhanced fat-suppressed T1-weighted (*C*), and sagittal enhanced fat-suppressed T1-weighted (*D*) MR images showing detachment of the vitreous (*arrows*). The vitreous base attachment to the retina at the optic disk is not detached. The hypointensity adjacent to the disk (*arrowhead* in *B*) is thought to be caused by hemorrhage.

space, the potential space between choroid and the sclera. Another potential space is the episcleral or Tenon's space, which is between the outer surface of the sclera and inner surface of the Tenon's capsule.

Posterior hyaloid detachment

Separation of the posterior hyaloid membrane from the sensory retina is referred to as "posterior vitreous" or "hyaloid detachment" [1,2]. In older patients, the vitreous tends to undergo degeneration and liquefaction. Extensive vitreous liquefaction leads to posterior hyaloid detachment. Accelerated vitreous liquefaction is associated with significant myopia, surgical or nonsurgical trauma, intraocular inflammation, post laser surgery of the eye, and persistent hyperplastic primary vitreous (PHPV). On CT and MR imaging, the detached posterior hyaloid membrane can be seen as a membrane within the vitreous cavity [see Fig. 2]. The detached membrane is separated from the disk (or may be attached to the disk by a thin band) and attached at the level of ora serrata [see Figs. 2 and 3]. There may be fluid in the retrohyaloid space, which shifts its location in the lateral decubitus position.

Retinal detachment

RD occurs when the sensory retina is separated from the RPE. RD resulting from a hole or tear in

the retina is referred to as "rhegmatogenous" (*rhegma* from Greek meaning to rent or rupture) RD. The sine qua non for a rhegmatogenous RD is vitreous liquefaction. Extensive vitreous liquefaction causes posterior hyaloid detachment, which in turn causes a tear at the site of vitreoretinal attachment or adhesion. The ensuing retinal break allows vitreous fluid to pass through the break into the subretinal space. Rhegmatogenous RDs are rare in pediatric patients. Most RDs in children are nonrhegmatogenous but are secondary to various ocular disease, such as retinoblastoma, PHPV, retinopathy of prematurity, Coats' disease [see Fig. 4], toxocariasis, and others. RD may be the result of retraction caused by a mass; a fibroproliferative disease in the vitreous, such as vitreoretinopathy of prematurity or vitreoretinopathy of diabetes mellitus; or accompanying an inflammatory process, such as *Toxocara* endophthalmitis [1,2]. Serous or exudative RD develops when the retinal-blood barrier is damaged. A breakdown of the retinal blood barrier with impairment of the RPE results in RD (nonrhegmatogenous RD). An increased fluid flow into the potential subretinal space (eg, in Coats' disease, scleritis, choroidal inflammation, choroidal mass, other intraocular tumor, or vitreous disease entities) may result in exudative RD. Exudative fluid may be shallow or bullous. Fluid may not extend all the way to the ora serrata [Fig. 5]. In severe cases the detached retina may be so bullous as to contact the posterior

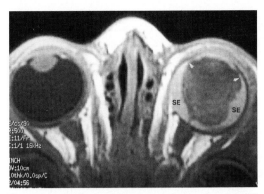

Fig. 4. Retinal detachment. Enhanced axial T1-weighted MR image in a child who has Coats' disease shows an exudative retinal detachment of the left eye. Note subretinal exudates (SE), which had the same signal intensity on unenhanced axial MR image. The detached sensory retina is limited at the ora serrata (*arrows*) and at the optic disk. The increased intensity of the left vitreous is related to protein leaking into the vitreous from abnormal retinal vessels.

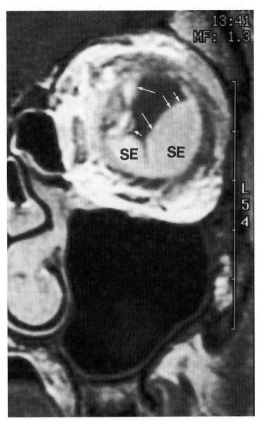

Fig. 6. Retinal detachment. Coronal enhanced T1-weighted MR image shows the characteristic corrugated retinal folds (*arrows*) on coronal view. The subretinal exudate (SE) signal was the same on unenhanced T1-weighted MR images.

lens surface [Fig. 6]. The common and uncommon causes of serous RD are summarized in Box 1. RD typically causes decreased vision. Other visual complaints, such as pain, photophobia, redness, sudden onset of tiny floating objects (floaters), and photopsia (flashes), may be present. The presence of sudden flashes of light and sudden appearance of floaters should cause serious consideration of RD. If RD is shallow, the diagnosis can be made easily with indirect ophthalmoscopy. If the retina is bullously detached, however, the diagnosis may be difficult [13]. Ultrasound, CT, and MR imaging can be used to make the diagnosis. In the authors' experience, MR imaging is superior to other imaging techniques to demonstrate features that could

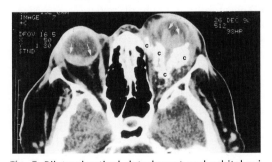

Fig. 5. Bilateral retinal detachment and orbital primary amyloidosis. Axial CT scan shows bilateral exudative retinal detachment (*arrows*). The detachment appears bullous on the left eye. The irregular calcifications (C) involving the left retrobulbar space are related to biopsy-proved amyloidosis. The cause of retinal detachment was not clear in this case.

differentiate different causes of RD. Exudative RD is characterized by shifting subretinal fluid, which assumes a dependent position beneath the retina. On CT and MR imaging, the appearance of RD varies with the amount of exudate, presence of hemorrhage, and organization of the subretinal materials. In a section taken at the level of the optic nerve disk, RD is seen with a characteristic V-shaped configuration with the apex at the optic disk and its extremities toward the ora serrata [see Fig. 4]. When total RD is present and the entire vitreous cavity is ablated, the leaves of the detached retina may touch at the center of the eye and appear as a folding membrane extending from the optic disk to the posterior surface of the lens, simulating Cloquet's canal. The MR imaging signal intensity of subretinal fluid depends on the protein content and presence or absence of hemorrhage. The subretinal fluid of an exudative RD is rich in protein, giving higher CT attenuation values and stronger MR imaging signal intensities (on T1-weighted MR images) [see Fig. 4] than those seen in the subretinal fluid

Box 1: Common and uncommon causes of serous retinal detachment

Common conditions
Coats' disease
Retinoblastoma
Retinopathy of prematurity
Choroidal tumors (primary or secondary)
Posterior scleritis
Vogt-Koyanagi-Harada syndrome
Exudative age-related macular degeneration
Postsurgical (associated with choroidal detachment)
Central serous chorioretinopathy

Uncommon conditions
Orbital inflammation (pseudotumor, cellulitis)
Infectious retinochoroiditis (toxoplasmosis, syphilis, cytomegalovirus, cat-scratch disease)
Uveal effusion syndrome
Vasculitis (polyarteritis nodosa, systemic lupus erythematosus, Goodpasture's syndrome)
Acute vascular or hemodynamic compromise (hypertensive crisis, toxemia of pregnancy, nephropathy)
Nanophthalmos (eyes with thick sclera and short axial length)
Optic nerve pits, colobomas, and morning glory anomaly
Familial exudative vitreoretinopathy
Sympathetic ophthalmia
Orbital arteriovenous malformation[a]

[a] In orbital inflammation and arteriovenous malformation the venous flow from the eye may be compromised by vascular engorgement. This results in exophthalmos and further vascular compromise. This can lead to retinal and choroidal effusion.
Modified from Anand R. Serous detachment of the neural retina. In: Yanoff M, Duker JS, editors. Ophthalmology. St. Louis (MO): Mosby; 1999. p. 8:40.1–40.6; with permission.

(transudate) of a rhegmatogenous detachment. In rhegmatogenous RD, produced by a retinal tear and subsequent ingress of vitreous fluid into the subretinal space, the signal of subretinal transudate is almost isointense to vitreous, making visualization of detached retina more difficult. RD is seen on coronal CT and MR images as a characteristic folding membrane, representing corrugated retinal folds [Fig. 6].

Choroidal detachment and choroidal effusion

CD is caused by the accumulation of fluid (serous CD) or blood (hemorrhagic CD) in the potential suprachoroidal space [1,2,10,14–16]. Serous CD frequently occurs after intraocular surgery, penetrating ocular trauma, or inflammatory choroidal disorders [14]. Ocular hypotony is the essential underlying cause of serous CD. Ocular hypotony may be the result of ocular inflammatory diseases (uveitis, scleritis); accidental perforation of the eye; ocular surgery; or intensive glaucoma therapy. The pressure within the suprachoroidal space is determined by the intraocular pressure, the intracapillary blood pressure, and the oncotic pressure exerted by the plasma protein colloids [17]. The capillaries of the choroid are fenestrated and these openings are covered by diaphragms, which permit the relatively free exchange of material between the choriocapillaris and the surrounding tissues [18]. Ocular hypotony results in increased permeability of the choriocapillaris, and this in turn leads to the transudation of fluid from the choroidal vasculature into the uveal tissue causing diffuse swelling of the entire choroid (choroidal effusion). As the edema of the choroid increases, fluid may accumulate in the potential suprachoroidal space, resulting in serous or exudative CD [14–16]. Other causes of choroidal effusion include inflammatory disorders of the eye, myxedema, photocoagulation, retinal cryopexy, Vogt-Koyanagi-Harada syndrome, nanophthalmos, and idiopathic uveal effusion syndrome. Nanophthalmos is an autosomal-recessive disorder in which there is bilateral short axial length globes, normal-sized lenses, and thick sclerae. As a result of scleral thickening, the scleral outflow channels and transscleral passage of vortex veins become impaired. This can lead to choroidal congestion, choroidal thickening, and eventually choroidal effusion [see Fig. 7]. The management of choroidal effusion in nanophthalmos and idiopathic choroidal effusion is surgical and consists of sclerotomy (scleral window operation) to decompress the vortex veins [13]. Hemorrhagic CD is a serious condition that may be associated with permanent loss of vision [19]. Both localized and massive choroidal hemorrhage may occur as a complication of most forms of ocular surgery and ocular trauma. Choroidal hemorrhage may occur in association with hemoglobinopathies, in patients receiving anticoagulant therapy, or spontaneously [19]. Intraoperative choroidal hemorrhage may progress to expulsion of intraocular tissues (expulsive choroidal hemorrhage) [19]. Clinically, the CD appears as a smooth gray–brown elevation of the choroid, extending from the ciliary body to the posterior segment [14,15]. Ophthalmoscopic visualization of the fundus may be precluded by hyphema (blood in the anterior chamber) or vitreous hemorrhage. Even when the other ocular media are clear, in pigmented eyes it is difficult to differentiate between serous and hemorrhagic CD with ophthalmoscopy [14,15]. Localized choroidal hemorrhage may be mistaken for a choroidal melanoma, particularly when it presents as a discrete, dark posterior ocular

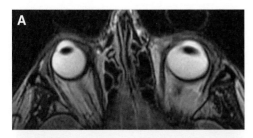

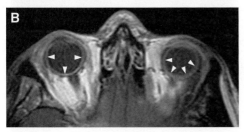

Fig. 7. Nanophthalmos and associated choroidal effusion. Axial T2-weighted (*A*) and enhanced axial T1-weighted (*B*) MR images. Note bilateral short axial length globes and marked thickened sclerae (*A*), and increased uveal enhancement (*arrowheads*), the left being greater than the right.

semilunar area of variable attenuation values. The degree of CT attenuation depends on the cause but is generally greater with inflammatory disorders of the eyeball. Hemorrhagic CD appears as either a low or high mound-like area of high density on CT. In a fresh hemorrhagic CD, the choroid and hematoma are isodense. In chronic hematoma, however, it may be possible to differentiate detached choroid and suprachoroidal fluid accumulation [see Figs. 8 and 9]. Serial CT, MR imaging, and ultrasonography reveal diminishing size over a period of several weeks or months. MR imaging is an excellent method to evaluate the eye in patients who have CD, particularly if ultrasonography or CT in conjunction with the clinical examination has not provided sufficient information [1]. On MR imaging, a limited choroidal hematoma appears as a focal, well-demarcated, smooth dome-shaped or lenticular mass [Fig. 8]. It is important to realize that this characteristic configuration usually does not change as the hematoma ages [16]. A decrease in the size of the choroidal hematoma, however, may be observed. Multiple lesions may be present [see Fig. 9]. The signal intensity of choroidal hematoma depends on its age. Within the first 48 hours, the hematoma is isointense to slightly hypointense relative to the normal vitreous on T1-weighted MR images but is markedly hypointense on T2-weighted MR images. After few days, its signal intensity changes, being relatively hyperintense on T1-weighted and hypointense on T2-weighted MR

mass [19]. Ultrasonography can be very useful for the diagnosis of CD, however, ultrasonography has certain limitations in examining traumatized eyes. The appearance of serous CD and limited or diffuse hemorrhagic CD on CT has been described [14]. It appears as a smooth, dome-shaped,

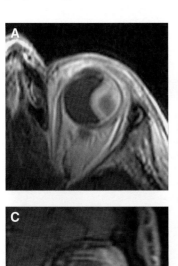

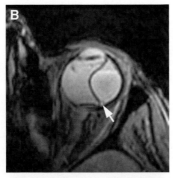

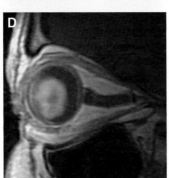

Fig. 8. Hemorrhagic choroidal detachment. Axial T1-weighted (*A*), axial T2-weighted (*B*), coronal T1-weighted (*C*), and sagittal T1-weighted (*D*) MR images showing a chronic hemorrhagic choroidal detachment. Note that the detached choroid is restricted at the expected level of the vortex vein or posterior ciliary artery (*arrow*). Note that the detached choroid extends to the ciliary body.

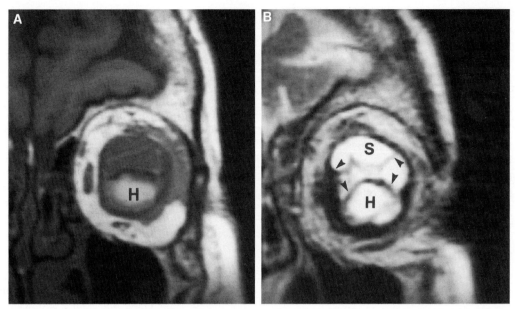

Fig. 9. Serous and hemorrhagic choroidal detachment. Coronal T1-weighted (*A*) and T2-weighted (*B*) MR images showing an inferior hemorrhagic (H) and superior serous (S) choroidal detachment. Note detached choroid (*arrows*), which is restricted at the expected level of vortex veins.

images. Chronic choroidal hematoma (3 weeks or older) become hyperintense on T1-weighted and T2-weighted MR images [see Figs. 8 and 9]. Serous CD and choroidal effusion have a different MR appearance compared with choroidal hematoma. The fluid in the suprachoroidal space in serous CD is often hypodense on CT, and its MR appearance is that of an exudate [Fig. 9]. At times, the appearance of CD and RD may be confused. Scleral attachments of the vortex veins restrict further detachment of the choroid beyond the anchoring point of the vortex veins, however, and similarly beyond the short posterior ciliary arteries and nerves. This restriction usually results in a characteristic appearance of the leaves of the detached choroid, which unlike the detached retinal leaves do not extend to the region of the optic nerve [see Figs. 8 and 9]. In addition, unlike the detached leaves of the retina, which end at the ora serrata, the detached choroid can extend to the ciliary body and also result in ciliary detachment [see Fig. 10].

Ocular inflammatory disorders

The eye may be affected by known or idiopathic inflammatory processes. A host of infectious diseases may affect the globe. Viral infections include herpes simplex, herpes zoster [Fig. 10], cytomegalovirus [Fig. 11], rubella, rubeola, mumps, variola, varicella, and infectious mononucleosis [1]. Bacterial diseases include tuberculosis, syphilis, Lyme disease, brucellosis, leprosy, cat-scratch disease, *Escherichia coli* infection, and other agents.

Fungal infections, particularly candidiasis, may involve the globes in diabetic and immunocompromised patients [1]. Parasitic infections, particularly *Toxocara canis,* cause granulomatous chorioretinitis with an eosinophilic abscess.

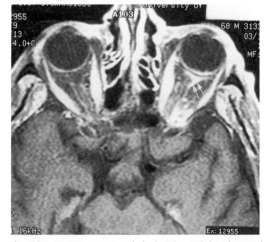

Fig. 10. Herpes zoster ophthalmitis. Axial enhanced fat-suppressed T1-weighted MR image shows abnormal enhancement along the left optic nerve sheath (*arrows*). Note also increased enhancement of left posterior globe.

Scleritis

The sclera may be the site of a number of inflammatory or noninflammatory processes. Episcleritis is a relatively common idiopathic inflammation of a thin layer of loose connective tissue between the sclera and the conjunctiva. Episcleritis is usually self-limited and resolves within 1 or 2 weeks [20]. Imaging is not indicated in episcleritis. In contrast to episcleritis, scleritis is a rare condition, and a more serious disorder. Scleritis can occur as an idiopathic condition (50%) or in association with rheumatoid arthritis, other connective tissue diseases, or with a group of other disorders, such as Wegener's granulomatosis, relapsing polychondritis, inflammatory bowel disease, Crohn's disease, Cogan's syndrome, and sarcoidosis [1]. In scleritis, histopathology may demonstrate granulomatous or nongranulomatous inflammation, vasculitis, and scleral necrosis [20]. Histopathologically, posterior scleritis is classified into two forms: nodular and diffuse. The term "posterior scleritis" refers to scleral inflammation behind the equator. Patients who have posterior scleritis may develop exudative RD, disk swelling, and CD [20,21]. Scleritis may be associated with uveitis (iritis, choroiditis) and increased intraocular pressure. Inflammatory debris may block scleral emissary veins, resulting in elevated episcleral venous pressure and hence elevated intraocular pressure. Ciliary body detachment adjacent to active anterior scleritis may cause angle closure glaucoma. If scleritis is associated with uveitis, the trabecular meshwork may be clogged with inflammatory debris and cells, causing glaucoma. On CT scans and MR images, posterior scleritis results in thickening of the sclera [Fig. 12]. There may be associated thickening of Tenon's capsule (sclerotenonitis) and secondary serous RD or

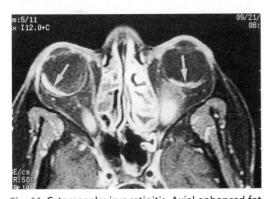

Fig. 11. Cytomegalovirus retinitis. Axial enhanced fat-suppressed T1-weighted MR image shows marked enhancement of posterior globes (*arrows*) in this immunocompromised patient who has bilateral cytomegalovirus retinitis.

serous CD. In general, it is easier to see these changes related to posterior scleritis on CT scans rather than MR images. Posterior nodular scleritis is a focal or zonal necrotizing granulomatous inflammation of the sclera. On imaging this entity may mimic choroidal malignant melanoma or ocular lymphoma.

Uveitis

Inflammation of the uvea (uveitis) may be limited to the anterior uvea (iritis), ciliary body (cyclitis), the posterior uvea, or the choroid (choroiditis, posterior uveitis). Posterior cyclitis (pars planitis) is referred to as "intermediate uveitis." Inflammatory diseases of the uvea are seldom limited to this vascularized layer of the eye. The sclera and retina are usually involved [1]. Posterior uveitis may be focal, multifocal, diffuse choroiditis, chorioretinitis, or neurouveitis [22]. The etiology of uveitis is often unknown. Traumatic iridocyclitis is the most common cause of anterior uveitis. Most intermediate uveitis is idiopathic [22]. The most common causes of panuveitis are idiopathic and sarcoidosis. Uveitis may be seen in patients who have juvenile rheumatoid arthritis, seronegative spondyloarthropathies, and herpetic keratouveitis. Uveitis may be caused by a specific organism, such as *Toxoplasma*. Other causes include bacterial posterior uveitis including Whipple's disease; viral uveitis (cytomegalovirus, herpes simplex, Coxsackie virus); fungal uveitis; and parasitic uveitis. Some forms of uveitis, such as sarcoidosis, Vogt-Koyanagi-Harada syndrome, and Behçet's syndrome, have strong ethnic association. Vogt-Koyanagi-Harada syndrome is an idiopathic bilateral chronic granulomatous uveitis, with exudative choroidal effusion and nonrhegmatogenous RD associated with alopecia, vitiligo, hearing problems, meningeal signs, pleocytosis in the cerebrospinal fluid, and poliosis. Behçet's syndrome is a multisystem vasculitis of unknown cause. Patients usually present with a history of oral and genital ulcerations. Vogt-Koyanagi-Harada is a cell-mediated autoimmune disease. It is often a self-limiting disease. Sympathetic uveitis is a rare bilateral autoimmune-related uveitis that develops after penetrating injury to the eye. Larval uveitis results from ingestion of the eggs of the nematode *T canis* or *Toxocara cati*. Imaging is not indicated in classic nontraumatic anterior uveitis. Patients who have granulomatous uveitis or posterior uveitis of unclear cause may benefit from ultrasound, CT, or MR imaging to assess the degree of choroidal or scleral thickening, masses (eg, abscess), and to evaluate for the presence of RD, choroidal effusion, or intraocular foreign bodies, particularly in patients who have media opacities [Figs. 13 and 14]. Optic disk enhancement on MR imaging and CT scans

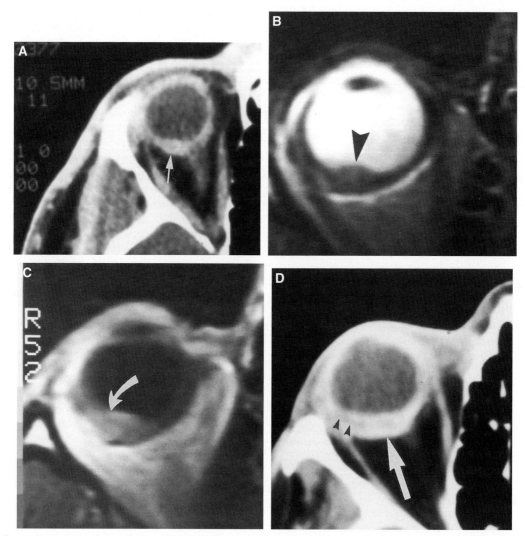

Fig. 12. Posterior nodular scleritis. (*A*) Axial enhanced CT scan shows abnormal enhancement along the posterior aspect of the right globe (*arrow*). Axial T2-weighted (*B*) and axial enhanced T1-weighted (*C*) MR images showing a mass-like lesion (*arrowhead* in *B* and *arrow* in *C*) compatible with posterior nodular scleritis. This CT and MR imaging appearance may not be differentiated from a choroidal mass. Patient responded well to a course of steroid therapy. (*D*) Enhanced axial CT scan in another patient who has necrotizing keratitis and scleritis showing thickening of the Tenon's capsule (*arrow*), fluid in the episcleral space (*arrowheads*), and marked thickening and increased enhancement of the sclera.

may be seen in patients who have pseudotumor cerebri [Fig. 15], simulating posterior uveitis, uveoneurol retinitis of cat-scratch disease, and retinal and choroidal tumors.

Endophthalmitis

Endophthalmitis refers to an intraocular infectious or noninfectious inflammatory process predominantly involving the vitreous cavity or anterior chamber. It is a serious complication following intraocular surgery, nonsurgical trauma, or systemic infection [23]. The visual outcome despite aggressive

treatment in many cases remains poor. In exogenous endophthalmitis, the organisms gain access to eye by surgical or nonsurgical trauma (mostly from patient's lid and conjunctival flora), or may gain access to the eye hematogenously (endogenous endophthalmitis) from an infectious focus, such as endocarditis, urinary tract or bowel infections, or an infected intravenous line or shunt. A predisposing factor may be present, such as prematurity, leukemia, lymphoma, disseminated carcinoma, drug abuse, immunocompromise, and long-term use of corticosteroids [23]. Phacoanaphylactic endophthalmitis is

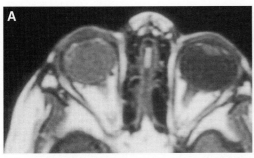
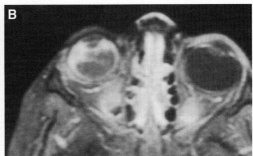

Fig. 13. Granulomatous uveitis. Axial T1-weighted (*A*) and enhanced fat-suppressed axial T1-weighted (*B*) MR images in a 3-year-old child showing marked enhancement of the right globe, predominantly adjacent to the ciliary body. Note increased intensity of the vitreous in precontrast T1-weighted image (*A*), representing leakage of protein into the vitreous or associated vitreous inflammation.

a granulomatous infection that results from autoimmunity to exposed lens protein. In endogenous bacterial and fungal endophthalmitis, septic emboli are lodged in the choriocapillaris and retinal arterioles. Bruch's membrane is disrupted and organisms gain access into the retina and vitreous. The organisms most frequently isolated in endophthalmitis are *Staphylococcus epidermidis, Staphylococcus aureus,* streptococcal species, and *Candida.* Parasitic granulomatosis refers to ocular inflammation as a result of infection with helminthic parasite. The most common of these are *T canis* or *T cati, Cysticercus cellulosae,* and microfilariae of *Onchocerca volvulus.* Toxocariasis result in granuloma formation in the posterior pole or periphery, and endophthalmitis. Cysticercosis may occur anywhere in the eye or around the eye. The CT and MR imaging findings in endophthalmitis include increased density of the vitreous on CT and increased signal intensity of the vitreous on T1-weighted and flair MR images because of increased protein from leaking retinal or choroidal vessels. The uvea may be thickened and demonstrates increased enhancement or focal enhancement (abscess) [Fig. 16]. Associated CD, RD, and posterior vitreous detachment may be delineated on CT and MR imaging.

Ocular calcifications

Calcification is commonly found in normal and abnormal ocular tissues. The presence of calcifications on CT scans can be used to correctly diagnose the type of pathology [Figs. 17–19] [24–26]. Idiopathic scleral calcification is seen in many patients older than 70 years of age. CT scan shows these calcified plaques near the insertions of lateral and medial rectus muscles. The calcified plaques may be in the posterior aspect of the sclera. Calcification may occur at the level of the ciliary body or in the choroid. Ciliary body calcification may be seen after trauma; after inflammation [see Fig. 17]; or in teratoid medulloepithelioma of the ciliary body. Choroidal calcification often follows severe intraocular inflammation or trauma. Choroidal osteoma is an unusual but distinct cause of choroidal calcification. The osteoma is a rare, well-defined, benign tumor (choristoma) that is found mainly in otherwise healthy young women [24]. It typically arises in the choroid adjacent to the optic nerve head of one or both eyes [Fig. 18]. Detection of calcification plays an important role in the diagnosis of malignant intraocular tumors, such as retinoblastoma and medulloepithelioma (see articles on retinoblastoma and medulloepithelioma elsewhere in this issue).

In published histopathologic series, calcium depositions have been seen to occur in necrotic areas of 87% to 95% of retinoblastoma. CT scan demonstrates calcification in more than 90% of retinoblastoma [1,2]. CT demonstration of calcification may be helpful for differentiating retinoblastoma from PHPV, retinopathy of prematurity, Coats' disease, and a variety of other nonspecific causes of leukocoria [1,2]. In children younger than 3 years of age, CT detection of appropriate intraocular calcification suggests that retinoblastoma is the most likely diagnosis. In children older than 3 years of age, however, detection of calcification has less differential value, because some other entities including PHPV, retinopathy of prematurity, and Coats' disease can also produce calcification in older children [24]. Calcification is often absent in PHPV. In older patients, however, calcification may be found in the crystalline lens or focally in a totally detached retina. Retinopathy of prematurity is a bilateral ocular disorder resulting in abnormal proliferation of fibrovascular tissue in the retina of premature infants who previously received oxygen therapy. The abnormal tissue extends into the vitreous cavity where it causes tractional RD. Calcification in the lens,

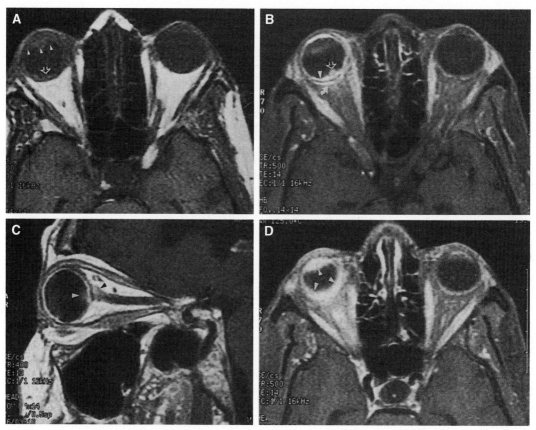

Fig. 14. Ocular sarcoidosis panuveitis. (*A*) Unenhanced axial T1-weighted (500/13 TR/TE) MR image shows nodular thickening of the posterior aspect of the right globe (*arrow*) and thickening of the anterior segment (*arrowheads*) of the right globe. (*B*) Enhanced axial fat-suppressed T1-weighted (500/13 TR/TE) MR image shows nodular enhancement of the posterior aspect of the right globe (*arrowhead* and *open arrow*) related to granulomatous involvement of the choroid. Note enhancement of the anterior segment of the right globe. Notice abnormal enhancement of Tenon's capsule (*curved arrow*). (*C*) Enhanced sagittal T1-weighted (400/13 TR/TE) MR image shows granuloma at the optic disk (*white arrowhead*) and involvement of the optic nerve (*black arrowhead*). (*D*) Enhanced axial fat-suppressed T1-weighted (500/14 TR/TE) MR image shows enhancement of markedly thickened uveal tract (*arrowheads*). (*From* Mafee MF, Dorodi S, Pai E. Saroidosis of the eye, orbit, and central nervous system. Role of MR imaging. Radiol Clin North Am 1999;37:74.)

choroid, and retrolental tissue has been reported in children who have late stage of this disease [24]. Coats' disease is a unilateral exudative RD that mainly affects boys between 18 months and 18 years of age. The disease is an idiopathic congenital disorder of the retinal vessels (telangiectases). Abnormal retinal vessels can occur either in the periphery or the central retina; leakage of lipid-rich serum from telangiectatic vessels into the subretinal space results in RD [see Fig. 4]. The retina may be shallowly detached or become bullously detached. Patients who have Coats' disease occasionally may have calcification in the retina. This calcification may be submacular and result from metaplasia of the RPE [2,24]. RPE is capable of metaplastic calcification or bone formation [Fig. 19]. Calcification

may also be detected on CT in patients who have microphthamos with or without colobomatous cyst. The calcification in these eyes most likely occurs in the choristomatous glial tissue [24]. Retinal astrocytic hamartoma is another lesion that may cause retinal calcification [2]. These hamartomas most frequently occur in tuberous sclerosis, but also may be noted in neurofibromatosis. Cytomegalovirus retinitis is a common infection in patients who have AIDS [see Fig. 11]. In cytomegalovirus retinitis, calcification may be seen in the necrotic portion of the retina, or in areas of healed retina [24]. Retinal drusen is a common cause of calcification of the RPE. Drusen are well-defined excrescences that form under the RPE in aging eyes, and are often associated with age-related macular degeneration.

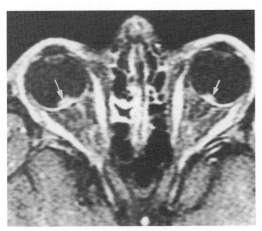

Fig. 15. Pseudotumor cerebri. Axial enhanced fat-suppressed T1-weighted MR image in a patient who has pseudotumor cerebri showing abnormal enhancement at the level of both optic discs (*arrows*).

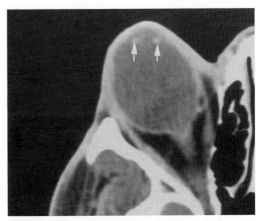

Fig. 17. Axial CT scan shows enlarged right globe caused by axial myopia. Note calcification of ciliary body (*arrows*). Lens has been removed.

Retinal drusen are very small and cannot be visualized by CT scanning. Subretinal neovascular membranes are fibrovascular proliferations that arise from the choroid and extend into the subretinal space, causing serous and hemorrhagic RDs. Numerous conditions may result in subretinal neovascular membranes, but age-related macular degeneration is the most common cause of subretinal neovascular membranes. Long-standing neovascular membranes may become calcified.

Drusen of the optic nerve are acellular accretions of hyaline-like material that occur on or near the surface of the optic disk. They are often seen in the prelaminar optic nerve. When drusen affect the papilla, the optic nerve head is elevated and shows blurred disk margins. Unlike retinal drusen, CT scans can readily detect optic disk drusen. Trauma in one series [24] was the single most common cause of ocular calcification. The calcification typically occurs many years after the initial trauma, when the damaged globes are in varying stages of atrophy or phthisis.

Ocular tumors

Most primary and metastatic ocular neoplasms in adults involve the uveal tract and in particular the choroid. Malignant melanoma is the most common tumor to involve the uvea [25–30]. Most primary ocular neoplasms in children, however,

Fig. 16. Endophthalmitis. Axial enhanced T1-weighted MR image shows marked thickening and enhancement of the entire uveal tract (*arrows*).

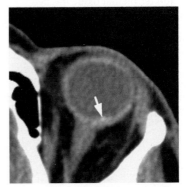

Fig. 18. Choroidal osteoma. Axial CT scan shows a calcified mass, compatible with presumed choroidal osteoma (*arrow*).

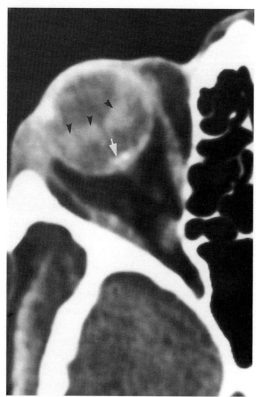

Fig. 19. Chronic retinal detachment. Axial CT scan shows retinal detachment. Note calcification at the optic disk (*arrow*). The increased thickening of the detached retina (*arrowheads*) is related to reactive retinal gliosis.

involve the retina. Retinoblastoma is the most common tumor to involve the retina (see the article on retinoblastoma and simulating lesions elsewhere in this issue) [31–33]. Retinal astrocytic hamartoma is another rare lesion involving the retina. These hamartomas most frequently occur in tuberous sclerosis, but also may be found in neurofibromatosis. On pathologic examination, these hamartomas show focal benign astrocytic proliferation that usually contains calcium [24].

Medulloepithelioma is an embryonic neoplasm derived from primitive neuroepithelium, presenting as a mass behind the pupil and iris [33]. It typically arises from the ciliary body epithelium, but may also occur as a posterior mass in the retina or optic nerve (see the article on medulloepithelioma of the ciliary body and optic nerve elsewhere in this issue) [33,34].

Malignant uveal melanoma

Malignant uveal melanomas are the most common primary intraocular tumor in adults. Some of these tumors may originate from pre-existing nevi [30]. Choroidal hemangioma, choroidal nevi, CD, choroidal cysts, neurofibroma and schwannoma of the uvea, uveal leiomyoma, ciliary body adenoma and adenocarcinoma, medulloepithelioma, juvenile xanthogranuloma, RD, disciform degeneration of the macula, and metastatic tumors are some of the benign and malignant lesions that may be confused with malignant uveal melanoma [27–30,34]. Because of their anatomic location, tumors of the uveal tract are not accessible to biopsy without intraocular surgery. Consequently, the diagnosis must often be made on the basis of clinical examination and judicious use of ancillary diagnostic procedures, such as fluorescein angiography, ultrasonography, CT, and MR imaging. This article only considers the role of MR imaging in the diagnosis of uveal melanoma. The MR imaging techniques for ocular lesions have been described in several prior publications [1,2,30]. The MR imaging characteristics of melanotic lesions are thought to be related to the paramagnetic properties of melanin [27]. Unlike most tumors, melanomas have short T1 and T2 relaxation time values. Most uveal melanomas appear as areas of high signal intensity on T1- and proton-weighted MR images [Fig. 20]. On T2-weighted MR images, melanomas appear as areas of moderately low signal intensity [Figs. 20 and 21]. The tumor may be dome-shaped [Fig. 21], mushroom-shaped, plaquoid [see Fig. 20], ring-shaped, or diffuse. Although in general the paramagnetic property of melanin plays an important role in MR imaging signal characteristics of melanomas, the histologic features of tumors undoubtedly contribute to their MR imaging features [30]. Melanomas are often arranged in tightly cohesive bundles and are highly cellular (short T2 relaxation time). Necrosis and hemorrhage are not uncommon [1,2,27,30]. At times, uveal melanomas may appear partially or completely hyperintense on T2-weighted MR images. Exudative or hemorrhagic RD may be present [see Fig. 20]. Extensive extraocular extension may be present even in the presence of a small intraocular malignant melanoma [Fig. 22]. Gadolinium diethylenetriamine pentaacetic acid contrast material is very useful in the diagnosis of uveal melanomas, certain ocular pathology, and, in particular, for evaluation of optic nerve and retrobulbar extension of ocular tumors [see Fig. 20]. Uveal melanomas demonstrate moderate enhancement on postgadolinium T1-weighted MR images [see Fig. 20].

Melanocytoma is a deeply pigmented benign tumor that may occur in the uvea and in the substance of the optic nerve. Approximately 50% of melanocytomas develop in blacks, whereas the incidence

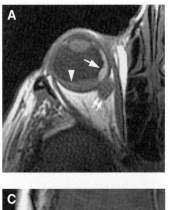

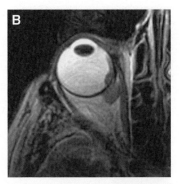

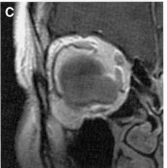

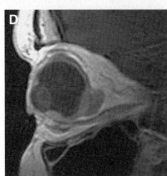

Fig. 20. Malignant choroidal melanoma. Axial T1-weighted (*A*), axial T2-weighted (*B*), coronal enhanced T1-weighted (*C*), and sagittal enhanced T1-weighted (*D*) MR images showing a plaquoid choroidal melanoma (*large arrow*), subretinal exudate (*arrowhead*), and extraocular extension of tumor (*small arrows*).

of malignant uveal melanoma in blacks is less than 1%. The MR imaging appearance of melanocytoma is similar to uveal melanoma [Fig. 23].

Choroidal hemangioma

Choroidal hemangiomas are congenital vascular hamartomas typically seen in middle-aged to elderly individuals [35,36]. Two different forms have been reported: a circumscribed or solitary type not associated with other abnormalities; and a diffuse angiomatosis often associated with facial nevus flammeus or variations of the Sturge-Weber syndrome [1–3,6,37]. The solitary choroidal hemangioma is confined to choroid, shows distinct margins, and characteristically lies posterior to the equator of the globe [36]. It is typically seen as a tumor located in the juxtapapillary or macular region of the fundus [36]. In contrast, the hemangioma associated with Sturge-Weber syndrome is a diffuse process that may involve the choroid, ciliary body, iris, and, occasionally, nonuveal tissues, such as the episclera, conjunctiva, and limbus [37]. CT, including dynamic CT, has been shown to be useful for the diagnosis of choroidal hemangioma [Figs. 24 and 25] [36,38]. MR imaging has been shown to be superior to CT for evaluation of uveal melanomas, choroidal hemangioma, and simulating lesions [1,2,27,37,38]. On T1-weighted MR images, the choroidal hemangiomas appear as isointense to slightly hypertense lesions with respect to the vitreous. They appear hyperintense on T2-weighted MR images [Fig. 26], so they become isointense to vitreous on these pulse sequences. They demonstrate intense contrast enhancement on enhanced T1-weighted MR images [Figs. 26 and 27].

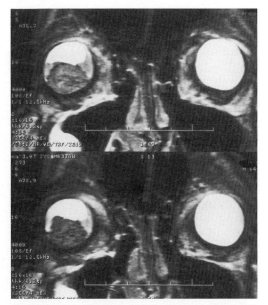

Fig. 21. Malignant choroidal melanoma. Coronal T2-weighted MR images showing a large mound-shaped choroidal melanoma (*arrows*). The MR images were obtained on a 3-T MR imaging unit using quadrature head coil.

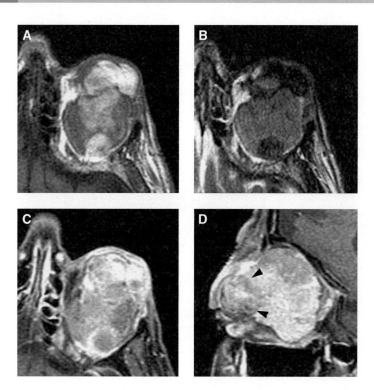

Fig. 22. Presumed ocular melanoma. Unenhanced axial T1-weighted (*A*), axial T2-weighted (*B*), enhanced axial (*C*), and sagittal T1-weighted (*D*) MR images showing an enhancing mass within the left globe (*arrowheads*) and a large retrobulbar mass. Eye examination showed a large intraocular mass. The patient was found to have multiple liver masses.

Uveal metastases

Uveal metastasis can be confused clinically and radiologically with uveal melanoma. Embolic malignant cells reach the globe by means of the short posterior ciliary arteries. The route of spread may be the reason why most of the metastases involve the posterior half of the globe [27]. The most common sources of secondary tumor within the eye are the breast and lung. Both eyes may be affected in about one third of the cases. Signal intensity of uveal melanomas and uveal metastases may be similar [Figs. 28 and 29].

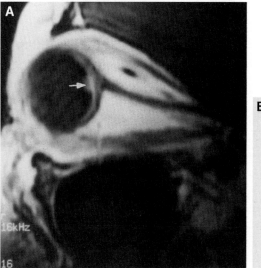

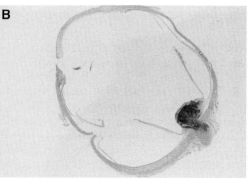

Fig. 23. Melanocytoma and melanoma of the optic disk. (*A*) Sagittal T1-weighted MR image shows a mass (*arrow*) at the optic disk. (*B*) photomicrograph of the eye showing the mass at the optic disk. This was considered to be a melanoma arising from a melanocytoma.

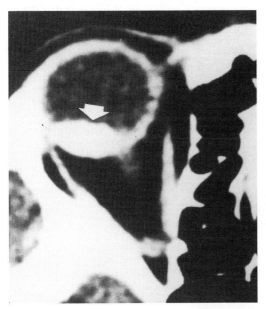

Fig. 24. Circumscribed choroidal hemangioma. Enhanced CT scan shows an intensely enhancing choroidal hemangioma (*arrows*).

Other uveal tumors

Choroidal lymphoma and leukemic infiltration of the uveal tract can be mistaken for choroidal tumor. The process often is bilateral. On MR imaging its signal characteristics are similar to uveal melanoma [27]. Neurofibroma and schwannoma of the choroid and ciliary body, adenoma and adenocarcinoma of the ciliary body, leiomyoma of the ciliary body, and other rare lesions can also be confused with uveal melanoma on MR imaging [1,2,27].

Choroidal hematoma

Choroidal hematoma, CD (serous and hemorrhagic), and posterior scleritis may simulate choroidal melanoma, particularly on CT scans [Fig. 30].

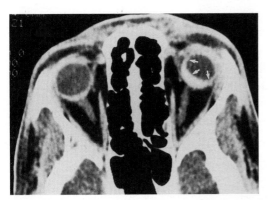

Fig. 25. Diffuse choroidal hemangioma. Enhanced CT scan shows a diffuse choroidal hemangioma (*arrows*).

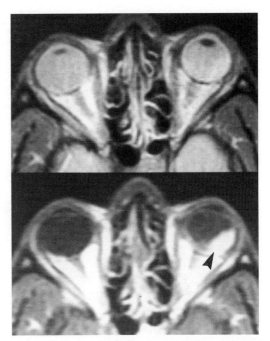

Fig. 26. Choroidal hemangioma. Proton-weighted (*top*) and enhanced T1-weighted (*bottom*) MR images showing an intensely enhancing choroidal hemangioma (*arrowhead*).

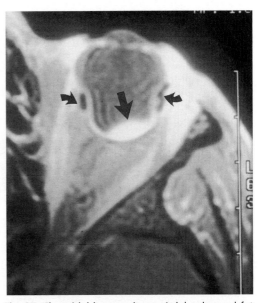

Fig. 27. Choroidal hemangioma. Axial enhanced fat-suppressed T1-weighted MR image shows an intensely enhancing choroidal hemangioma (*straight arrow*). Note scleral buckling (*curved arrows*) for the repair of retinal detachment. The cause of retinal detachment was not clear until MR imaging was performed.

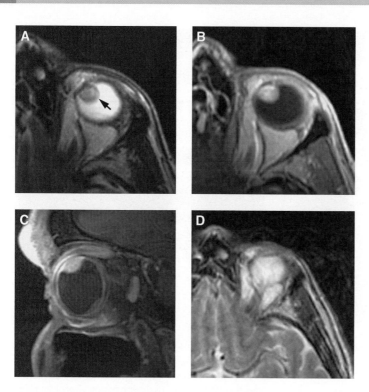

Fig. 28. Ocular metastasis. Axial T2-weighted (*A*), axial enhanced fat-suppressed T1-weighted (*B*), sagittal enhanced fat-suppressed T1-weighted (*C*), and post–proton beam treatment axial T2-weighted (*D*) MR images showing a mass (*arrow*) compatible with biopsy-proven metastatic hypernephroma. Note satisfactory response following proton beam treatment (*D*).

Summary

Since the development of CT and MR imaging, significant progress has been made in ophthalmic imaging. As the technology advanced and MR imaging units improved their ability in term of spatial resolution, the role of MR imaging in ophthalmic imaging has increased accordingly. This article considers the role of MR and CT imaging in the diagnosis of selected pathologies of the eye.

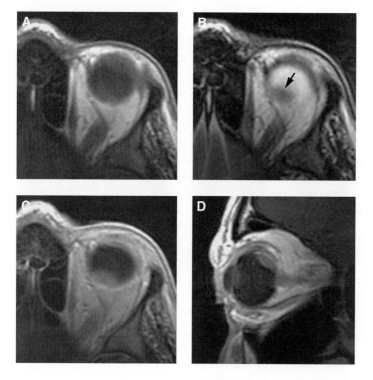

Fig. 29. Ocular metastasis. Axial T1-weighted (*A*), axial T2-weighted (*B*), enhanced axial (*C*), and sagittal T1-weighted (*D*) MR imaging showing a metastatic mass (*arrow*) from primary malignant thymoma.

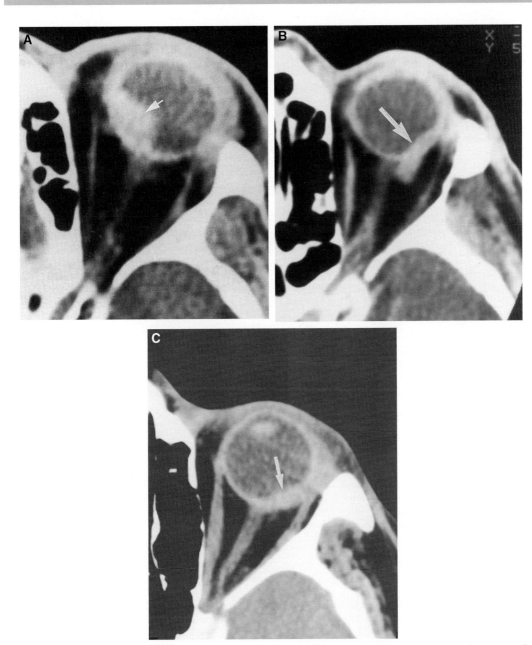

Fig. 30. Choroidal hematoma, simulating choroidal melanoma. (*A*) Axial CT scan shows a hyperdense mass (*arrow*) compatible with choroidal hematoma. (*B*) Axial CT scan shows a hyperdense mass (*arrow*) compatible with choroidal melanoma. Note extraocular extension of this melanoma. (*C*) Enhanced axial CT scan shows focal thickening of the eyeball caused by a choroidal melanoma.

Acknowledgments

The authors are grateful to Dr. Kiarash Mohajer for helpful literature research, Aura Smith for secretarial assistance, and Yasir Aich for technical support.

References

[1] Mafee MF. The eye. In: Som PM, Curtin HD, editors. Head and neck imaging. 4th edition. St. Louis (MO): Mosby; 2003. p. 441–527.

[2] Mafee MF. The eye and orbit. In: Mafee MF, Valvassori GE, Becker M, editors. Imaging of the head and neck. 2nd edition. Stuttgart (Germany): Thieme; 2005. p. 137–294.

[3] Warwich R, Williams PL. Gray's anatomy. 35th British edition. Philadelphia: WB Saunders; 1973.

[4] Snell RS, Lemp MA, editors. Clinical anatomy of the eye. Boston: Blackwell Scientific; 1989.

[5] Reech MF, Wobij JL, Wirtschapter JD. Ophthalmic anatomy: a manual with some clinical

applications. San Francisco: American Academy of Ophthalmology; 1981.

[6] Mafee MF, Putterman A, Valvassori GE, et al. Orbital space occupying lesions: role of computed tomography an magnetic resonance imaging. An analysis of 145 cases. Radiol Clin North Am 1987;25:529–59.

[7] Rtumin U. Fundus appearance in normal eye. I. The choroid. Am J Ophthalmol 1967;64:821–57.

[8] Nakaizumi Y. The ultrastructure of Bruch's membrane. II. Eyes with a tapetum. Arch Ophthalmol 1964;72:388–94.

[9] Park KL. Anatomy of the uvea. In: Yanoff M, Duker JS, editors. Ophthalmology. St. Louis (MO): Mosby; 1999. p. 10:2.1–2.2.

[10] Mafee MF, Peyman GA. Retinal and choroidal detachment: role of MRI and CT. Radiol Clin North Am 1987;25:487–507.

[11] Mafee MF. Magnetic resonance imaging: ocular anatomy and pathology. In: Newton TH, Bilanuik LT, editors. Modern neuroradiology, vol. 4. Radiology of the eye and orbit. New York: Clavadel press/Raven press; 1990. p. 2.1–3.45.

[12] Mafee MF, Goldberg MF, Valvassori GE, et al. Computed tomography in the evaluation of patients with persistent hyperplastic primary vitreous (PHP's). Radiology 1982;145:713–4.

[13] Anand R. Serous detachment of the neural retina. In: Yanoff M, Duker JS, editors. Ophthalmology. St. Louis (MO): Mosby; 1999. p. 8: 40.1–40.6.

[14] Mafee MF, Peyman GA. Choroidal detachment and ocular hypotony: CT evaluation. Radiology 1984;153:697–703.

[15] Peyman GA, Mafee MF, Schulman JA. Computed tomography in choroidal detachment. Ophthalmology 1984;92:156–62.

[16] Mafee MF, Linder B, Peyman GA, et al. Choroidal hematoma and effusion: evaluation with MR imaging. Radiology 1988;168:781–6.

[17] Capper SA, Leopold IH. Mechanism of serous choroidal detachment. Arch Ophthalmol 1956; 55:101–13.

[18] Siegelman J, Jakobiec FA, Eisner G, editors. Retinal diseases: pathogenesis, laser therapy and surgery. Boston: Little, Brown; 1984. p. 1–66.

[19] Kapusta MA, Lopez PF. Choroidal hemorrhage. In: Yanoff M, Duker JS, editors. Ophthalmology. St. Louis (MO): Mosby; 1999. p. 41.1–8:41.4.

[20] Goldstein DA, Tessler HH. Episcleritis, scleritis and other scleral disorders. In: Yanoff M, Duker JS, editors. Ophthalmology. St. Louis (MO): Mosby; 1999. p. 5:13.1–13.9.

[21] Chaques VJ, Lam S, Tessler HH, et al. Computed tomography and magnetic resonance imaging in the diagnosis of posterior scleritis. Ann Ophthalmol 1993;25:89–94.

[22] Forster DJ. Basic principles: general approach to the uveitis patient and treatment strategies. In:

Yanoff M, Duker JS, editors. Ophthalmology. St. Louis (MO): Mosby; 1999. p. 10:3.1–3.6.

[23] Marx JL. Endophthalmitis. In: Yanoff M, Duker JS, editors. Ophthalmology. St. Louis (MO): Mosby; 1999. p. 10:21.1–21.6.

[24] Yan X, Edward DP, Mafee MF. Ocular calcification: radiologic-pathologic correlation and literature review. International Journal of Neuroradiology 1998;4:81–96.

[25] Zeffer HJ. Calcification and ossification in ocular tissue. Am J Ophthalmol 1983;101:1724–7.

[26] Bullock JD, Campbell RJ, Waller RR. Calcification in retinoblastoma. Invest Ophthalmol Vis Sci 1976;11:252–5.

[27] Mafee MF, Peyman GA, McKusick MA. Malignant uveal melanoma and similar lesions studied by computed tomography. Radiology 1985;156: 403–8.

[28] Mafee MF, Peyman GA, Grisolano JE, et al. Malignant uveal melanoma and simulating lesions: MR imaging evaluation. Radiology 1986;160: 773–80.

[29] Mafee MF, Peyman GA, Peace JH, et al. MRI in the evaluation and differentiation of uveal melanoma. Ophthalmology 1987;94:341–8.

[30] Mafee MF. Uveal melanoma, choroidal hemangioma, and simulating lesions. Radiol Clin North Am 1998;36:1083–99.

[31] Mafee MF, Goldberg MF, Greenwald MJ, et al. Retinoblastoma and simulating lesion: role of CT and MR Imaging. Radiol Clin North Am 1987;25:667–81.

[32] Mafee MF, Goldberg MF, Cohen SB, et al. Magnetic resonance imaging of leukokoric eyes and use of in vitro proton magnetic resonance spectroscopy of retinoblastoma. Ophthalmology 1989;96:965–76.

[33] Kaufman LM, Mafee MF, Song CD. Retinoblastoma and simulating lesions: role of CT, MR imaging and use of Gd-DTPA contrast enhancement. Radiol Clin North Am 1998;36:1101–17.

[34] Chavez M, Mafee MF, Castillo B, et al. Medulloepithelioma of the optic nerve. J Pediatr Ophthalmol Strabismus 2004;41:48–52.

[35] Enochs SW, Petherick P, Bogdanova A, et al. Paramagnetic metal scavenging by melanin: MR imaging. Radiology 1997;204:417–23.

[36] Mafee MF, Ainbinder DJ, Hidayat AA, et al. Magnetic resonance imaging and computed tomography in the evaluation of choroidal hemangioma. International Journal of Neuroradiology 1995;1:67–77.

[37] Mafee MF, Atlas SW, Galetta SL. Eye, orbit, and visual system. In: Atlas SW, editor. Imaging of the brain and spine. 3rd edition. Philadelphia: Lippincott Williams & Wilkins; 2002. p. 1433–524.

[38] Mafee MF, Miller MT, Tan W, et al. Dynamic computed tomography and its application to ophthalmology. Radiol Clin North Am 1987;25:715–31.

MAGNETIC
RESONANCE
IMAGING CLINICS

Magn Reson Imaging Clin N Am 14 (2006) 271–285

Acute Injury to the Immature Brain with Hypoxia with or Without Hypoperfusion

P. Ellen Grant, MD[a],*, David Yu, MD[b]

The most common nontraumatic mechanisms of brain injury in the neonate and young child are quite different than in the older child and adult. In this age group global brain hypoxia with or without hypoperfusion is a common mechanism of injury. Etiologies include neonatal asphyxia, choking, near drowning, sudden infant death syndrome, nonaccidental injury, severe asthma, and pneumonia. This is much different than in adults, where the most common nontraumatic brain injury is caused by focal ischemic events (from focal arterial occlusion), and when global brain hypoperfusion occurs, it is usually caused by cardiac arrest without preceding hypoxia.

When immature brain is injured because of hypoxia with or without hypoperfusion, the acute imaging findings and evolution of the imaging findings are different than the typical adult ischemic stroke. In the adult, acute ischemic stroke results in predominantly acute necrotic cell death.

In the immature brain, hypoxia with or without hypoperfusion often results in a significant component of delayed cell death [1]. Although these differences may be caused in part by the different mechanisms of injury, it is also possible that programmed cell death mechanisms that are primed for the developmental process of neuronal pruning are activated more easily in the immature brain. To understand brain injury in the immature brain and the differences between the immature and mature brain, it is important to understand the possible pathways for cell death and the implications for imaging, particularly with diffusion-weighted imaging (DWI). The four major pathways for cell death are as follows [2,3]:

1. *Acute necrosis:* This occurs if there is an overwhelming insult to the cell causing unrecoverable energy failure and immediate cell death by necrosis. These injuries present as bright DWI and dark apparent diffusion coefficient

This article was originally published in *Radiologic Clinics of North America* 2006;15(1):63–77. This article was supported by grant K23 NS42758 to Dr. Grant and in part by the National Center for Research Resources (P41RR14075) and the Mental Illness and Neuroscience Discovery (MIND) Institute.
[a] Division of Pediatric Radiology, Massachusetts General Hospital, Boston, MA, USA
[b] Shields MRI Health Care Group, Brockton, MA, USA
* Corresponding author. Division of Pediatric Radiology, Massachusetts General Hospital, Ellison 237, Boston, MA 02114.
E-mail address: egrant2@partners.org (P.E. Grant).

doi:10.1016/j.mric.2006.06.004

(ADC) lesions (decreased ADC) within minutes. On follow-up imaging, these regions progress to volume loss with increased T2 signal caused by gliosis or cystic encephalomalacia.

2. *Delayed necrosis:* This occurs when the insult is not severe enough to cause immediate energy failure with oxygen and blood flow returning before the cell shuts down its energy mechanisms. The recovery is only transient, however, and cell death occurs by delayed necrosis. In clinical cases with histories of hypoxia or hypoperfusion and initially normal DWI studies but delayed ADC decreases, it is suspected that delayed necrosis is occurring. In these clinical scenarios, DWI abnormalities appear within hours to days of the insult. It is presumed that the ADC reductions occur for the same reasons as in immediate necrosis. Similar imaging sequelae of volume loss with gliosis or cystic encephalomalacia are expected.

3. *Delayed apoptosis:* This occurs when oxygen and blood flow return before the cell shuts down its energy mechanisms. The severity of the injury is less than with delayed necrosis because the energy metabolism recovers, but the insult is severe enough to cause the cell to undergo delayed cell death by apoptosis. To the authors' knowledge, no studies assessing the DWI signature of apoptosis have been performed because of the difficulty in developing a pure apoptotic model. This is further complicated by the fact that there are at least two different types of apoptosis: caspase dependent and caspase independent. Not only is the DWI signature unknown but there may also be more than one DWI signature for apoptosis. Given that apoptosis is a form of programmed cell death not accompanied by ATP loss and not always accompanied by sodium-potassium pump failure, it is presumed that the process of apoptosis can occur when DWI is normal. In clinical cases with progressive volume loss over weeks without an ADC decrease, it is presumed that cell death by apoptosis has occurred.

4. *Delayed aponecrosis or necroapoptosis:* This is a mixed cell death phenotype with morphologic and biochemical features of both apoptosis and necrosis that may result when apoptotic death programs are initiated and the cell energy metabolism fails, inducing necrosis; or may be a result of concomitant activation of mixed cell death mechanisms in ischemic or traumatically injured brain cells.

The primary importance of understanding these concepts of delayed cell death as an imager, is that cell death is a dynamic process with the delay in appearance of a DWI signal abnormality determined by mechanism and severity of injury and regional vulnerability. Delayed cell death is common in global brain hypoxia or hypoperfusion as blood flow and oxygen are typically restored. In these cases, the extent and severity of DWI abnormalities can change drastically over time because of variable regional vulnerability and resulting regional variations in delay to cell death. DWI within the first day can often detect the pattern of injury but is a poor predictor of the final injury. Rarely, DWI may never show significant decreases and yet long-term volume loss is observed. These scenarios are very different than the typical arterial ischemic stroke, where the lesion seen on acute DWI is very close to the final lesion volume and most cells in the DWI abnormality proceed to cell death by necrosis.

This article reviews the imaging features and evolution of immature brain injury caused by hypoxia with or without hypoperfusion in the neonate and young child. Clinical presentations and available literature on mechanisms and clinical outcomes are discussed. In many of these cases, DWI does not show the full extent of the injury but detects a pattern of injury that is important in guiding clinical care. Awareness of the delayed cell death mechanisms outlined previously is essential to understand DWI sensitivity and evolution and to provide the most accurate clinical interpretation, especially in cases of hypoxia with or without hypoperfusion.

Brain injury in the neonate

Although CT may be used acutely to rule out hemorrhage or bony fractures, MR imaging is the study of choice for assessing parenchymal brain injury in the neonate [4]. The role of MR imaging with DWI and MR spectroscopy is to provide early detection of injury (usually by day 1) [5], to determine the pattern of injury, and to assess the severity and extent of the injury. Early detection of perinatal brain injury allows the clinical team to determine if the acute brain injury is the cause of the clinical symptoms. The pattern of injury can give clues to the potential mechanisms of injury, and when combined with the severity or extent of the brain injury, this information may help manage the expectations for clinical outcome.

The imaging protocol for acute neonatal brain injury should include the following:

1. *Axial T1-weighted images:* The authors prefer axial three-dimensional spoiled gradient recalled echo with 25-degree flip angle because of its improved gray-white contrast and high

resolution. If motion is a problem, fast spin or turbo spin echo T1 images are used.

2. *Axial T2-weighted images:* The authors prefer T2-weighted fast spin or turbo spin echo because of its faster scan times, although some centers use dual echo spin echo proton density and T2-weighted sequences because of higher sensitivity to T2 change. Longer TEs improve contrast and a TE around 205 milliseconds should be used for fast spin echo T2 and 120 millisecond for spin echo T2.

3. *Axial gradient echo images:* The authors routinely perform gradient echo to detect subtle hemorrhages and venous engorgement. This is more important in centers that elect to perform fast spin or turbo spin echo over routine spin echo T2 because these are notoriously insensitive to deoxyhemoglobin and intracellular methemoglobin.

4. *Axial DWI (with calculation of ADC maps):* At pediatric centers the maximum b value used in the calculation of ADC values ranges from 700 to 1000 s/mm^2. The authors prefer a b value of 1500 s/mm^2 because of the improved contrast to noise [6]. It is helpful to have both DWI and ADC maps, because early deep gray nuclei injuries are occasionally better seen on ADC maps.

5. *MR spectroscopy of the basal ganglia and thalami and centrum semiovale on at least one side:* Longer echo times are used to assess lactate (TE of 144 or 270 milliseconds). Shorter echo times are used to assess N-acetyl aspartate (NAA) and lipid levels (TE of 35 or 144 milliseconds). Three-dimensional whole-brain sequences are preferred but time constraints and patient motion typically limit one to single voxel acquisitions.

Although fluid-attenuated inversion-recovery (FLAIR) may be useful to detect glial scarring in the chronic phase or to look for ventricular debris in acute infection, it is insensitive to acute edema in the newborn [Fig. 1].

Imaging should be performed as soon as clinically possible to assess for the presence and pattern of injury. In most cases, neonatal hypoxic-ischemic brain injury can be detected on DWI within 23 hours of life but the sensitivity of DWI changes over time [5,7,8]. There have been reports of negative studies in the first 24 hours [9] but often this is a moot point because most of the time the neonate is too unstable for MR imaging within 24 hours or the clinical symptoms that lead to the MR imaging occur after 24 hours. In the six neonates on whom the authors have performed DWI within 24 hours, all have been positive. Often a second MR imaging between day 5 and 8 is helpful to rule out progression and determine the evolution of injury, because delayed white matter involvement may not be evident until this time. If transportation is difficult or scanner availability is limited, MR imaging should be performed between days 2 and 4 when DWI changes because the primary injury is easily appreciated and the pattern of injury can be identified. Although T1- and T2-weighted images often show abnormalities as early as day 1, these findings are much more subtle and DWI is essential to confirm the presence and better determine the pattern of injury. After day 8, DWI is often insensitive but in neonates presenting with perinatal encephalopathy, T1- and T2-weighted abnormalities are typically easily identified [10,11].

There are primarily three patterns of brain injury that can be identified on acute neonatal DWI, which are similar to patterns that have been described on subacute to chronic routine MR imaging:

- *Central pattern:* Involvement of the ventrolateral thalamus, corticospinal tract, or perirolandic cortex [Fig. 2].
- *Peripheral pattern:* Involvement of cortex and white matter but sparing of the ventrolateral thalamus, corticospinal tract, and perirolandic cortex [Fig. 3].
- *Focal pattern:* Vascular territory lesions [Fig. 4].

Central and peripheral patterns

If the global brain injury in the central and peripheral patterns is acute and severe, the neonate may present with clinical features of perinatal encephalopathy (often called hypoxic-ischemic encephalopathy). Perinatal encephalopathy is a specific clinical syndrome that requires the following criteria to be met [12]:

1. Profound metabolic or mixed acidemia (pH < 7 on umbilical cord artery blood sample if obtained).
2. One- and 5-minute Apgar scores of 0 to 3.
3. Neurologic manifestations, such as seizures, coma, or hypotonia.
4. Multisystem organ dysfunction (typically cardiovascular, gastrointestinal, renal, hematologic, or pulmonary).

When neonates meet the criteria for perinatal encephalopathy, they are more likely to have a central pattern of injury [13]. In many cases where injury is identified on DWI, however, the neonate does not meet the full criteria for perinatal encephalopathy. In fact, a neonate can have normal Apgar scores but present with seizure-like activity and have diffuse abnormalities on DWI. Perinatal encephalopathy (or hypoxic-ischemic encephalopathy) is not an imaging diagnosis and evidence

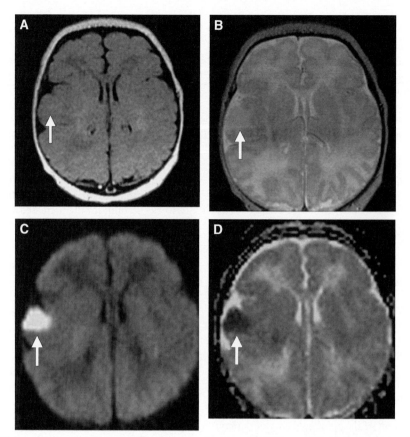

Fig. 1. Insensitivity of FLAIR. (*A*) Axial FLAIR, (*B*) T2 fast sin echo, (*C*) DWI, and (*D*) ADC map at level of bodies of lateral ventricles on day 2 of life in a term infant presenting with focal seizures. The focal vascular territory ischemic injury that is easily identified on DWI and ADC images (*arrow*) is not seen on the FLAIR image (*arrow*), but is visible on the T2 fast spin echo image (*arrow*).

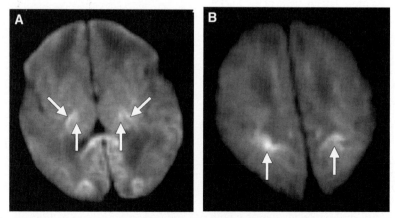

Fig. 2. Central pattern of DWI injury. Bright DWI signal involves (*A*) the posterior limb internal capsule (*angled arrows*), the ventrolateral thalamus (*vertical arrows*), and (*B*) the perirolandic cortex (*arrows*). The margins of the DWI lesions are often indistinct.

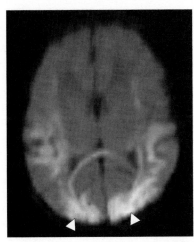

Fig. 3. Peripheral pattern of DWI injury. Bright DWI signal involves diffuse regions of white matter and cortex (*arrowheads*). The margins of the DWI bright lesions are often indistinct.

of brain injury may be present on MR imaging in the absence of clinical perinatal encephalopathy.

Neonatal hypoxic-ischemic injury is associated with many risk factors. Antepartum associations include maternal hypotension, infertility treatment, and thyroid disease. Intrapartum associations include forceps delivery, breech extraction, cord prolapse, abruptio placentae, and maternal fever. Postpartum risks include severe respiratory distress, sepsis, and shock [14].

The central pattern is thought to result when there is global profound lack of oxygen and blood flow (hypoxia and ischemia) to the brain for a relatively short period of time (minutes) resulting in injury of regions of high energy demand [1]. Pathologic studies of term neonates who succumbed to a profound hypoxic ischemic event show relative cortical sparing and deep gray matter injury particularly involving hippocampi, lateral geniculate nuclei, putamen, ventrolateral thalami, and dorsal mesencephalon. These regions have high concentrations of excitatory amino acids (glutamate, aspartate) and corresponding N-methyl-D-aspartate receptors. Excessive uptake of excitatory amino acids by N-methyl-D-aspartate receptors results in depolarization of neuronal membranes, excessive calcium influx, activation of second messenger systems, mobilization of internal calcium stores, activation of lipases and proteases, generation of free fatty acids and free radicals, mitochondrial dysfunction, depletion of energy stores, and ultimate neuronal death. Mature deep gray nuclei also contain myelin and are also undergoing active myelination with high-energy requirements at term. The combination of increased excitatory amino acids and N-methyl-D-aspartate receptors and active myelination may

cause these regions to be more susceptible to injury following profound asphyxia [11].

Profound asphyxia before 32 weeks gestational age results in injury to thalami, basal ganglia, and brainstem. Compared with profound asphyxia in term infants, perirolandic cortex is spared. Thalamic involvement is similar but basal ganglia involvement is less, with decreased scarring. Basal ganglia begin to myelinate at 33 to 35 weeks gestational age compared with thalami at 23 to 25 weeks. Barkovich and Sargent [10] speculate that the higher energy demands from active myelination within the thalami but not the basal ganglia before 32 weeks account for the increased susceptibility of the thalamus to profound asphyxia at this gestational age. In addition, the basal ganglia, which have a lower white matter content and delayed onset of myelination compared with thalami, may suffer less injury and develop less scarring because of presence of fewer cells that are able to mount an astroglial response. Without an astroglial response, brain reacts to injury by resorption resulting in volume loss and cavitation, which is seen in the basal ganglia.

The peripheral pattern is thought to result from a global brain hypoxia and ischemia that is more prolonged (hours) but less profound and is often termed *partial asphyxia* [10,13,15]. This pattern of injury primarily involves cortex and white matter that is not actively myelinating. It is thought that the immature white matter is more vulnerable to ischemia-related injury than mature white matter. In particular, preoligodendrocytes and oligodendrocyte progenitor cells are more susceptible to antioxidant depletion and free radical exposure than mature oligodendrocytes. Oligodendrocyte

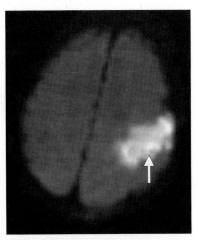

Fig. 4. Focal pattern of DWI injury. Bright DWI signal is seen in a focal region corresponding to an arterial vascular territory. Typically, the margins of the DWI bright lesion are sharp (*arrow*).

progenitor cells express glutamate receptors including α-amino-3-hydroxy-5-methyl-4-isoxazole propionic acid (AMPA) and kainite receptors making them vulnerable to excess activation by glutamatergic neurotransmission and cell death by excitotoxicity [14].

There is variation in the peripheral pattern depending on gestational age that is thought to depend on the maturation of the brain and vascular supply at time of insult. In premature neonates, periventricular white matter is supplied by ventriculopetal arteries coursing inward from the cerebral cortex. With maturity, ventriculofugal arteries develop coursing peripherally from the ventricular wall. Ventriculofugal arteries develop between 32 and 44 weeks gestational age. Development of ventriculofugal arteries is believed to shift the watershed region in neonates from periventricular at earlier ages to cortical at term, explaining the centrifugal shift of injury with brain maturity. In the immature nervous system, damaged tissue undergoes liquefaction necrosis and is resorbed. Repair process with astrocyte mitosis and growth is believed to begin developing only at 28 weeks, explaining why earlier injury is not accompanied by gliosis [16]. Although the changing watershed zone may play a significant role in this pattern of injury, more recently a role for inflammatory mediators and altered innate immunity has been postulated [17]. The authors have also begun to question if hypoxia may play a larger role than hypoperfusion. The physiologic mechanisms behind these types of injury are not completely understood.

DWI abnormalities in central patterns of injury caused by profound insults may underestimate the degree of injury on follow-up but typically brainstem involvement on acute DWI or markedly decreased ADCs in the posterior limb internal capsule portend a poorer prognosis [Fig. 5] [18,19]. Subtle diffuse increased T2 signal and bright T1 signal can often be seen in the putamen and thalami by 2 days [20]. By 6 or 7 days decreased T2 signal is often seen in the putamen and thalami. The T1 changes become more focal by about 8 to 10 days [20].

In peripheral patterns of injury, regions of bright DWI signal and decreased ADC involve both white matter and cortex [see Fig. 3]. Often loss of gray-white distinction can be seen by 2 days on T2-weighted images in areas with cortical involvement but T2 images underestimate the extent of white matter involvement. Follow-up imaging studies show a spectrum of outcomes with the T2- and T1-weighted abnormalities often involving a smaller region than the initial DWI abnormality [Fig. 6]. Reports of preterm infants suggest that the DWI abnormalities primarily involve the white matter in infants less than 36 weeks [7].

Because of the difficulties in predicting tissue outcome based on DWI and ADC maps at any one point in time, the authors avoid the term "stroke" or "infarct" when describing these lesions to the neonatal intensive care team. These terms imply that the area with bright DWI signal and low ADC is irreversibly injured with all cell types in the abnormal region undergoing necrosis. The authors have adopted the term "metabolic stress or insult" to imply that the tissue with the abnormal DWI signal has experienced a severe enough insult to at least alter its energy metabolism and to allow for the possibility that some or all of the cellular

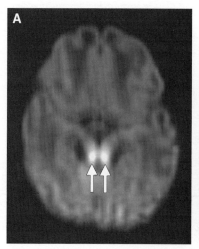
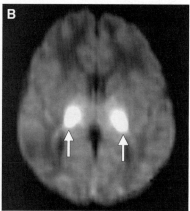

Fig. 5. Central pattern with brainstem involvement. Bright DWI signal (*A*) in the posterior brainstem (*arrows*) and (*B*) in the ventrolateral thalamus (*arrows*) on day 1 in a neonate that died within 1 week after presenting with Apgar scores of 0, 0, and 0 at 1, 5, and 10 minutes, respectively.

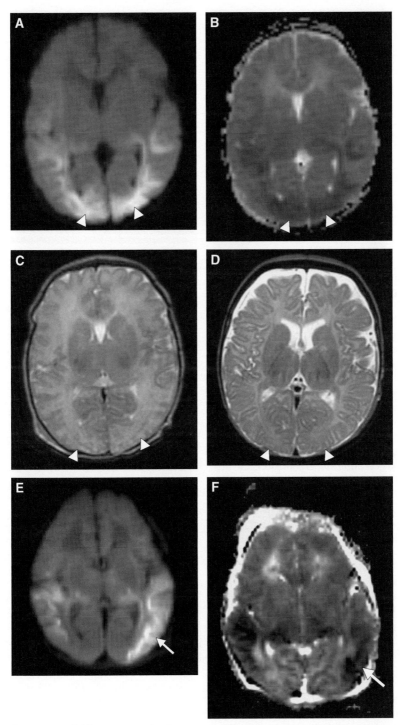

Fig. 6. Peripheral pattern variable outcomes. In the top row (*A*) diffuse bright DWI signal, (*B*) corresponding decreased ADC, and (*C*) increased T2 in the cortical gray matter on day 2 (*arrowheads*) results in (*D*) mild diffuse volume loss and a smaller region of subtle ulegyria in the occipital regions on T2 4 months later. (*E*) Bilateral but asymmetric DWI signal worse on the left (*arrow*), (*F*) corresponding to decreased ADC, slightly more extensive on the left (*arrow*), and (*G*) associated with loss of gray-white distinction on the left (*arrow*) progresses to (*H*) more extensive volume loss on T2 (*arrow*) 4 months later.

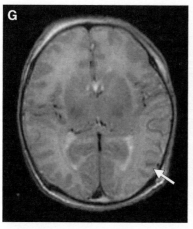
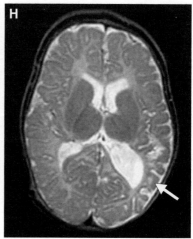

Fig. 6. (continued)

elements may recover and that selective cellular death may occur instead of full-thickness injury.

Lactate is often identified in the basal ganglia and thalamic region in encephalopathic neonates and may be helpful in short-term prognosis [21,22]. The role of MR spectroscopy in neonates that are not encephalopathic and in preterm infants is less clear. When present in the acute stage it suggests that mitochondrial function has been impaired and anaerobic metabolism is occurring. Because of the frequent association of hypoxic-ischemic brain injury with rebound hyperperfusion, the absence of lactate does not exclude anaerobic metabolism because the authors have found that rebound hyperperfusion can decrease tissue lactate levels.

Unlike in adult ischemic stroke, in neonatal hypoxic-ischemic injury, reperfusion occurs before the cells begin to undergo immediate necrosis. In immediate necrosis, failure of ATP production and glutamate-mediated toxicity result in influx of sodium and calcium with cellular edema and rupture. This is the typical result of ischemic infarction in adults. In neonates suffering from hypoxic-ischemic injury reperfusion occurs and if the mitochondria have not been irreversibly injured, the cells can once again produce ATP. In this context, cell death is not necessarily averted but cell death pathways may be converted from immediate necrosis to delayed cell death by either necrosis, apoptosis, or a combination of both [2,3]. This explains the delayed nadir in ADCs and the appearance of new areas of decreased ADC seen in the first few days after an insult that has been reported [8,9,19,23,24].

Currently, there is still little information on the correlation between MR imaging findings in the first week of life and outcome at school age when the full impact on neuropsychologic function begins to become apparent. Outcome studies based on entrance criteria of perinatal distress are applicable only to that population. The outcome for neonates presenting with DWI abnormalities in the absence of perinatal distress cannot be determined from these studies.

Focal pattern

Arterial strokes are most common in term infants. Risk factors include history of infertility, preeclampsia, prolonged rupture of membranes, and chorioamnionitis with marked increases when multiple risk factors are present [25].

The focal pattern is caused by focal arterial occlusions. In most cases the cause is unknown, but possibilities include emboli, thrombosis, or transient spasm. Typically, these are focal events on an otherwise normal brain with no evidence of global brain involvement [26,27]. As expected, most of these neonates are not encephalopathic and typically present within the first few days of life not with focal neurologic deficits but with a focal seizure. The typical history is a newborn with normal delivery and normal Apgar scores presenting with focal seizure activity around day 2 of life. Although it is commonly thought that these injuries occur at or around the time of birth, the reasons for the delay in overt seizure activity are unclear.

In the few cases the authors have studied with perfusion imaging, hyperperfusion when imaged on day 2 is commonly seen. In addition, preliminary data suggest that the region of tissue with T2 abnormalities on follow-up may be slightly smaller than the initial DWI abnormality, consistent with these injuries reperfusing more rapidly than is typical for adult strokes and delayed mechanisms of cell death may play a larger role. The role of apoptosis in neonatal stroke has been also supported by animal models [28].

Outcomes are typically quite good in these lesions compared with the diffuse injuries. Concomitant involvement of basal ganglia, corpus callosum, and posterior limb of the internal capsule has been reported to predict the development of hemiparesis, with no child with one or two of these structures involved developing hemiparesis [29].

Brain injury in the young child

Drowning, choking, and nonaccidental trauma are among the most common forms of brain injury in the young child. In near drowning and choking and often in nonaccidental trauma, hypoxic hypoxia occurs followed by reoxygenation when resuscitated. If the hypoxia is prolonged, cardiac dysfunction or arrest may occur, resulting in a period of decreased or absent perfusion and hypoxia. With resuscitation, reoxygenation and reperfusion occur. MR imaging plays an important role in the assessment of cerebral injury because often the child is sedated in the field, limiting the clinical examination on arrival to the emergency room, or the history is not forthcoming.

When imaging in the young child exposed to a hypoxic or anoxic event with or without associated cardiac arrest the authors recommend that the protocol include the following sequences:

1. Axial T1-weighted
2. Axial T2-weighted fast spin echo
3. Axial DWI
4. MR spectroscopy with TE of 35 or 144 ms, including the lentiform nucleus and occipital cortex
5. Perfusion (optional)

At the authors' institution, imaging is preformed at the earliest feasible time to assess for the presence or absence of injury and to detect the pattern and severity of the injury. If normal, a second study at approximately 48 hours is performed to determine if there is delayed injury. When transportation is difficult, imaging between 2 and 4 days is likely most helpful for diagnosis of injury and for prognosis.

Anoxia and hypoperfusion

In children following asphyxia (anoxia) and subsequent cardiorespiratory arrest, those who have vegetative outcomes or succumb to the injury typically have abnormal MR imaging with DWI and MR spectroscopy within the first 12 to 24 hours. The actual time at which the imaging becomes abnormal is not well documented but it probably depends on the severity of the insult, with most severe anoxic

hypoperfusion injuries becoming abnormal within 12 hours [Fig. 7]. The initial abnormalities are bright DWI low ADC in the posterior lateral lentiform and ventrolateral thalamus (as in the neonate) within approximately 12 to 24 hours, which precede T1 and T2 signal changes. If dynamic susceptibility contrast perfusion-weighted MR imaging is performed at this time, the authors have noted marked increases in relative cerebral blood volume in these regions of decreased ADC indicating rebound hyperperfusion in this area. Unlike neonatal profound hypoxia and hypoperfusion with reperfusion and unlike the deep gray injury in most adult cases of cardiac arrest, however, the injury shows significant progression over time. By approximately 48 hours, the entire basal ganglia and thalamus become involved and the perirolandic and visual cortex [see Fig. 7], with MR spectroscopy in DWI-abnormal cortical areas showing elevated lactate and glutamate. Between 48 and 72 hours, the entire cortex becomes involved and diffuse cerebral swelling is evident. White matter ADCs decrease and cortical ADCs normalize. Abnormalities on routine MR imaging sequences and MR spectroscopy by day 2 portents a poor prognosis but a normal study cannot rule out injury until day 3 or 4. Best correlation for MR imaging and MR spectroscopy findings with outcome was at 3 to 4 days with 100% positive and negative predictive value for poor outcome [30]. The predictive values of DWI and perfusion have not been determined, but in the authors' experience [31], DWI abnormalities within 12 to 24 hours have a poor prognosis. A similar progression with time has also been documented on CT, although the detection of the initial findings does not occur until after 24 hours, and on MR imaging with MR spectroscopy [16,30]. At 4 to 6 days, hemorrhage may develop within the basal ganglia or cortex. MR imaging with DWI shows massive cerebral swelling; normalization of cortical ADCs (likely caused by vasogenic edema); and marked white matter ADC decreases. MR spectroscopy shows significant loss of all metabolites in the cortex and lactate. In some cases where mannitol has been given, mannitol may be detected as a peak at 3.9 ppm [Fig. 8].

Hypoxia-anoxia with maintained perfusion

For short durations, isolated hypoxia or anoxia without ischemia is better tolerated both clinically and pathologically. With isolated hypoxia there is preservation of cerebral blood flow allowing continued supply of nutrients and removal of toxic products [32]. In cases with respiratory arrest that do not progress to cardiac arrest, the cerebral injury is primarily caused by hypoxic hypoxia with reoxygenation during recovery or resuscitation.

Imaging findings with isolated hypoxic hypoxia are not well documented, with most studies focusing on ischemic hypoxia. In the authors' (albeit limited) experience, it seems that delayed injury with selective involvement of the white matter (postanoxic leukoencephalopathy) may be under-appreciated. In the authors' cases, respiratory arrest was documented or significant respiratory compromise was highly suspected but no cardiac arrest or dysfunction occurred. In the literature, similar

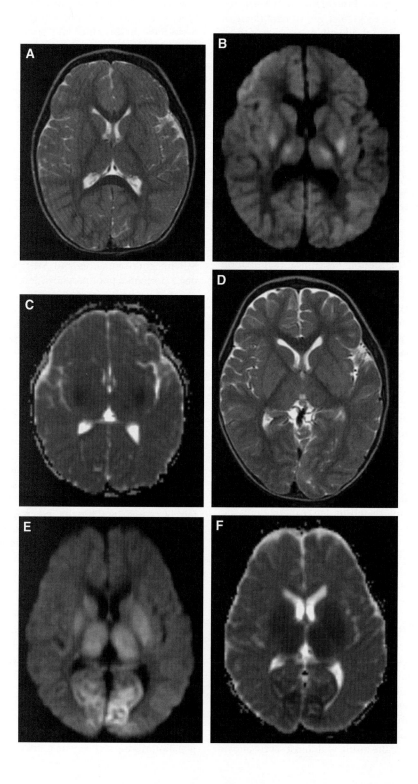

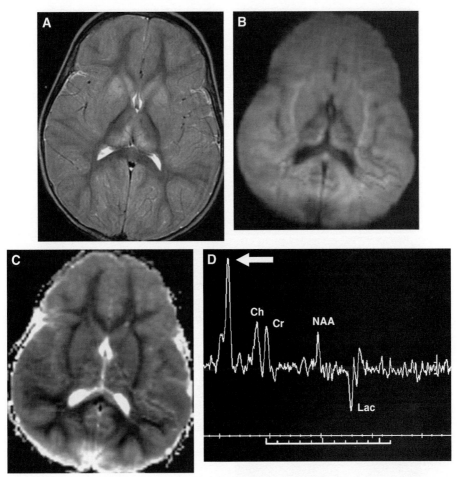

Fig. 8. Severe anoxia and hypoperfusion. Four days after cardiorespiratory arrest caused by near drowning in another toddler, (*A*) the T2 fast spin echo shows diffuse cerebral swelling with increased T2 in gray matter. (*B*) DWI shows increased signal throughout the brain. (*C*) On the ADC map the gray matter ADCs are close to normal but the white matter ADCs are markedly reduced. (*D*) MR spectroscopy in the parietal lobe gray matter shows markedly reduced choline (Ch), creatine (Cr), and NAA peaks indicating profound tissue injury, the presence of lactate (Lac) indicating anaerobic metabolism, and an unusual peak of 3.9 ppm corresponding to mannitol (*arrow*).

injuries can be seen in adults with respiratory arrest, carbon dioxide poisoning, cyanide poisoning, cardiac arrest, or drug overdose [33]. Initial MR imaging with DWI and MR spectroscopy is typically normal but by approximately day 2 (in the adult literature it may be many days later), marked ADC decreases throughout the white matter are noted [Fig. 9] [31]. These injuries evolve to diffuse volume loss often with abnormally increased T2 on long-term follow-up.

Because these children are so young, clinical evidence of the diffuse white matter injury is often not obvious. Without imaging identification of the white matter injury that becomes apparent approximately 2 days after the insult, significant risk to cognitive function may not have been

Fig. 7. Severe anoxia and hypoperfusion. (*A*) Eighteen hours after cardiorespiratory arrest secondary to choking the T2 fast spin echo shows no abnormality but (*B*) DWI shows abnormally bright signal in the posterior putamen and ventrolateral thalamus. (*C*) The corresponding ADC map shows that the DWI bright regions have decreased ADC. Two days after cardiorespiratory arrest in the same toddler, (*D*) only subtle increased T2 signal is noted in the basal ganglia, thalami, and occipital cortex on T2 fast spin echo, whereas (*E*) the DWI shows marked increased signal in these regions and in the perirolandic cortex (not shown). (*F*) These areas correspond to regions of decreased ADC on the ADC map. The cause of the brain volume loss between (*A*) and (*D*) is unknown but is likely caused by mannitol and other medical interventions.

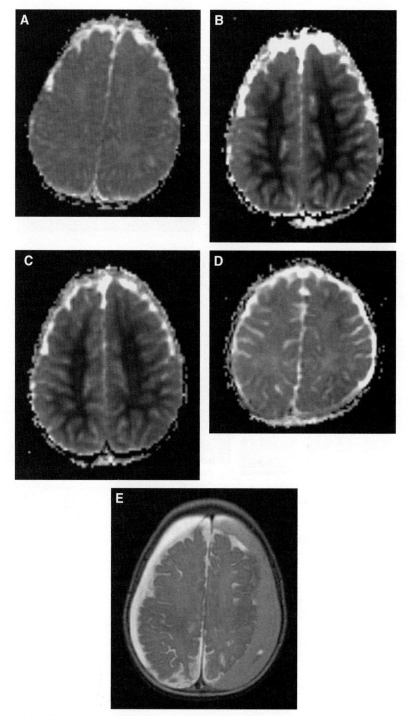

Fig. 9. Hypoxia with delayed white matter injury. Progression of injury on ADC maps with (*A*) normal ADC at 18 hours, (*B*) maximal white matter ADC decrease at 2 days, (*C*) less marked but persistent white matter ADC decrease at 4 days, (*D*) elevation of white matter ADCs at 8 days, and (*E*) an axial T2-weighted image showing marked volume loss 2 months after event with secondary bilateral subdural collections.

identified and early intervention may not have occurred.

Limitations of diffusion-weighted imaging

As a result of the authors' experience in the adult stroke population, where cell death occurs predominantly by acute necrosis, it is common to assume that the DWI obtained during the acute phase represents the full extent of the cerebral injury. If normal, an acute injury is ruled out. Although a normal DWI rules out acute necrosis, it does not rule out activation of delayed cell death pathways. Unlike in the adult, in the infant and young child cerebral insults associated with hypoxia with or without hypoperfusion followed by reoxygenation with or without reperfusion commonly occur. The immature brain has primed delayed (or programmed) cell death pathways used for normal

processes of neuronal pruning that can become overactivated after an insult. In addition, the reoxygenation and reperfusion results in restored energy supply, which may avert acute necrotic cell death in favor of delayed apoptosis, necrosis, or mixed cell death. A normal DWI in the acute setting or regions with normal DWI signal in the acute setting does not rule out significant injury and impending cell death. In fact, in one example, despite the presence of an acute cerebellar reversal sign on CT (suggesting an anoxic insult), multiple DWI studies in the first week were normal with only a minimal decline in the ADCs in the right visual cortex on day two. On follow-up imaging, diffuse cerebral volume loss was noted [Fig. 10] [31]. This case suggests that volume loss, suggestive of apoptotic cell death, may occur in the absence of significant ADC decreases.

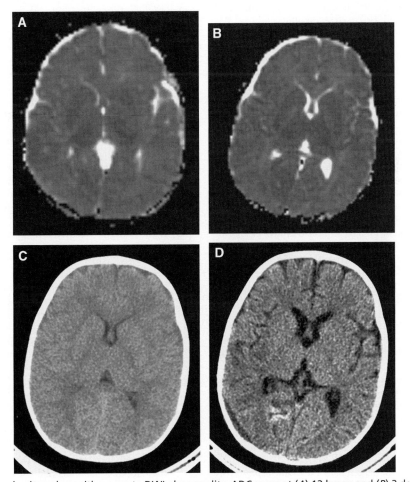

Fig. 10. Cerebral volume loss with no acute DWI abnormality. ADC maps at (*A*) 12 hours and (*B*) 3 days compared with (*C*) CT before cerebral insult and (*D*) CT 18 days after the insult. Despite near normal ADC maps, interval volume loss can be seen by comparing CT scans, where the study 18 days after the insult (*D*) shows not only a small region of increased attenuation likely representing early calcification in the right visual cortex but also diffuse volume loss despite lack of diffuse ADC changes.

Summary

Hypoxia with or without hypoperfusion is a common mechanism of injury in the immature brain and can result in normal or minimally abnormal imaging studies in the first 12 hours. Often, injury progresses over time suggesting a central role for delayed cell death pathways. An awareness of the patterns of injury associated with different mechanisms of injury and the central role of delayed cell death pathways in injury evolution is important for the radiologist to understand the significance and potential outcome of these injuries.

References

[1] Johnston MV, Trescher WH, Ishida A, et al. Neurobiology of hypoxic-ischemic injury in the developing brain. Pediatr Res 2001;49:735–41.

[2] Leist M, Jaattela M. Four deaths and a funeral: from caspases to alternative mechanisms. Nat Rev Mol Cell Biol 2001;2:589–98.

[3] Yakovlev AG, Faden AI. Mechanisms of neural cell death: implications for development of neuroprotective treatment strategies. Neurorx 2004; 1:5–16.

[4] Ment LR, Bada HS, Barnes P, et al. Practice parameter: neuroimaging of the neonate: report of the Quality Standards Subcommittee of the American Academy of Neurology and the Practice Committee of the Child Neurology Society. Neurology 2002;58:1726–38.

[5] Barkovich AJ, Westmark KD, Bedi HS, et al. Proton spectroscopy and diffusion imaging on the first day of life after perinatal asphyxia: preliminary report. AJNR Am J Neuroradiol 2001; 22:1786–94.

[6] Pectasides M, Pienaar R, Matsuda KM, et al. Optimizing diffusion weighted imaging in neonatal vascular territory injuries. Presented at the International Society for Magnetic Resonance in Medicine 13th Annual Scientific Meeting and Exhibition. Miami Beach, Florida, May 7–13, 2005.

[7] Inder T, Huppi PS, Zientara GP, et al. Early detection of periventricular leukomalacia by diffusion-weighted magnetic resonance imaging techniques. J Pediatr 1999;134:631–4.

[8] Takeoka M, Soman TB, Yoshii A, et al. Diffusion-weighted images in neonatal cerebral hypoxic-ischemic injury. Pediatr Neurol 2002;26:274–81.

[9] Robertson RL, Ben-Sira L, Barnes PD, et al. MR line-scan diffusion-weighted imaging of term neonates with perinatal brain ischemia. AJNR Am J Neuroradiol 1999;20:1658–70.

[10] Barkovich AJ, Sargent SK. Profound asphyxia in the premature infant: imaging findings. AJNR Am J Neuroradiol 1995;16:1837–46.

[11] Barkovich AJ. MR and CT evaluation of profound neonatal and infantile asphyxia. AJNR Am J Neuroradiol 1992;13(3):959–72. [discussion 973–5].

[12] The American College of Obstetricians and Gynecologists' Task Force on Neonatal Encephalopathy and Cerebral Palsy and the American College of Obstetricians and Gynecologists and the American Academy of Pediatrics: criteria required to define an acute intrapartum hypoxic event as sufficient to cause cerebral palsy. In: Neonatal encephalopathy and cerebral palsy: defining the pathogenesis and pathophysiology. Washington DC: American College of Obstetricians and Gynecologists; 2003. p. 74–80.

[13] Sie LT, van der Knaap MS, Oosting J, et al. MR patterns of hypoxic-ischemic brain damage after prenatal, perinatal or postnatal asphyxia. Neuropediatrics 2000;31:128–36.

[14] Ferriero DM. Neonatal brain injury. N Engl J Med 2004;351:1985–95.

[15] Barkovich AJ, Truwit CL. Brain damage from perinatal asphyxia: correlation of MR findings with gestational age. AJNR Am J Neuroradiol 1990;11:1087–96.

[16] Barkovich A. Pediatric neuroimaging. 3rd edition. Philadelphia: Lippincott, Williams & Wilkins; 2000.

[17] Lassiter HA. The role of complement in neonatal hypoxic-ischemic cerebral injury. Clin Perinatol 2004;31:117–27.

[18] Hunt RW, Neil JJ, Coleman LT, et al. Apparent diffusion coefficient in the posterior limb of the internal capsule predicts outcome after perinatal asphyxia. Pediatrics 2004;114: 999–1003.

[19] Wolf RL, Zimmerman RA, Clancy R, et al. Quantitative apparent diffusion coefficient measurements in term neonates for early detection of hypoxic-ischemic brain injury: initial experience. Radiology 2001;218:825–33.

[20] Barkovich AJ, Westmark K, Partridge C, et al. Perinatal asphyxia: MR findings in the first 10 days. AJNR Am J Neuroradiol 1995;16:427–38.

[21] Barkovich AJ, Baranski K, Vigneron D, et al. Proton MR spectroscopy for the evaluation of brain injury in asphyxiated, term neonates. AJNR Am J Neuroradiol 1999;20:1399–405.

[22] Kadri M, Shu S, Holshouser B, et al. Proton magnetic resonance spectroscopy improves outcome prediction in perinatal CNS insults. J Perinatol 2003;23:181–5.

[23] McKinstry RC, Miller JH, Snyder AZ, et al. A prospective, longitudinal diffusion tensor imaging study of brain injury in newborns. Neurology 2002;59:824–33.

[24] Soul JS, Robertson RL, Tzika AA, et al. Time course of changes in diffusion-weighted magnetic resonance imaging in a case of neonatal encephalopathy with defined onset and duration of hypoxic-ischemic insult. Pediatrics 2001;108: 1211–4.

[25] Lee J, Croen LA, Backstrand KH, et al. Maternal and infant characteristics associated with

perinatal arterial stroke in the infant. JAMA 2005;293:723–9.

[26] Matsuda KM, Krishnamoorthy KS, Grant PE. ADC changes in neonatal brain injury and outcome. In: 48th Annual Society of Pediatric Radiology, May 3–7, 2005. New Orleans (LA): Springer; 2005. p. S70–1.

[27] Matsuda KM, Lopez CJ, Pectasides M, et al. Apparent diffusion coefficients (ADC) in neonatal brain injury: patterns of injury and outcome. Presented at the American Society of Neuroradiology 43rd Annual Meeting. Toronto, Canada, May 23–27, 2005.

[28] Manabat C, Han BH, Wendland M, et al. Reperfusion differentially induces caspase-3 activation in ischemic core and penumbra after stroke in immature brain. Stroke 2003;34:207–13.

[29] Boardman JP, Ganesan V, Rutherford MA, et al. Magnetic resonance image correlates of hemiparesis after neonatal and childhood middle cerebral artery stroke. Pediatrics 2005;115:321–6.

[30] Dubowitz DJ, Bluml S, Arcinue E, et al. MR of hypoxic encephalopathy in children after near drowning: correlation with quantitative proton MR spectroscopy and clinical outcome. AJNR Am J Neuroradiol 1998;19:1617–27.

[31] Pectasides M, Buckley AW, Krishnamoorthy KS, et al. Respiratory ± cardiac arrest: delayed ADC decreases. In: 48th Annual Society of Pediatric Radiology, May 3–7, 2005. New Orleans (LA): Springer; 2005. p. S72.

[32] Singhal AB, Topcuoglu MA, Koroshetz WJ. Diffusion MRI in three types of anoxic encephalopathy. J Neurol Sci 2002;196:37–40.

[33] Chalela JA, Wolf RL, Maldjian JA, et al. MRI identification of early white matter injury in anoxic-ischemic encephalopathy. Neurology 2001;56:481–5.

MAGNETIC
RESONANCE
IMAGING CLINICS

Magn Reson Imaging Clin N Am 14 (2006) 287–291

Index

Note: Page numbers of article titles are in **boldface** type.

doi:10.1016/S1064-9689(06)00044-4